Fontographer
Type by Design

FONTOGRAPHER

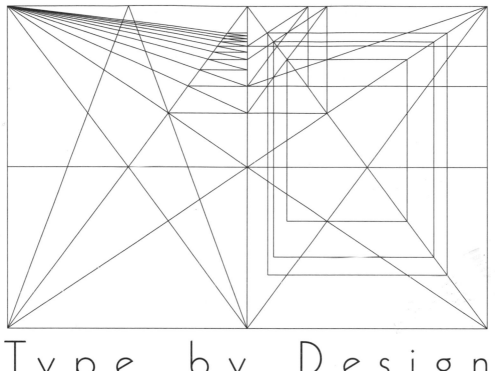

Type by Design

Stephen Moye

MIS:
PRESS

A Subsidiary of
Henry Holt and Co., Inc.

First Edition—1995

Library of Congress Cataloging in Publication Data
Moye, Stephen.
   Fontographer : type by design / written & illustrated by Stephen Moye.
   p. cm.
   Includes bibliographical references.
   Fontographer.
Font editors.
Z250.8.F65M69 1995   686.2/2544536 20   95-324
ISBN 1-55828-447-8   CIP

Printed in the United States of America

10 9 8 7 6 5 4 3 2 1

MIS:Press books are available at special discounts for bulk purchases for sales promotions, premiums, fund-raising, or educational use. Special editions or book excerpts can also be created to specification.

For details contact: Special Sales Director
                            MIS:Press
                            115 West 18th Street
                            New York, NY 10011

Associate Publisher: Paul Farrell

Managing Editor: Cary Sullivan

Technical Editor: Dan Margulis

Copyedit Manager: Shari Chappell

Copy Editor: Suzanne Ingrao

Design, Page Layout, Illustration, and
    Typography: Stephen Moye

Table of Contents ❏

v

Acknowledgments

O ONE EVER WRITES a book entirely alone. The informally collaborative process includes friends, colleagues and all those who have contributed to the subject at hand. They sit patiently at your elbow, offering advice, encouragement and the not infrequent "tsk-tsk." It is now my happy task to thank those who have helped me so generously in this endeavor.

I have Earl Allen — formerly Technical Support at Altsys, now Remote Support Specialist for Scitex America Corp. — to thank for suggesting this project to me. Several years ago, I asked him if there were a book available that discussed techniques of type design with Fontographer. "No," he said, "so why don't you write one? You might learn something." I should also thank him for not laughing when he reviewed my first attempts. Andrew Meit, also formerly of Altsys where he was Mac font products tester, has been extremely generous in sharing his time and knowledge with me.

I am extremely grateful to Richard Beatty not only for thoroughly reviewing the book in its preparation and offering sterling advice on it, but also for the magnificent typefaces — Goudy Italian Oldstyle and his own design Livingston — in which the book is set. In addition, he very generously catered to a whim of mine and altered the lowercase *y* so that its tail was more in line with the prevailing descender line. His friendship, courtesy, kindness and encouragement have been a very real treat.

I also want to extend to Judith Sutcliffe my deepest appreciation for taking the time to engage in a thorough examination of this book at an early stage. Her criticisms and suggestions — and support — set me on the right path, resulting in much clarification, reorganization and rethinking.

Thanks also to friends and colleagues at Brown University Graphic Services for their support: Larry Carr, Director; Diane Greaves, Assistant Director; Deb Berlo, Manager; and Brenda Sousa, Coordinator. Greg Kazarian, Departmental Computing Coordinator at the Watson Institute at Brown University, provided a lively interest and support.

I owe a tremendous debt of gratitude to Dan Margulis for reviewing the final draft in breathtaking detail. Dan's extraordinary talents are beautifully shown off in his own book *Professional Photoshop* (John Wiley and Sons, Inc., 1995): It is an essential resource volume if you ever use Photoshop. His criticism brought to light many, many lapses on my part, and millions of typos.

One last word of thanks. Were it not for Paul Farrell, Associate Publisher of MIS: Press, it is quite likely that *Fontographer: Type by Design* might never have seen the light of day. His engaging though sure lightness of touch and thought-provoking conversation encouraged me to improve the book in a multitude of ways, and made me entirely comfortable with the demanding process of bringing the work to press. I am also grateful for the kind assistance of Cary Sullivan, Managing Editor, and Andrew Neusner, Assistant to the Publisher.

Through the good and generous offices of these people, and many more, I can offer you a much improved book, far better than I could have ever produced entirely on my own.

Stephen Moye
Providence, Rhode Island
The Feast of All Fools, 1995

Introduction ❑

MY PURPOSE IN THIS BOOK is to supply you with information and tools that will help to make your use of Fontographer both more enjoyable and productive. I also want to indicate to you new approaches to the craft of font design, and to indicate that such design does not exist in a vacuum: every aspect of it has an intimate relationship with every other aspect of typographic design. It is precisely the infinite possibilities that arise out of this synergy that makes typography so fascinating and absorbing.

Fontographer is, essentially, a simple tool but that very simplicity makes it useful for virtually any purpose the mind can conceive. The resulting interplay of tool and purpose can, and often does, give rise to great complexity of design, though the complexity is often hidden by the presence of a unifying artistic vision and sense of purpose.

My approach to elucidating this complexity follows that of Donald Knuth. Some paragraphs are marked with a ❖ or ❖❖, and the type is a bit smaller. This is meant to indicate that the material so marked is more advanced, and not necessarily intended for people just starting out. As you gain experience and knowledge, you will start to delve into the ❖ and then into the ❖❖ sections.

One very important piece of advice I would give is this: read the Fontographer *User's Guide*. It is excellent, and I have made no attempt to repeat material here that is already there. With respect to advanced topics, the *User's Guide* sections on creating Multiple Master fonts and hinting are essential reading if you are going to work in those areas.

Above all: Enjoy.

I dedicate this work to —

My mother, who would have found it interesting;

My father, who will be pleased with this evidence of
utility from his errant son;

And Steven, without whom I could not and would
not have done this thing.

Warning: Type design can be hazardous to
your other interests. Once you get hooked,
you will develop intense feelings about
letterforms; the medium will intrude on the
messages you read. And you will perpetually
be thinking of improvements to the fonts
that you see everywhere, especially those of
your own design.   *Donald E. Knuth*

O wondrous type! O vision fair...
Latin 15c. hymn, Hymnal 1982, No. 136

Drawing in PostScript

THE BASIC PROCESS of drawing in Fontographer is this: Locate the important points on the desired shape — call them critical points; attach drawing points to the critical points in a process that has been aptly compared to "connecting the dots" in which the lines connecting the dots are alive; finally, adjust and fine-tune the drawn shape. Simple.

PostScript requires us to analyze an object in terms of its shape, and then to locate the critical points on the shape, and to attach drawing points at those critical points. From each drawing point there issues a straight-line handle with a Bézier Control Point (BCP) at its end, indicated (in Fontographer) by a small cross. Using the *BCPs*, we adjust the curve that we are drawing to match the given shape. The drawing points *anchor* the curve to the template shape at the critical points, while the BCPs *shape* the curve accurately to the template, or desired, shape. Fontographer provides a complete toolbox for drawing, and version 4.1 goes even further. Figures 1.1 and 1.2 show a typical working environment in Fontographer version 3.x and the expanded toolbox palette of version 4.1 respectively — don't worry, some of the things you see there we haven't discussed yet. You might also cast a glance at Figure 1.3 for a visual explanation of some of the terms used thus far.

FIGURE 1.1   FONTOGRAPHER 3.X

The tools in the toolbar can be accessed with Command-#, where # is the number given after the tool. Especially for keyboards with a numeric keypad, this is an enormous time-saver.

The overshoot lines should be included in your Guideline layer to help you attain consistent character shapes through hinting when printing at low resolution. Overshoot is typically 1% – 2% of the em-square, and can be as much as 4%.

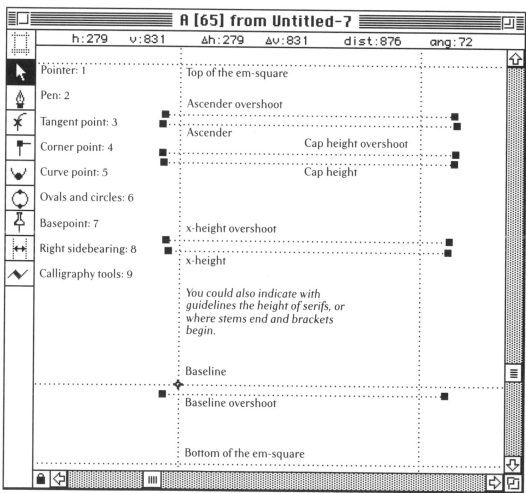

FIGURE 1.2   FONTOGRAPHER 4.1

Fontographer 4.1 offers an entire palette of new tools, very similar to those of Macromedia FreeHand, another of Altsys' offspring.

1) The pointer. It selects and moves points.
2) Rectangles. Double-clicking on this will give you a dialogue box that allows you to set the roundness of the corners. Hold down the Shift key to constrain to a square, and the Option key to draw from the center.
3) Circles and Ellipses. Hold down the Shift key to constrain to a circle, and the Option key to draw from the center.
4) Freehand tool. Double-click to get a dialogue box that determines type and width of stroke, and the angle of the pen for calligraphic effects.
5) Knife tool. This intelligent tool works in three ways. Click on a path with it and it will split the path at that point. Click-and-drag across one or more paths, and a line is drawn that causes the path to be split where the line intersects with the path. Option-click-and-drag across one or more paths, and a line is drawn which causes the path segment to be deleted when the line intersects with the segment.
6) Corner-point tool. Adds a corner point.
7) Rotation tool. Rotates a selected object. Use with the mouse, or double-click to get the Transform... dialogue box.
8) Scale tool. Scales a selected object. Use with the mouse, or double-click to get the Transform... dialogue box.
9) Measurement tool. Click-and-drag between two points to measure the distance. A useful, elegant, and well-implemented tool.
10) Perspective tool. Distorts a character by altering the perspective from which it is seen. New in version 4.1.

11) Hand. The hand tool is simply a quick way of navigating around the screen, rather than using the scroll bars.
12) Polygon and Stars. Draws polygons and stars. Double- click to get a dialogue box that allows you to specify the shape of the object.
13) Line. Draws straight lines.
14) Pen. Combines the function of corner and curve tools. Click and a corner point is added; click-and-drag and the control points are dragged out of the drawing point while dragging, thus making a curve point.
15) Curve. Adds a curve point.
16) Tangent. Adds a tangent point.
17) Flip tool. Reflects a shape across an axis. Use with the mouse, or double-click to get the Transform... dialogue box.
18) Skew tool. Distorts a shape by means of a kind of stretching. Use with the mouse, or double-click to get the Transform... dialogue box.
19) Magnify. Enlarges at the click point.
20) Arc tool. This automates drawing arcs, and draws a variety of them. New in version 4.1.

Fontographer 4 sports a new information bar at the top of the drawing window. 1) Distance of the pointer from the origin; 2) distance of a selected point from the origin; 3) distance of the pointer from a selected point; 4) distance of the pointer from the basepoint; 5) distance of a selected point from the basepoint; 6) number of points in the character; 7) number of selected points.

1	2	3	4	5	6	7
662,236.8	461.4,344.7	200.5,−108	662,236.8	461.4,344.7	4	1

FIGURE 1.3   ANATOMY OF A BEZIER CURVE

Bézier curves are used by PostScript (and therefore by Fontographer) to draw curves. Bézier curves can conform to virtually any shape with a minimum of drawing points, and the curve itself can be computed relatively quickly and easily.

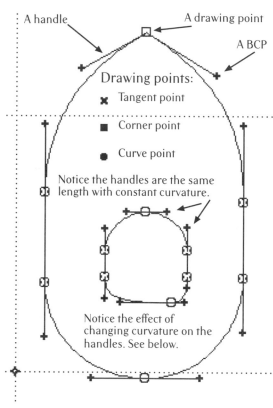

A handle   A drawing point   A BCP

Drawing points:

✗   Tangent point

■   Corner point

⬗   Curve point

Notice the handles are the same length with constant curvature.

Notice the effect of changing curvature on the handles. See below.

BCPs (Bézier Control Points) are found at the other ends of the handles (indicated by small crosses) from the drawing points. Grab a BCP with the pointer to control the length and direction of a handle—see the illustration.

Nomenclature: I usually refer simply to 'handles' and 'points' (i.e., drawing points): 'moving a handle' implies moving the BCP attached to it.

2. How drawing points control shape.
Drawing points are distinguished by the way the handles attached to them behave. All drawing points have two handles, although one or both handles may be of zero length and so not visible.

Curve points have handles that move see-saw fashion about the drawing point.

The handles for a *Corner point* move independently and so are useful for producing curves with discontinuities.

Tangent points have handles that are extensions of straight-line segments, and so are useful when a curve must blend seamlessly into a straight line.

The Pen tool is capable of creating Curve or Corner points. Click to produce a corner point; Click & drag to produce Curve points; Option-Click & drag to produce Corner points at the end of a curved path segment.

1. Controlling the shapes.
There are three things that control the shape of a Bézier curve:
1. Drawing points
2. Handles
3. BCPs

Drawing points are placed where you click the mouse; there are three kinds:
1. Tangent
2. Corner
3. Curve
Look at the illustration for a key and examples.

Handles extend from the drawing points and determine the shape of the curve.

3. How handles control shape
A section of a Bézier curve (that is, a section of the curve between two drawing points) is controlled by two handles. To the extent that curvature is constant along the segment, the two controlling handles will be of equal length; to the extent that it changes, they will be of unequal length, with shorter handles associated with increasing curvature.

An important characteristic of the curve with respect to the handles is this—the curve is always tangent to the handle at the drawing point: that is, the curve and the handle will have the same slope at the drawing point.

What to draw in Fontographer? Just about anything you Orthogonal
like. Alphabets, of course, are the most common candidates. But if Bézier curves
you think of Fontographer as a kind of graphics database, you will
begin to see new possibilities. *Anything* can be put into the 'letter'
slots such as pictures, ornaments, road signs, architectural elements,
musical notes and symbols… the list could go on forever. Just use
your imagination and have fun.

1. *Overview and terminology.* We note the critical points on the
shape; that is, where we will click the mouse to place drawing points.
Critical points are often on parts of the curve that are momentarily
parallel to either the baseline — the x-axis in math — or the left
sidebearing — the y-axis in math. For the sake of convenience we
will use the mathematical term *orthogonal* to describe those places at
which the given shape is parallel to one of the axes. By 'axes' I mean
the x and y axes, both of which are at right angles to each other; if I
am referring to a specific axis, I will make that clear. Critical points
also occur where the curve changes direction or where it comes from,
or goes to, a straight line segment.

Drawing points have handles, and at the ends of the handles
are Bézier Control Points (BCPs). The BCPs are the things you drag
with the pointer in order to adjust the length and direction of the
handles, and thus the shape of the curve you are drawing.

❖   **2. *Bézier curves.*** PostScript, and therefore Fontographer, uses Bézier
curves for the rendering of curved forms. Bézier curves are supple shapes
that can be molded to almost any possible shape. Their principle is simple: The
curve that we are drawing comprises a series of drawing points, i.e., points
located on the curve itself, while the shape of the curve between the drawing
points is altered by the handles and the BCPs attached to them. Figure 1.4A
shows a curve with only its drawing points visible; Figure 1.4B shows the same
curve with both drawing points and handles visible. By altering the orientation
of the handles, we can alter the shape of the curve. Figure 1.4C: Note that the
drawing points remain in the same place.

FIGURE 1.4   SIMPLE BÉZIER CURVES

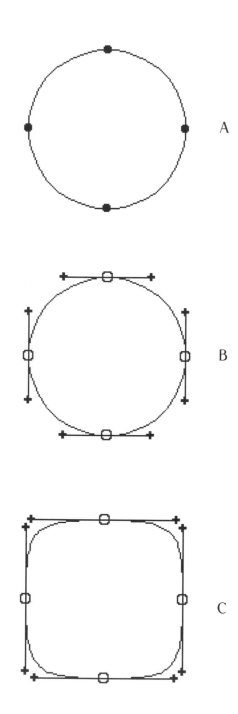

3. Critical points.　So the first problem is to determine where to place the drawing points. Broadly speaking they are placed at what are called "inflection points" — that is, where the curve we wish to draw changes direction. Most often, these points are the highest or lowest, left-most or right-most points on the curve: For the mathematically minded, these changes of direction are more properly termed x/y minima and maxima. Points of inflection are not always x/y minima and maxima: Sometimes they are at changes of direction or where a curve blends into a straight line segment.

Critical points

Drawing points: corner, curve, tangent

What does all that mean? Look at Figure 1.5A. The grayed circle is the shape that we are trying to trace with Bézier curves. Notice that we have placed drawing points at noon, 3 o'clock, 6 o'clock and 9 o'clock. These are the x/y minima and maxima: The four points attached to the circle represent its greatest and least x and y values. Because the circle that we are tracing is a TIFF or PICT template, we have a useful guide to placing the drawing points: Where the template shows a perfectly horizontal or vertical arrangement of pixels, that is where we should place a drawing point (Figure 1.5B). Figure 1.6 shows some more complex curve templates and the location of the necessary drawing points on them.

4. Drawing points.　Drawing points in Fontographer come in three kinds: *curve, corner* and *tangent.* The *Curve* tool adds a curved segment to the shape under construction. The *Corner* tool adds a corner to the shape. The *Tangent* tool adds a drawing point that allows a smooth transition to or from a curved line and a straight line segment. Figure 1.7 shows each kind of point in use. (In the patois of TrueType, drawing points are called "on-curve" points because they are placed on the template curve.)

FIGURE 1.5   SHAPES & ORTHOGONALITY

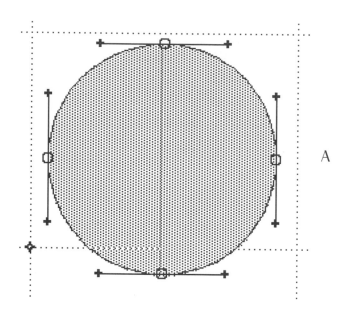

A

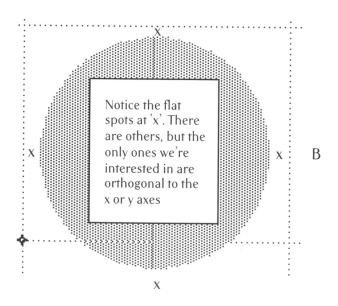

B

FIGURE 1.6   LETTERS AS SHAPES

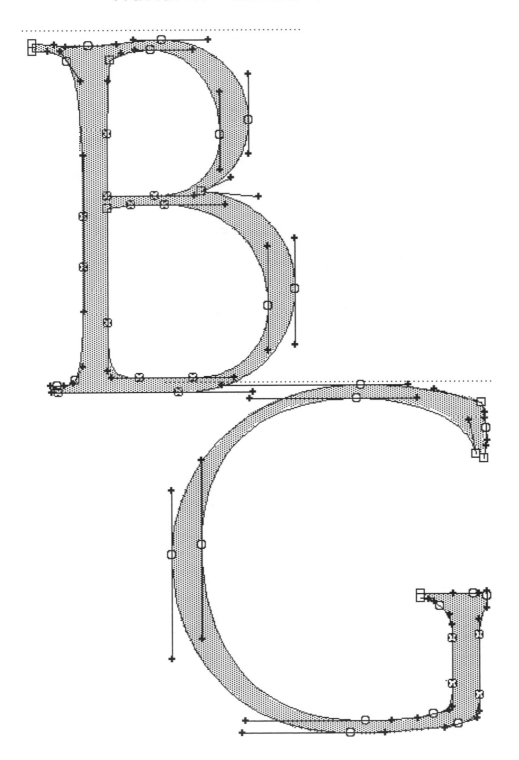

FIGURE 1.7   VARIETIES OF DRAWING POINTS

The drawing points in this example
are shown as they appear
when they are selected.

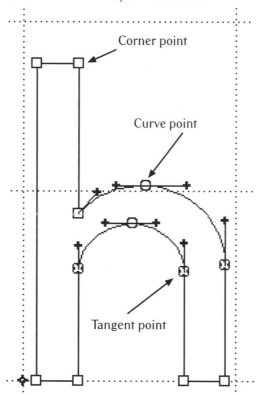

Corner point

Curve point

Tangent point

5. *Handles and BCPs.* Each drawing point has two *handles,* and at the end of each is a Bézier Control Point (BCP). The handles and BCPs control the shape of the curve being drawn, the process that was begun by placing drawing points at certain, critical locations on the template. It is important to remember the following: The Bézier curve is always tangent to the handle at that handle's associated drawing point. Keeping this fact clearly in mind will go far to make the adjustment of the handles and BCPs easy and predictable. (Again, in TrueType parlance BCPs are referred to as "off-curve" points because they are not usually found *on* the template curve.)

The handles of a drawing point behave differently depending on the tool being used. The curve tool lays down drawing points that have two handles associated with each. The handles are hooked together and act like a see-saw with the drawing point at the fulcrum: Move one of the handles, and the other moves in the opposite direction (Figure 1.8A). The corner tool can also have two handles associated with each drawing point it lays down, but they are independent of each other: Move one, and the other remains stationary (Figure 1.8B). The tangent tool lays down a drawing point that has only one visible handle associated with it: If the tangent drawing point is at the end of a straight line segment (as it most often is), its BCP seems to grow out of that line segment, thus making the curve flow smoothly into the straight line (Figure 1.8C).

FIGURE 1.8   DRAWING POINTS & THEIR HANDLES

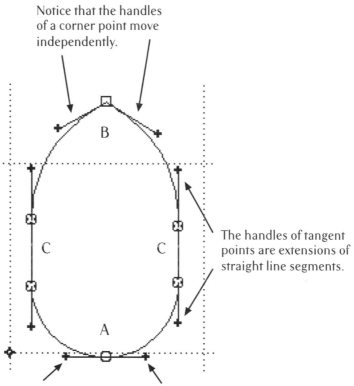

Notice that the handles
of a corner point move
independently.

The handles of tangent
points are extensions of
straight line segments.

The handles of a curve point see-saw around that point.

6. *Four rules for drawing a typeface.*   We are now in a position to discuss the four basic rules of PostScript drawing:

> **The Bump rule**   Drawing points are placed at inflection points (we've discussed this one already).
>
> **The Rule of one-third**   The distance between a drawing point and one of its associated BCPs should be roughly one-third of the length of the curve being drawn. There are many exceptions to this rule, but it is a good place to start.
>
> **The Conciseness rule**   Use only the smallest number of drawing points that you need to create the shape you require. The fewer the points, the smaller the file, the faster is it imaged, and the easier it is to edit.
>
> **The Orthogonality rule**   The handles should be orthogonal (i.e., perpendicular to, or at right angles). This is particularly true for stems and curve segments that will benefit from the effects of hinting.

Although these rules are given for use in drawing typefaces, they are also extremely useful in doing any kind of PostScript drawing. My own work in Illustrator, Freehand and Canvas is quicker and more efficient by virtue of having a definite approach to the placement of drawing points and their manipulation. Refer to Figure 1.9 for examples and further insights.

FIGURE 1.9   THOU SHALT, & THOU SHALT NOT...

Note: It has been my experience that these guidelines for PostScript drawing can be applied to the use of any program that uses Bézier curves, such as FreeHand, Illustrator or Canvas: You place drawing points more quickly and confidently, and the resulting drawings are easier to edit and more compact in size.

Right   Wrong

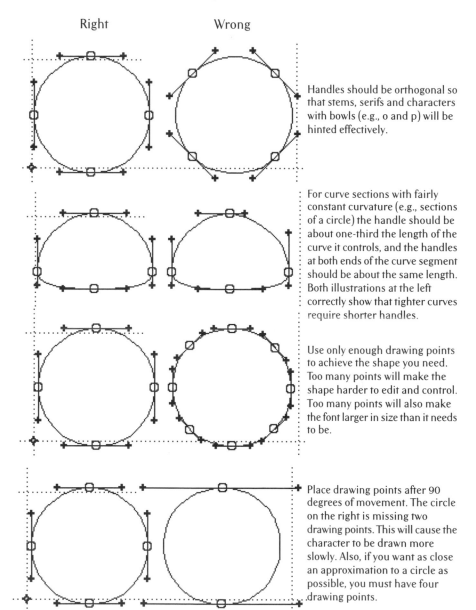

Handles should be orthogonal so that stems, serifs and characters with bowls (e.g., o and p) will be hinted effectively.

For curve sections with fairly constant curvature (e.g., sections of a circle) the handle should be about one-third the length of the curve it controls, and the handles at both ends of the curve segment should be about the same length. Both illustrations at the left correctly show that tighter curves require shorter handles.

Use only enough drawing points to achieve the shape you need. Too many points will make the shape harder to edit and control. Too many points will also make the font larger in size than it needs to be.

Place drawing points after 90 degrees of movement. The circle on the right is missing two drawing points. This will cause the character to be drawn more slowly. Also, if you want as close an approximation to a circle as possible, you must have four drawing points.

7. *Measuring distances.* With all of this talk about dimensions, we should review the tools that Fontographer gives you to indicate position and dimensions. The most straightforward is the Location … command in the Point menu (also Command-L). This command tells you the location of the selected point *with respect to the origin of the x-y coordinate system.* That is fine for the location of one point, but suppose that you want to find out how far one point is from another (e.g., for a stem width)? You could get out a pencil and paper, use Command-L for the two points, and subtract the two appropriate locations. Or…

You can use the Basepoint tool. The location of the cursor (shown in the information bar at the top of the character outline window) is given relative to the current location of the Basepoint. The principle is simple: Select the Basepoint tool, click on some point that you want to be your reference point (this moves the Basepoint to that point), move the cursor to the other point you are measuring, and read the distance between the two points in the information bar. The information is given in two forms: 1) Cartesian, in which the distance is shown as a difference in the x- and y-coordinates; and 2) Polar, in which the distance is shown as the straight-line distance between the points, and the angle that line makes with respect to the x axis.

Finally, of course, there is the measuring tool in Fontographer 4 — a really well-thought-out and useful tool. Refer to Figure 1.2 for more about the point-information window.

Tip: Use AutoSnap when measuring distances with the Basepoint tool. If you want the Basepoint to be located *precisely* where a given point is, turn on AutoSnap. This will cause the basepoint to be placed exactly on the drawing point closest to the cursor at the time. This will also cause the measurements shown in the information bar to freeze when the cursor is at or near other drawing points; that is, the measurement 'snaps to' drawing points.

8. *Orthogonal handles.* Look for a moment at Figure 1.10, the letter *p*. There are some parts of this letter that we would like to be standardized: the stem, the thick part of the bowl, the thin part of the bowl and the serifs. Handles that are orthogonal to the prevailing coordinate system act as signals to the PostScript interpreter, indicating that the curves to which they are attached should be treated in a special manner. Notice in the figure, too, some handles that are not orthogonal where the bowl connects to the stem. It is not as important visually to maintain a perfect uniformity in such cases, so there is no need for orthogonal handles. See Figure 1.11 for examples.

FIGURE 1.10   ORTHOGONALITY & HANDLES

The orthogonality of the handles indicates to the
PostScript interpreter that the curves to which they
are attached are to be treated specially when hinting
is applied; specifically, that strokes so marked are to
be of uniform width. Where the stroke width is not
critical, the handles need not be orthogonal.

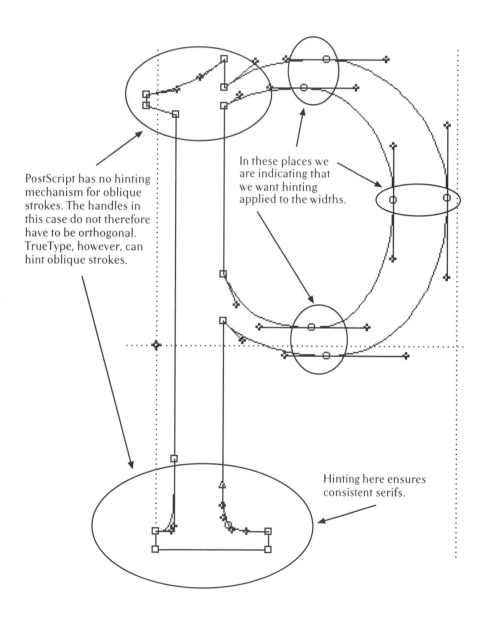

PostScript has no hinting
mechanism for oblique
strokes. The handles in
this case do not therefore
have to be orthogonal.
TrueType, however, can
hint oblique strokes.

In these places we
are indicating that
we want hinting
applied to the widths.

Hinting here ensures
consistent serifs.

FIGURE 1.11   MORE ORTHOGONALITY & HANDLES

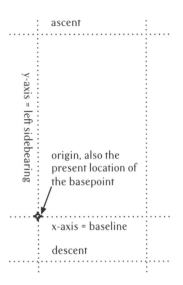

ascent

y-axis = left sidebearing

origin, also the present location of the basepoint

x-axis = baseline

descent

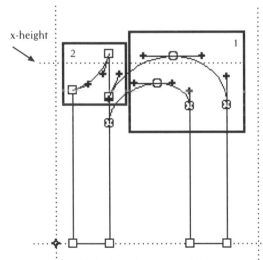

x-height

2

1

Here we have a useful, if not overly elegant lowercase *n*. The curves in box 1 are drawn with their handles as orthogonal: this is as it should be, so that the PostScript hinting mechanism will cause the stem and curve to print correctly at low resolution.

Box 2, however, shows handles that are not orthogonal: this is OK because we are more concerned with the correct **shape** than the **width**.

Notice how the curve and point overshoot the x-height. This is necessary to avoid making the character seem too short. The same thing would happen at the baseline. Overshoot is typically 1% to 2% of the em square.

❖ **9. The PostScript interpreter.** The PostScript interpreter is a very interesting device. One of its most interesting characteristics is that it is both demanding and unfriendly. It insists that PostScript code be extremely clean, and when the code is otherwise, the interpreter stops everything it's doing and shuts down — in some cases it may even turn itself off and on again just to clear itself completely.

❖ The font-rasterizing subsection of the PostScript interpreter is, if anything, even more demanding. I suppose that this stems from Adobe's original assumption that only Adobe and its licensees would be creating PostScript typefaces, thus assuring the quality and purity of the PostScript code for fonts. The interpreter expects drawing points to be placed at extrema and it does not handle the drawing of such curves very well when there are missing drawing points. It also expects the handles to be well-behaved: They should not usually point at each other and they must never cross each other.

❖ **10. Type 1, Type 3 and TrueType.** These are the basic font formats. Type 1 fonts are handled in a special way by the PostScript interpreter (see above), and must strictly conform to stringent rules. Type 3 fonts are, in essence, little EPS (encapsulated PostScript) files. They may be virtually as complex as you like, be drawn in virtually any way you like, and may contain gray-scale images. There is yet another important distinction: The PostScript interpreter will only darken printer or screen pixels that lie _entirely inside_ the outline of a Type 1 character; whereas any fraction of a pixel that lies _on_ the outline of a Type 3 character will be darkened. The result is that Type 3 fonts look heavier or darker than their Type 1 counterparts. Additionally, of course, Type 3 fonts cannot be imaged with Adobe Type Manager.

❖ ❖ **11. About hinting.** Orthogonal handles engage the PostScript hinting mechanism. Hinting allows characters to be attractively rendered even at medium to low resolution. As printers gain in resolution, hinting becomes less important. It will always be important for rendering PostScript fonts on a viewing screen. Fontographer does a superb job of calculating the hinting for a roman typeface with little or no intervention from the user. Hinting is a cultural matter, or application-specific, in that the same hinting mechanism that works well for roman type is not suitable for Japanese Kanji or graphic figures such as dingbats: In those cases you might have to tweak the values chosen by Fontographer.

Overshoot

Automatic
Curvature

Avoid open
paths

❖ ❖ Another concept to which you will see frequent mention is *overshoot*, and this applies to characters that have either curves or points at either their tops or bottoms. Curved and pointed tops must extend somewhat higher than the tops of flat letterforms, and similarly shaped bottoms must extend a little below the baseline. The reason for this is that in the absence of this sort of compensation, the tops of characters will not appear high enough, and the bottoms will appear to sit above the baseline. This adjustment to compensate for certain shapes is called overshoot. It is important because PostScript Type 1 fonts allow you to use overshoot, but *hint* the overshoot in such a way so that it does not become exaggerated at small font sizes printed at low to medium resolution. Please refer to the glossary for this work, Chapter 9, if there are any terms that puzzle you as you read.

12. *Automatic curvature.*

One feature of Fontographer's Curve, Corner and Tangent tools deserves particular mention: automatic curvature. That is, Fontographer makes a guess about the location of the BCPs associated with the drawing points. This is a time-saver particularly as Fontographer's guesses are usually quite good.

13. *A few things to avoid.*

It is easy to forget that a PostScript printer is really a computer hooked up to a device that puts marks onto paper or film. The computer can, like any computer, suffer a system error, in which case it stops working altogether. There are, indeed, some things that it is possible to do in drawing a typeface in Fontographer that will cause the PostScript interpreter to 'crash.' Naturally, it would be good to avoid these things. So, the following situations should be noted with care.

First, make sure that all of the paths are closed — open paths are the most common cause of a font failing to print, and it only takes one character with an open path to cause such a failure. This is also one of the hardest problems to track down. I have found them in my own work by looking carefully at the printout that Fontographer produces. Usually there is a weird jagged stroke on a character or a long thin line that comes from nowhere to indicate the presence of an open path.

Second, do not create *kinks* with the BCPs. This is a mildly difficult notion to explain, and yet it is a fairly common error. A kink is created when 1) adjacent control handles cross each other, 2) or when a line drawn from (and extending colinearly from) one handle crosses an adjacent handle. The first instance is very bad indeed and can cause the PostScript interpreter to fail. A third case can also be discerned, although it is not technically a kink: when two adjacent drawing points have a critical point between them, but no attached drawing point. See Figure 1.12 for examples of these.

FIGURE 1.12   KINKS

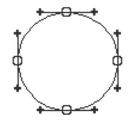

Here is a circle drawn with the
Circle/Oval tool. All of the
points and handles are placed
correctly.

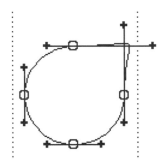

A VERY BAD KINK: one handle
intersects another issuing from
an adjacent drawing point.
Curves should not cross the handles that control them. To be
avoided at all costs.

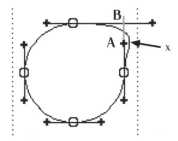

ALSO A VERY BAD KINK: A line drawn from and extending the
handle at 'A' (shown in gray) intersects at 'B' with an adjacent
handle. Notice that the curve crosses the line extending from
'A'. Also much to be avoided. Worse, there is a spot on the
curve, at x, which is orthogonal but which has no drawing
point.

Third, do not create *overlapping paths*—either the same path overlapping itself, or one path overlapping another. This is a fairly frequent error and leads to typefaces that will not print. It can come about as a result of forgetting to use the *Remove overlap* command; by drawing an extremely complex character and losing track of the path; or by using the *Change weight* command to create a heavier face — if you use this command, review each character outline carefully.

Fourth, do not place one drawing point directly on top of an adjacent one. It is impossible for the PostScript interpreter to make sense of this circumstance, and usually results in a crash. This can be a difficult problem to track down as there is no indication that the problem exists in the Fontographer drawing window.

❖ ❖ *14. Avoiding long paths.* Finally, avoid excessively long and/or complex paths. To see why, read the following passage from *Adobe Type 1 Font Format*: "Many versions of the PostScript interpreter have an internal limit of 1500 flattened path elements per character; exceeding this bound results in a limitcheck error. *Each character outline in a given font design must not exceed this limit when rendered.*" (Italics mine) If you absolutely must have characters that exceed this limit, you might consider making a font in the Type 3 format, which is not subject to the specialized restrictions of the type-imaging section of the PostScript interpreter.

❖ ❖ What does that mean? PostScript doesn't really draw curves, as such. Instead, it approximates curved line segments with a large number of invisibly small straight line segments. But PostScript needs a way to judge just how closely the straight line segments are to conform to the shape of the curve, and for this it uses the concept of *flatness* in the form of the PostScript operator *setflat*. The flatness (which is set by setflat) is a measure, in device (or printer) pixels, of the maximum distance between the given curve and the straight line segment that approximates it. In the *PostScript Language Reference Manual* this is called the 'flatness error tolerance', which is a good way of thinking about the concept. The larger the flatness error tolerance, the fewer line segments are required to approximate the curve, and the less accurate will the curve

Avoid overlapping paths

Avoid coincident points

Avoid overly long, complex paths

PostScript

Setflat

1500 flattened
segments
per path

Dealing with
complex
paths

appear. On the other hand, the smaller the flatness error tolerance, the more line segments are required to approximate the curve, which results in a better approximation of the curve.

❖ ❖ It is crucially important to bear in mind that this limitation of 1500 flattened path elements is influenced by two things: (1) the resolution of the printer, and (2) the size (and/or the complexity) of the character(s) being printed. One pixel on an imagesetter might be 1/2540 inch while on a LaserWriter it would be 1/300 inch: The same flatness setting would result in a much larger number of line segments on the Linotronic than on the LaserWriter. Similarly, a 200-point size character will result in a larger number of straight line segments than a 12-point character.

❖ ❖ The bottom line is that complex characters are very likely to run into this limitation, particularly at high resolution on an imagesetter and/or at large sizes. You have four options in this case. 1) You can simplify the character; 2) You can break the character up into parts, place the parts in different character slots and give the slots either no width or kern the parts so that they overlap; 3) Make the character part of a Type 3 font format file; 4) For the adventurous, you can alter the printer's default value by using the setflat operator.

15. *Putting it all together.* Let's start with a simple example: a circle. Using the rules that we enumerated, we place the drawing points (Figure 1.13A). Notice that we are leaving the BCPs visible. Note the fact that the BCPs are connected to their drawing points by lines that are parallel/perpendicular to the x or y axis. Also note that the fit is quite good.

Next, we'll do an ellipse (Figure 1.13B). The same observations hold true, including the fit of the curve.

Now we'll trace the same ellipse, after it has been rotated by 20° (Figure 1.13C). Notice the placement of the drawing points: at the flat spots in the template. Now the fit of the curve is terrible with respect to the template. Notice, however, that the lines that connect the drawing points with their BCPs are no longer orthogonal. To make them orthogonal, we simply make them visible and click on

them with the mouse while holding down the Shift key. When we
have thus adjusted all four sets of BCPs we end up with a virtually
perfect fit after all (Figure 1.14A).

Finally, a more complex figure: a blob (Figure 1.14B). The
purpose of this figure is simply to introduce the following topic.

16. Template stairstepping.   If you magnify the template of
Figure 1.14B, you get Figure 1.14C. This segment of the template is
a hump that is thrust to the left: The approach on the left hand side
is quite steep, while the right hand side slopes more gently. Notice
the flat spots: These are the x-y maxima/minima. Now look at the
stairsteps immediately before and after. The drawing point should
be placed at the n*1.75 pixel, where n is the length of the stairstep
immediately preceding the flat spot.

FIGURE 1.13   SIMPLE APPLICATIONS

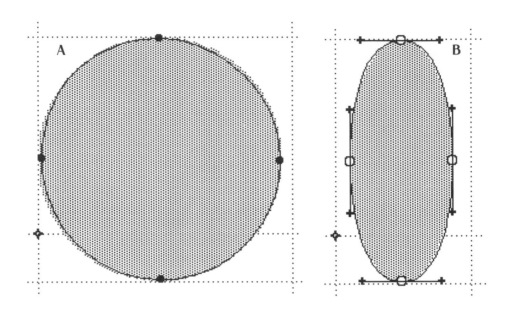

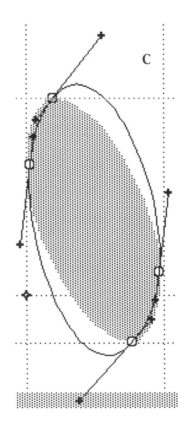

FIGURE 1.14 MORE COMPLEX APPLICATIONS

A

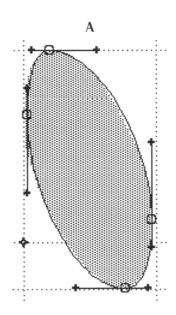

B

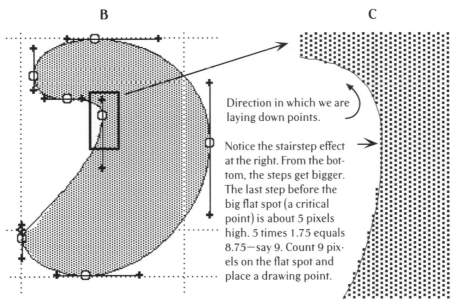

C

Direction in which we are laying down points.

Notice the stairstep effect at the right. From the bottom, the steps get bigger. The last step before the big flat spot (a critical point) is about 5 pixels high. 5 times 1.75 equals 8.75—say 9. Count 9 pixels on the flat spot and place a drawing point.

If math and pixel-counting are not your style, then imagine a curve drawn through the shape: the drawing point will be placed at the deepest point on the curve.

x and y min-
ima and
maxima

17. *The concept of x-y minima/maxima.*   As you move along a curve that you are tracing with drawing points, the curve becomes momentarily parallel to one or another of the axes — the x-axis or the y-axis. It is at those points that you lay down most of the drawing points. Other drawing points are found at discontinuities where the curve shifts suddenly in direction: these points are usually corner points. Look again at Figure 1.14B for an example of this. Figure 1.15 shows a more complex example, showing corner points with handles that are *not* orthogonal.

FIGURE 1.15   ANOTHER COMPLEX SHAPE

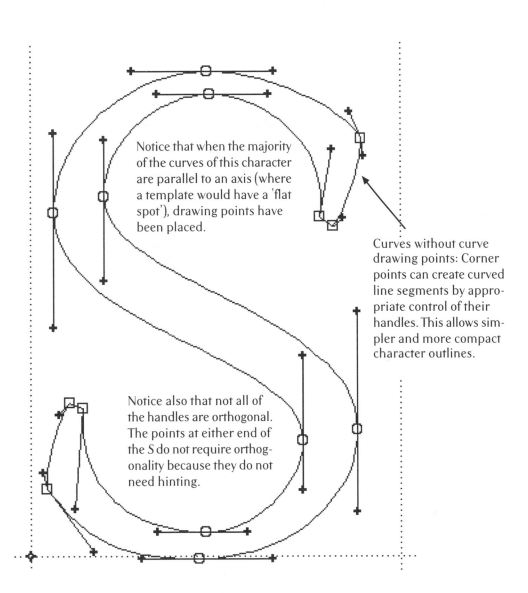

Notice that when the majority of the curves of this character are parallel to an axis (where a template would have a 'flat spot'), drawing points have been placed.

Curves without curve drawing points: Corner points can create curved line segments by appropriate control of their handles. This allows simpler and more compact character outlines.

Notice also that not all of the handles are orthogonal. The points at either end of the S do not require orthogonality because they do not need hinting.

Drawing
process:

1. Place points.

2. Orthogo-
nalize the
handles.

3. Adjust BCPs.

4. Check path
directions.

18. *A working procedure.* The simple demonstrations that we have just carried out lead us to formulate an efficient procedure that can be applied to almost any drawing problem in Fontographer:

Place the drawing points. Using the correct tools, place the drawing points at the appropriate critical points. The drawing points are placed on the outermost layer of template pixels (unless you are compensating for ink squeeze or a flaw in the character). Outermost paths should be drawn in a clockwise direction; after that, successively inner paths should alternate counterclockwise and clockwise.

Orthogonalize the handles. Make the handles and BCPs visible (either by clicking on their drawing points or using Select All in the Edit menu), and, *holding down the Shift key*, click on one of the BCPs of a curve-pair, or on each BCP of a corner-pair. This applies *only* to those sections of curve that are tangent to lines orthogonal — some drawing points will have handles that are not orthogonal. At this point (if you have placed the drawing points correctly) you should see a terrific improvement in the shape of the curve you have drawn.

Adjust the BCPs for fit. You will probably need to make some minor adjustments of the BCPs. Be sure that you maintain orthogonality by holding down the Shift key as you move the BCPs. Again, the object is to make the curve you are drawing conform as closely as possible to the outermost layer of template pixels.

Path directions. Make sure that you have the paths going in the right direction by using the Check path direction command in the Path menu. This can be done when you finish each character, or when you have finished the typeface.

Refer to Figure 1.16 for a valuable insight into checking the quality of your work: This technique uses the drawing elements of the character itself to reveal hidden or potential strengths and weaknesses of the character and/or its rendering. On occasion you will find that you misjudged a particular curve and that you must insert a drawing point between two that you have already laid down. You might also find that you can get two drawing points to do the work of three.

Figure 1.16 Patterns

We spend so much time adjusting drawing points, fiddling with control points and twisting itsy-bitsy bits of curves, that we can fall prey to the error of neglecting to observe the harmonies and rhythms of the whole. Fortunately, Fontographer (and any other PostScript program such as FreeHand or Illustrator) provides a perfect mechanism for avoiding this myopia. The technique itself is simple: just **Select All** so that all the control points (and

their handles) as well as all the drawing points, are visible: now you can observe the control and drawing points in relation to each other to insure that their relationship maintains or reflects the rhythm of the character itself. That sounds just frightfully too artsy, doesn't it? Well, it's really quite practical and a good check to see that all is as it should be. Some examples:

Simple relationships

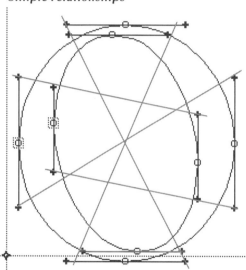

The variations share the relationships

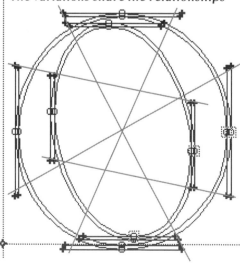

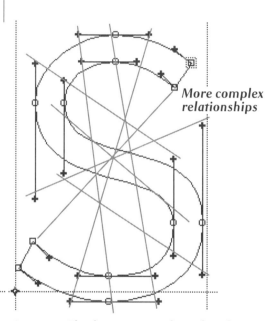

More complex relationships

Important: *The characters were drawn first, then analyzed. That is, design preceded analysis, not the other way around: the letters were not drawn in such a way as merely to prove a point.* The gray lines show the ways in which the control points and handles reveal the underlying rhythm of the outline, the relationship of the parts to the whole. Where this rhythm can be seen to break down, this might indicate some basic—perhaps intended, perhaps no— rhythmic lapse in the basic design; or it might indicate a flaw in rendering the intended shape; or both.

Notice that the lines indicating the relationships do not necessarily attach directly to a given set of control points. They simply serve to indicate the relationships, their nature and direction in a general way. Although good drawing will naturally show this phenomenon, I am grateful to Richard Beatty for formulating the matter so tellingly and for bringing it to my, and now your, attention.

19. Examples.   The following examples are intended to make clear the points we have made so far.

S Figure 1.17A   Notice that the drawing points are where they should be, but that the handles are not orthogonal: This is just as it should be because the curve at those points is not tangent to lines orthogonal.

h Figure 1.17B   Notice again where the curved segment attaches to the principal vertical stroke, that the control handles are not orthogonal. Notice the serifs: These particular serifs are interesting in that only two curve drawing points are needed to form them. Serifs are so important that they have their own chapter: see Chapter 4. Also notice the use of the tangent points to get the curved segment to flow seamlessly into the vertical stroke.

L Figures 1.17C & 1.17D   It can be needlessly time consuming to try to draw letters such as X, x and H as single continuous paths. Draw the individual parts first (Figure 1.17C), use Correct Path Direction from the Path menu, and finally use Remove Overlap from the Special menu (Figure 1.17D). This example was done using the pen tool: The character was drawn in its entirety and then the overlaps were removed by Fontographer. This is enormously handy because it can be tricky and time-consuming to get curved strokes that cross each other to preserve the correct width and direction when the two strokes are drawn as a single path. It is much better to draw the paths independently and to get Fontographer to deal with the overlaps by removing them.

FIGURE 1.17   A VARIETY OF SHAPES

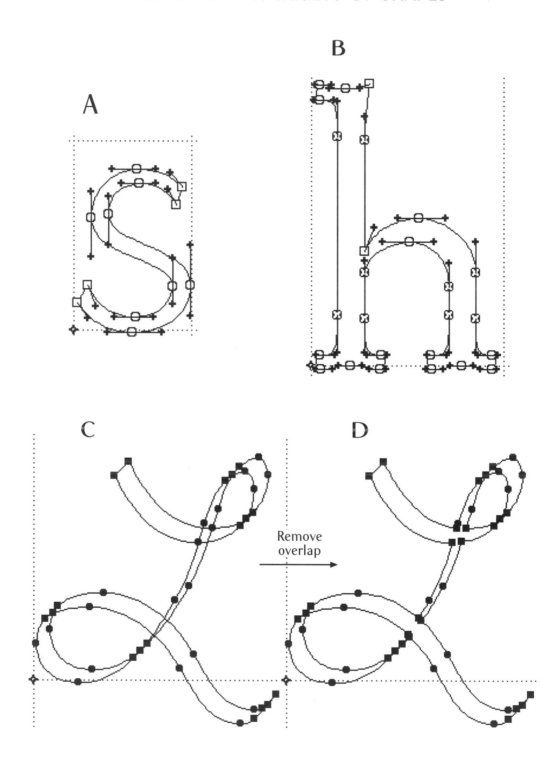

❖ ❖   **20. Remove overlap cautions.**   This very powerful function has been fine-tuned in Fontographer to make the production of type more efficient. Still, it is possible to ask the function to do too much, and in the process confuse it — you might end up with a lot of cleanup as a result. Before you do anything, use Correct Path Directions to make sure that all of the paths in the character have the right directions. Then, remember two important things that will let Remove Overlap work more efficiently. First, a common mistake is to select an entire character and to use Remove Overlap: instead, use the function to remove the overlap of only two paths at a time. Second, if the overlapping paths are very long and/or meet at either very large or very small angles, it might be best to insert points on the paths that are very close to where the paths intersect. (You can use Merge Points to remove the points added temporarily.) This limits the amount of computation that Remove Overlap has to perform, and increases the accuracy of the resulting path.

❖   **21. Drawing TrueType directly.**   TrueType is based on a different spline curve (quadratic splines, to be precise), one that is not nearly as supple as that used in PostScript (i.e., Bézier curves). There are, therefore, more drawing points required to produce a shape that conforms acceptably to the template shape. That would not be a problem, in and of itself, but the handles (in TrueType parlance the "off-curve" points) act together throughout the entire shape: move one control point and that one change ripples through the entire curve. Ugly. It is far better to draw in PostScript, using Bézier curves, and to have a program like Fontographer convert the Bézier paths into quadratic spline paths. The advantages to the TrueType format are that it is built into the Mac operating system and it is faster.

❖   Let me restate the above more succinctly and with a view to making an unexpected point: TrueType is not a design medium. The curves on which TrueType is based — quadratic splines — are feisty creatures that are difficult to control. A change in one on- or off-curve point ripples through the entire shape: not nice, not convenient, not fun. So, the best way to proceed is to design the type in PostScript using pliable and intuitively straightforward Bézier curves, translating PostScript into TrueType as a final step. Translation into TrueType will mean that most characters will have about twice as many drawing points as they originally had, *even when translated back into PostScript.*

TrueType as
typeface
protection

Zero-width
characters
& problem
spacing

Bézier curves

❖ An interesting side-effect of this, however, is that the conversion to TrueType can serve as a kind of copy protection in that the original shapes become so heavily laden with drawing points that they are virtually uneditable, *even in PostScript.* Remember that one of the reasons we use as few points as possible in drawing characters (the 'conciseness' rule) is so that it is easier to edit the shapes. In a sense, therefore, you can protect the shapes of the characters from most kinds of tampering. (See "Problem Solving," however, for a way to get around the problem of a multiplicity of points in TrueType.)

22. Zero-width characters. Some programs (Ready,Set,Go, Microsoft Word and Quark XPress, for example) require certain characters to have a width of 0 em-units, otherwise the spaces between letters will not be correct. The characters are: NULL (#0), TAB (#9) and CR (#13).

To do this in Fontographer, you should place 1 point *only* (any kind) at the origin, and set the width of the character to 0 em-units. Do this for the NULL, and paste copies of that into TAB and CR.

❖ ❖ *23. About Bézier curves.* In 1912, the Russian mathematician Sergei Bernstein published an account of a family of polynomials (later called Bernstein polynomials) that could be used to approximate data that were obtained from phenomena for which descriptive equations were unavailable. You could, for example, plot the growth of an organism over time, and use one of the Bernstein polynomials to give a curve that would fit the data. The equation that gave rise to the curve could also be used to interpolate or extrapolate data not found in the original data sample. In the 1960s, a French engineer working for the automobile firm of Renault, Pierre Bézier, discovered that a certain class of Bernstein polynomials (later called Bézier curves) could be used to describe curves to a computer that could, in turn, be made to control machinery that could shape material accordingly.

❖ ❖ A spline, in construction, is a thin strip of wood or metal that can be shaped to any specified curve. The mathematical equivalent is a curve — and its generating equations — that can conform to, shape itself to virtually any shape we might need. Bézier curves are a variety of spline curves. There are many others, but Bézier curves are supple, easy to shape, and easy to compute. Figure 1.18 shows the geometrical principles on which Bézier curves depend.

FIGURE 1.18   CONSTRUCTING A BÉZIER CURVE

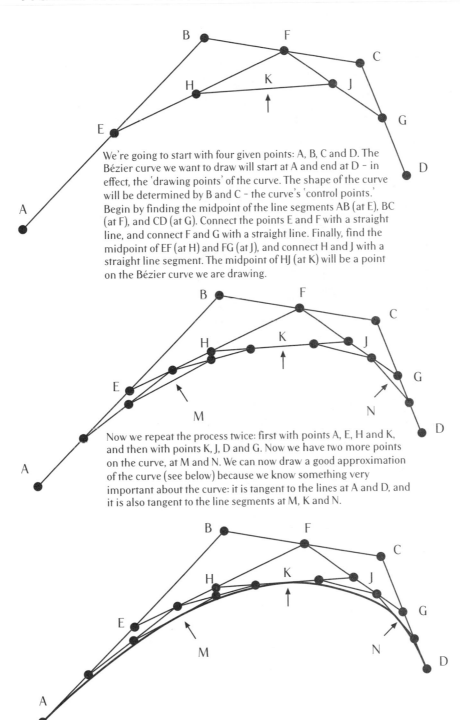

We're going to start with four given points: A, B, C and D. The Bézier curve we want to draw will start at A and end at D – in effect, the 'drawing points' of the curve. The shape of the curve will be determined by B and C – the curve's 'control points.' Begin by finding the midpoint of the line segments AB (at E), BC (at F), and CD (at G). Connect the points E and F with a straight line, and connect F and G with a straight line. Finally, find the midpoint of EF (at H) and FG (at J), and connect H and J with a straight line segment. The midpoint of HJ (at K) will be a point on the Bézier curve we are drawing.

Now we repeat the process twice: first with points A, E, H and K, and then with points K, J, D and G. Now we have two more points on the curve, at M and N. We can now draw a good approximation of the curve (see below) because we know something very important about the curve: it is tangent to the lines at A and D, and it is also tangent to the line segments at M, K and N.

❖ ❖ Mathematically, Bézier curves are relatively straightforward. Bézier curves have a degree that is 1 less than the number of control points used to describe the curve. The Bézier curves that are used in PostScript are cubic Béziers, because they use four control points – in the terminology used here, two drawing points and two control points.

❖ **24. Orphan points and open paths.** Work on complex characters can lead to two problems that need to be cleaned up before generating a typeface. Orphan points are unattached remnants of paths that have been altered or deleted. Open paths are simply paths that were not closed: This frequently happens when the Remove Overlap function is used. Figure 1.19 discusses how to find orphan points.

FIGURE 1.19   FINDING ORPHAN POINTS & OPEN PATHS

To track down orphan points and open paths, go into Preferences and make sure the following options are checked:

⊠ **Hilite the first point in each path**
⊠ **Hilite the ends of unclosed paths**
⊠ **Hilite adjacent points that overlap**

so that the examples at the top of the Preferences window look like this:

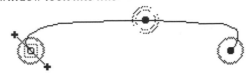

(Selected Point)   (Unselected Point)

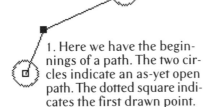

1. Here we have the beginnings of a path. The two circles indicate an as-yet open path. The dotted square indicates the first drawn point.

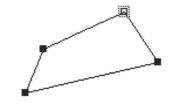

2. The path is now closed.

3. If we perform Cleanup Paths, Fontographer will decide which is the 'first point' by finding, first the right-most, and then the lowest point.

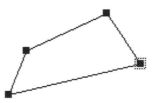

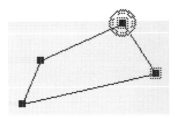

4. And here we see signs of trouble. On the same path there are two "first" points – an impossibility – and one of those is an open path (shown by the circle), sitting on, and so hiding or hidden by, another point. The stray point that we have found in this way is not part of an open path because there is only one point with a circle around it.

❖   The removal of orphan points is a little tricky* and what follows are two useful approaches that you might have to refine for your own use. The situation is this: You have a path, one point of which is sitting on top of — and thereby masking — an orphan point. You could select the path, and send it to the back (in the Arrange submenu of the Element menu); that would place the path *behind* the orphan point, which could then be clicked on, and deleted. Alternatively, you could select the path by double-clicking on it, then Shift-marquee select the entire path. This toggles the path selection *off*, while selecting the orphan point, which can then be deleted.

---

*   I hope that, in the not-too-distant future, the Clean Up Paths dialog box will have check boxes for "Delete Orphan Points" and "Close Open Paths".

Creating a Typeface ❑ 2

E ARE NOW READY to consider the decisions you might want to make when starting any typeface. We are going to look at how to use a template. Then we will consider some of the questions of creating a restoration or renovation of a typeface. Finally we will move on to consider the challenges of creating a typeface from scratch.

Two important points should be made at the outset. First — to put it simply — Fontographer is not just for alphabets. You are probably already aware of fonts such as Hermann Zapf's Dingbats but might not be aware of Richard Beatty's needle-point font — each 'letter' represents a different color of thread; or his breathtaking collection of borders and ornaments in font form; or Judith Sutcliffe's charming Petroglyph Hawaii which is based on stone drawings, or her Insecta sampled in Figure 7.7. Letraset has released a series of 'Design Fonts' in their Fontek series, and more are appearing from other vendors with increasing frequency.

Second, although what follows begins by an examination of the use of TIFF or PICT templates, it is by no means essential to begin your work with templates. By all means use Fontographer to design a typeface from scratch without a single template — see below for a few tips on approaching just such a project. Fontographer is a supple tool and can accommodate just about anything you want to do. The only requirement is that you should enjoy yourself and produce something you like in the process. Still, templates do give the beginning user a useful tool which teaches how best to manipulate drawing points and control points. Getting the Bézier curves to fit an arbitrary shape is good practice.

1. A method for working.   I want to set out a plan for the drawing of a typeface. This is not engraved in stone, but simply a suggestion, which you will want to alter to suit your own needs. The following list also sets out many of the topics that we will be discussing in the coming pages.

i.   ScanningFind, draw or otherwise create an original of the font (or representative letters from the font) that is clean and suitable for scanning. The letters should be about 200-400 scanner pixels in height: e.g., for a 300dpi scanner, the characters should be an inch or somewhat more in height. If you are not using templates — or, rather, if you are using, shall we say, *cerebral* templates — skip to number 5 below.

ii.   Scan the original, making sure that the scan is straight.

iii. Copy the letters from the scanning application (or the drawing program to which you have exported the scan). Be sure that you always use a selection rectangle of the same height to cut the character to the clipboard.

iv.   Paste the scanned character into Fontographer. Adjust the position of what is now your template character with respect to the baseline and left sidebearing. You might also make a preliminary adjustment of the width at this time.

v.   Trace the character manually or automatically. The drawing points will usually be placed on the outermost layer of template pixels. Make sure that the principle handles (for stems and bowls) are orthogonal. If you are not using a template, simply draw the characters as you wish, also checking for orthogonality. In any case, use guides for things like cap height, ascenders, descenders, x-height, overshoot, etc. The outermost path should be drawn *clockwise*, with successively 'inner' paths alternating counterclockwise/clockwise.

vi. Consult the Metrics window fairly frequently to check for uniformity of stem-width and serifs, good curve shapes, and consistent baseline placement. You can also make use of Fontographer 4.x's Preview function, making the drawing points invisible. Make a first approximation of letterspacing.

vii. Try to make your major design decisions early in the process of designing or tracing a typeface. It is easier to change your mind earlier in the process rather than later when you have drawn the entire face.

viii. Fine-tune the letterspacing.*

ix. Create the kerning pairs.*

x. Print an extensive sample.

2. *The shape and construction of letters.* You may well be wondering how to get a handle on how to shape letters. The best place to start is with calligraphy, whose conventions were accepted and transmuted over the centuries into typographic conventions. Get your hands, therefore, on one or more good books on calligraphy, those that contain a lot of good illustrations. Even if you do not feel yourself particularly gifted as a calligrapher, it will do you good to take pen in hand and try to recreate the forms you see. You will need this hand/eye coordination when you design and manipulate type. Who knows: you might find a hidden talent. Your use of the calligraphy tools in Fontographer will also, of course, become more informed.

The second place to look is in PostScript type files themselves. Look upon Fontographer as a teaching tool, in which the lessons of

---

* Fontographer 4.x will help you to arrive at a first approximation.

the masters can be observed, and from which much can be learned. A practical demonstration of this technique is found in Chapter 4, in which several examples of serifs are taken from standard typefaces and examined in detail.

3. *Templates.* Templates are extremely useful in getting a typeface into Fontographer for tracing. Anything you can put onto the Apple clipboard can be pasted in the Background layer of Fontographer, ready for tracing, either by hand or automatically.

The process is simple:

1 Enlarge the original to a convenient size, so that each letter is somewhere between 200 and 400 scanner pixels in height.

2 Scan the enlargements, preferably at 300 dpi or better.

3 Open the TIFF or PICT file that results from the scan, Copy and Paste the letters into Fontographer background layer.

The only problem that might arise is with #3. *You must be careful the area that you select to Copy is always the same size.* Fontographer scales the material pasted into the Background layer: usually to fit between the top and the bottom of the em-square. If you were to Copy/Paste, say, an uppercase X and lowercase x by drawing selection rectangles only just large enough to contain the characters, both *selection rectangles* would be sized to fit between the top and bottom of the em-square: the X and x would be scaled to be the same size. If you did this for each letter, when you finished drawing the outlines you would have to scale each letter individually, a tedious and time-consuming project.

It is much more efficient to draw the *same* selection rectangle around all of the template letters so that they will retain the correct sizes relative to each other when pasted in Fontographer's background layer. Two approaches are possible. You can draw a

rectangle in your illustration program, and drag it over the letters you · Em-square
want to copy, using it as a guide for sizing the template. Or you
can reposition the origin of your ruler and simply determine that all
selection rectangles will be, say, 2 inches by 4 inches, using the ruler
as a guide.

It is possible to bypass the automatic scaling that Fontographer
performs when it pastes a template into the background by holding
down the Option key while pasting. This is *not* recommended,
although it might seem like a good idea at first in that it bypasses
the problem of maintaining a consistent scale between the templates.
The problem is that when you then scale up the outlines you have
drawn, because of a kind of rounding error, the points (drawing or
control) will very likely not be located in the same relationship to
each other that they were previously. This means carefully checking
and editing each character after scaling. Boring.

4. Setting up the typeface.   When you begin work on a new
typeface there are a few decisions that you will have to make. The
first is the size of the em-square. The standard size is 1000 units on
a side: 1000 units wide, 800 units ascent and 200 units descent.
Using a larger em-square will gain you some accuracy in drawing,
but will result (in em-squares over 1600 units) in larger PostScript
files. For optimal efficiency a *TrueType* em-square should be a power
of two: 1024, 2048, 4096 units, etc., and 2048 units is said to be
optimal, according to the Apple TrueType specification. In the dialog
box that comes up when you choose *New...* from the File menu,
you will see a box for "Leading". This is simply extra space (in
em-units) that will be inserted between lines of text. It should be
ignored: Allow typographers to add the space they feel necessary.

Before you begin, you will want to decide on certain guidelines that you will draw in Fontographer's guideline layer. The primary guides you will draw are, among others:

1. The baseline (it is already drawn for you)
2. The x-height
3. The cap height
4. The ascender line
5. The descender line
6. The italic slant

In addition, you will also probably want to indicate the overshoot amounts for the baseline, x-height, cap height and ascenders. There are other guidelines that you might want to include such as serif height and stem width.

An average cap height would be approximately 700. The other quantities will follow as ratios based on the cap height. Also present in the guidline layer should be the following *overshoots*:

1. The baseline overshoot
2. The x-height overshoot
3. The cap height overshoot

The overshoot amounts are typically between 10 and 20 em units for a 1000-unit em-square. A final guideline layer might look like Figure 2.1. The overshoots are necessary for two reasons. First, characters with curves or vertices at their tops and/or bottoms have to overshoot the guideline they would normally reference: if they don't, they look too short and/or seem to sit above the baseline. This is confirmed by much analysis. Peter Karow (1988, p171) reports the following findings:

1. A square or circle appears optically correct when it is 1%±1% taller than it is wide.

2. A circle appears optically as tall as a rectangle when it has a cap and base overhang of 1.5%±0.5% taller than it is wide.

3. A triangle appears optically as wide as a rectangle when it is 5%±1% wider.

4. A sharp apex (A, V, W) appears to be as high as a rectangle only when the apex is 3%±1% longer than the square side.

Second, the hinting mechanism of PostScript — and therefore of Fontographer — allows for maintenance of the overshoot at low resolution so that the character set retains a consistent baseline, x-height, ascender height and cap height.

❖ **5. Hinting.** This important function within the PostScript (and TrueType) environments should be clearly viewed for what it is: an aid to printing at low resolution. Or, to put the matter another way: On a high resolution imagesetter, all faces — PostScript Type 1, Type 3 or TrueType — are created equal.

❖ PostScript fonts in Fontographer are hinted for stem-width and overshoot. A sampling of representative stems is taken and their widths measured. The most representative widths are chosen to be standards: These standard widths replace the widths closest to them in size when printing at low resolution. Fontographer surveys a large number of characters in its effort to establish the 'blue zone', that is, the overshoot regions. If you are planning a typeface, be aware that overshoot is typically in the region of 1% to 2%, and possibly up to 4%.

❖ ❖ You can view, alter or add to Fontographer's conclusions by accessing Hinting Setup... under the Expert submenu. You might, for instance want to add a descender overshoot (not normally needed) by specifying -182,-170 in the Vertical alignment zones box.

❖ What all this means is that the drawing of these characters should be done carefully and that any unintended and superfluous eccentricities of form should be avoided: Fontographer's decisions about the hinting process based on these characters will be propagated throughout the typeface. Control of TrueType hinting is not currently available in Fontographer.

❖   The TrueType hinting mechanism is, potentially, much more complex and subtle and can even extend to the possibility of optical scaling. For the present, one of the forms of hinting available in TrueType but not in PostScript is the hinting of diagonals.

❖   Hinting is not appropriate for every purpose to which Fontographer might be put. While roman typefaces and their italics are generally suited to hinting (indeed, the hinting process was designed with them specifically in mind), artwork (logos for instance) or Arabic script or Chinese characters or Japanese *hiragana* might not be appropriate candidates for hinting.

❖   ***6. Flex.***   A particular sort of hinting is referred to as *flex*. There are two common instances of this phenomenon. First, principal strokes (horizontal or vertical) are frequently drawn so that they have a calligraphic arch (a slight inward bending of the stroke) — Zapf's Optima is an example. Second, some serifs are cupped, having small indentations at their tops or bottoms.

❖   Low to medium resolution printing devices cannot render these characteristics acceptably, so PostScript has a mechanism for ironing them out. To do this, however, the arched curves (or cupped serifs) must conform to the following (see Figure 2.1):

1   The curve must consist of exactly three points;

2   The outer points must be placed identically, either horizontally or vertically. That is, they must have either the same x- or y-coordinate.

3   The middle point (which defines the height, depth or width of the curve) must be 6 em units or less (for a 1000-unit em-square) from the imaginary horizontal or vertical line that connects the outer points.

4   The middle point does *not* have to be exactly halfway between the two outer points.

❖   Flex can be a useful feature for getting good-looking and consistent print from a low-resolution printer. Be aware that it takes longer to print and results in larger PostScript files.

FIGURE 2.1   FLEX

This letter conforms to all of the requirements for the
application of 'flex' hinting.

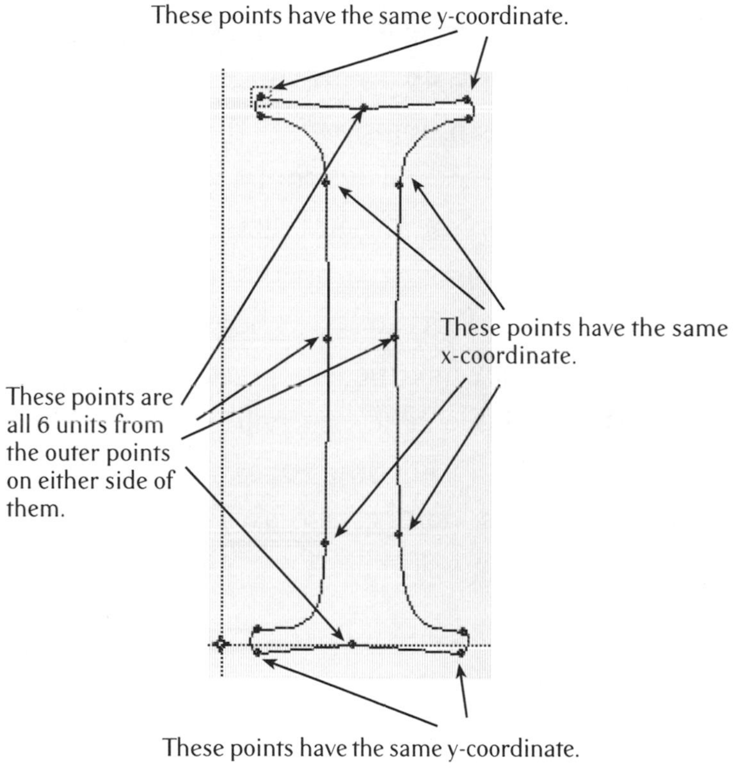

These points have the same y-coordinate.

These points have the same
x-coordinate.

These points are
all 6 units from
the outer points
on either side of
them.

These points have the same y-coordinate.

7. A word about AutoTrace. AutoTrace can be thought of as pre- and post-Fontographer version 4.0. Quite simply, version 4 has an AutoTrace that makes everything else pale into insignificance. AutoTrace seems to work best if the average character is about 300–400 scanner pixels in height. Characters that are about an inch in height should be scanned at 300 dpi, while characters that are 4 or 5 inches in height should be scanned at 72 dpi.

What is new in version 4 is the accuracy and fidelity of the trace. In addition, by means of some cleverness, you can even improve on the trace. Once you have autotraced the character you can apply Clean Up Paths to the resulting trace. For example, use a 'tight' autotrace on the template image — remember that Clean Up Paths works best when it has lots of information about the shapes. Then use Clean Up Paths (simplification set to 1–3) for virtually perfect outlines, and fully Type 1 conforming, at that.

I find that even after all of these operations there are often too many points on the outline. This can be further fixed by the judicious use of Merge points. Pick any intermediary point that looks not to be essential to the shape, and Merge it. You will often find that the fit of the curve is the same, and sometimes better. Also remember that the goal is to have the fewest number of drawing points while at the same time creating the best possible fit of the outline to the template.

8. Historical models. When you wish to create an exact reproduction of a type face, you really have very few options open. You will create a template, and draw the outlines exactly as you find them. Again, problems arise only when you attempt to print such a typeface on a low-resolution printer, particularly without hinting: The stems and curves will not in every case be the same as the original, particularly at small sizes. Bear in mind, too, the size the original designer intended — that is, was it designed to be a 12-point text type or 60-point display type? Another factor is the effect of the printing process on the historical sample from which you are making your template: to what extent does ink squeeze and paper absorbancy shape the template, and should you 1) compensate for it or 2) reproduce it? See Chapter 7.

In any event, a common first step is to find clean printed samples and to have those samples photographed and enlarged. This will help in discovering the extent to which ink-squeeze is a part — necessary or not — of the typeface. It also allows you to trace the outline of the face either with a pencil (strongly encouraged) as a first step, or with the mouse *via* the use of templates. You could scan the photographs and take the scans into Photoshop to be cleaned up, and then into Fontographer. This also allows you to examine multiple examples of the same letter, which will indicate the range of possibilities for drawing the final character.

9. Typefaces based loosely on historical models.   This is one step removed from the exact recreation of a given model. In this case you can begin by observing the salient points of the typeface: the shape of the serifs; the ratio of thick-to-thin strokes; cap-, ascender- and x-height and descender depth; the angle of stress; etc. Then with these raw materials you proceed as if you were drawing a typeface from scratch (*see next*). You will, of course continually check the original to see that you are remaining true to it within the limits that you have set for yourself. See Chapter 7.

10. Designing a typeface from scratch.   Even if you are not a type designer, it is a richly educational experience to design your own typeface. This section is not intended as a course in typographic aesthetics, but as a suggestion for a method of approaching the techniques and tools of typographic design. Bear in mind, though, that you are embarking on the design of at least 52 little works of

Creating a
typeface:
a suggested
approach

Numerals &
upper-
case, then
lowercase

Em-square size

Cap height

art that demand a lot of close attention to detail. They can be very recalcitrant or slippery. If you have a plan of action in mind before you begin, you will find the design process to be more efficient and pleasant than it might otherwise be.

The most important observation I can make at this point is this: Do not simply begin at *A* and slog your way through to *Z* by brute force. Take the time to decide what the finished product should look like, make your basic design decisions accordingly, and then proceed to draw the characters themselves.

To start with, you will want to begin by drawing the upper case, numerals and punctuation: This will give you a useful titling face, even if you decide not to provide an accompanying lower case. You must begin by making some decisions about the general aspect of your prospective typeface. The first decisions you must make are: 1) the size of the em-square and 2) the cap height.

11. The size of the em-square.   The size of the em-square will determine the accuracy with which you can carry out the drawing of the characters: The larger the em-square, the more accurately you can place the drawing points. The 1000-unit em-square is fairly standard. If you intend, at the outset, to create TrueType, the em-square should be some power of 2: 1024, 2048, 4096, etc. This speeds up the rasterizing process somewhat. The cap height will be some proportion of the em-square. Remember that the em-square includes both ascenders and descenders. In other words, all of the letters must be drawn within the em-square. The width of a letter should be drawn, as a rule, within 1.5 to 2 times the em-square.

12. Cap height.   A good starting place is approximately 600-650 em units in a 1000-unit em-square font. This provides for flexibility in case you decide to make the ascenders taller than the caps — very often the case.

Having made these basic decisions, you now proceed to the characters themselves. Once again, you should take the time to make some preliminary plans about the shape of the characters. The three broad areas of concern are: (1) the ratio of size of the thick strokes to the size of the thin strokes (think of the letter *V* for instance); (2) the size and shape of the serifs; (3) the way in which the main strokes connect to the serifs, i.e., the structure of the brackets; (4) Ascender and descender dimensions.

Thin/thick
strokes

Serifs

Brackets

Ascenders,
descenders

Ratio of thick
to thin

Stress

13. *Thick/thin.* This is an important decision, because upon it depends a number of other design elements. It will also be the principal determinant for typographic 'color' which is the overall impression that type gives. Bear in mind the following: Little distinction between thick and thin will give rise to a monotone (and possibly monotonous) letter, while extreme contrast will give rise to a fragile or brittle design. Both extremes tend to tire the eye when used in body text.

14. *Stress.* In the architecture of letters, stress is the degree to which the thick and thins of a character are (or are not) parallel/perpendicular to the prevailing baseline. Pictures are worth thousands of words, so let's look at examples. Figure 2.2A shows a modern-style character *o* in which the stress is vertical. Figure 2.2B shows an old-style character in which the thicks and thins lie at an angle to the baseline (about 15°). In calligraphy, this effect is obtained by holding the pen at an angle to the baseline. The effect can be difficult to reproduce in Fontographer (except, of course, for the calligraphic tools), but the following technique will give you a first approximation to the desired shape. Begin with the modern character in Figure 2.2A, but rotate the inner oval counterclockwise 12° (Figure 2.2B). You will notice that the control handles of the inner shape are not orthogonal. The next step is to cut the inner shape to the Clipboard, and paste it into the background layer (Figure 2.2C). You then use that as a template to re-draw the inner shape according to the orthogonal principles we have already discussed (Figure 2.2D). In point of fact, stress, from the standpoint of calligraphy, is rather more complex than I have indicated thus far. A good calligrapher will vary the angle of the pen according to the effect desired. It is also possible to increase the pressure on the pen-nib and thus widen the stroke subtly — another aspect of stress. Figures 2.3 and 2.4 have yet more information on stress and its formation. We will have more to say about these subjects in Chapter 5.

FIGURE 2.2   STRESS

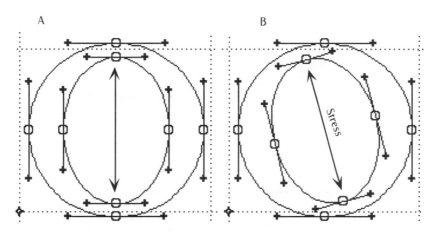

A

B

Modern-style characters are characterized by vertical stress: the thicks and thins of a character are parallel to the drawing axes.

Oldstyle characters show an angled stress. Begin by taking the inner oval of the modern character at the left and rotate it by, say, 15°. Notice that the handles are not parallel to the axes: very bad.

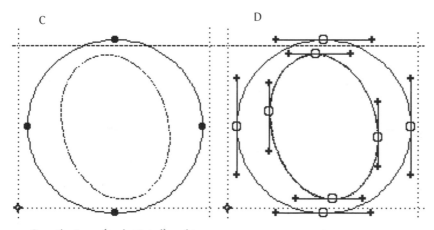

C

D

Copy the inner (and rotated) oval to the Background layer and paste it.

Now, using the rotated oval in the Background layer, trace the new oval in conformance to the principles of good PostScript drawing. Orthogonalize the handles (make them parallel to the axes), adjust them for fit, and apply the Correct path direction command in the Path menu. Done. *Note* – You could also apply Clean Up Paths... to the rotated oval.

Figure 2.3 Circles, Ellipses & Stress

In calligraphy, when a pen is held at some angle to the width of the paper (usually 45° or so) the thinnest and thickest parts of a stroke are at an angle to the vertical or horizontal axes. The letter *O* is a good example: if the pen is held parallel to the width of the paper, we get a character like the one at *B* below, where the thicks and thins are coincident with the x and y axes; if we hold the pen at an angle we get a character like that of *H*, where the thicks and thins are somewhat displaced from the horizontal and vertical. This is a characteristic of many oldstyle and transitional typefaces. The angle that the displaced thicks and thins make with the horizontal or vertical axes is called the 'stress angle.' The method for recreating this effect in Fontographer is simple and interesting, but not obvious.

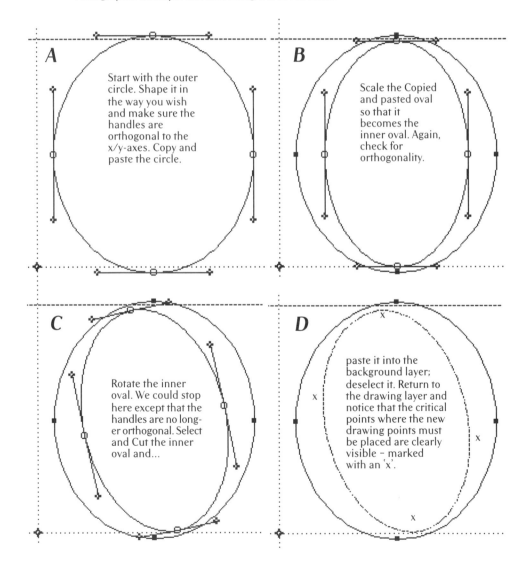

A Start with the outer circle. Shape it in the way you wish and make sure the handles are orthogonal to the x/y-axes. Copy and paste the circle.

B Scale the Copied and pasted oval so that it becomes the inner oval. Again, check for orthogonality.

C Rotate the inner oval. We could stop here except that the handles are no longer orthogonal. Select and Cut the inner oval and...

D paste it into the background layer; deselect it. Return to the drawing layer and notice that the critical points where the new drawing points must be placed are clearly visible – marked with an 'x'.

Figure 2.4   More Circles, Ellipses & Stress

Figure 'H' is interesting on a number of counts, and amply repays close inspection. Notice that the handles of the inner oval are shorter than those for the outer: naturally, because the inner oval is smaller than the outer. The inner oval has been rotated counterclockwise, but the left and right critical points seem to be rotated clockwise. Also notice that the top-most and bottom-most drawing points of the inner oval are *not* coincident with the stress-angle (indicated by the arrow), but seem rotated slightly counterclockwise (like the oval itself). A useful technique can be inferred: when drawing a rotated object, draw it first unrotated; then rotate it and trace the rotated version. Also notice the symmetrical pattern of the handles and control-points: not suprising, but interesting, and a useful visual confirmation of the process.

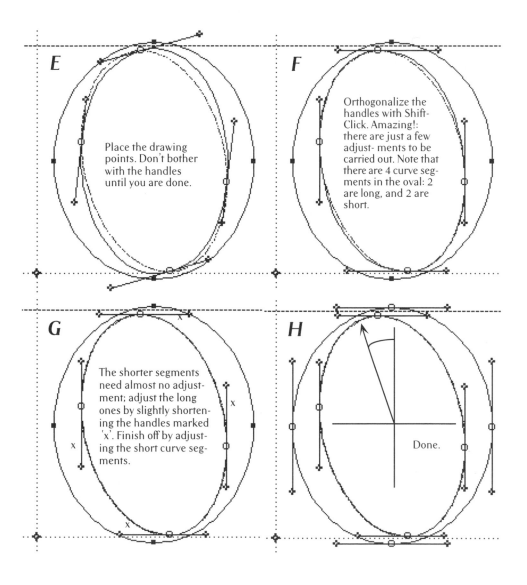

E Place the drawing points. Don't bother with the handles until you are done.

F Orthogonalize the handles with Shift-Click. Amazing!: there are just a few adjust- ments to be carried out. Note that there are 4 curve seg- ments in the oval: 2 are long, and 2 are short.

G The shorter segments need almost no adjust- ment; adjust the long ones by slightly shorten- ing the handles marked 'x'. Finish off by adjust- ing the short curve seg- ments.

H Done.

15. *Size/shape of serifs.* Serifs (if you are creating a serif typeface) are major contributors to the "style" of a typeface. They must be nicely judged: not too large so that they look like big feet in army boots, and not so small that the letter looks like it might tip over. The height of a serif is rather less than the width of a thin stroke (discussed above). The ends of the serif can be rounded, square or chiseled. A good starting point for the thickness of a serif is about the size of a thin principal stroke. The origin of the serif has been much discussed. It seems to have developed from the strokes necessary to finish off an engraved or pen-drawn stroke.

The serif is the distinguishing characteristic of a serif typeface. It must be very nicely judged: neither too heavy, too large, nor too small; functional (guiding the reader's eye effortlessly across the horizontal line of text) yet not obtrusive.

Here is a summary of the basic proportions of the strokes used in constructing a roman alphabet. The following table gives stroke dimensions as a percentage of cap height:

Uppercase thick stroke	13–15
Uppercase thin stroke	6–8
Lowercase thick stroke	6–8
x-height	40–70
Serif width, UC	40
Serif width, lc	35–37
Serif height	2–4

Logically, the height of the serif ought to fall somewhere between the width of the thick and thin principal strokes, and so is variable from face to face. The width of the serif, as noted above, is some 35%–40% of the cap height, and should not interfere with the fit of the letters.

16. *Joining strokes to serifs: brackets.* There are three possibil- Brackets ities: (1) There can be no brackets (examples: Serifa and Rockwell, Figure 2.5, #1); (2) the brackets join smoothly with both the principal strokes and the serifs (Figure 2.5,#2); (3) occasionally, the join between the bracket and the serif shows as a corner rather than as a smooth join: this gives a calligraphic or incised look to the faces (Figure 2.5, #3). See Chapter 4 which is devoted entirely to the serif.

FIGURE 2.5   SERIFS & THEIR BRACKETS

Brackets are the swellings at the ends of stems that serve to attach the serif to the stem. They serve the same function visually in a typeface that a bracket does in holding up up a shelf on a wall: a strengthening attachment that gives support and stability.

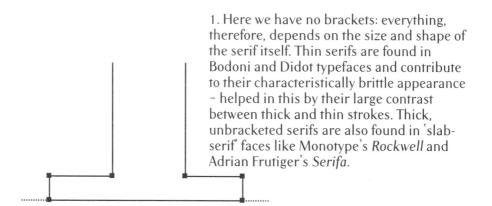

1. Here we have no brackets: everything, therefore, depends on the size and shape of the serif itself. Thin serifs are found in Bodoni and Didot typefaces and contribute to their characteristically brittle appearance – helped in this by their large contrast between thick and thin strokes. Thick, unbracketed serifs are also found in 'slab-serif' faces like Monotype's *Rockwell* and Adrian Frutiger's *Serifa*.

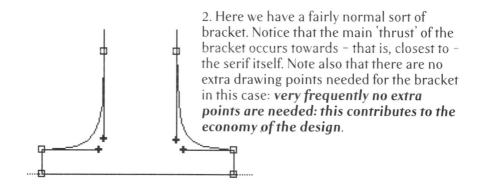

2. Here we have a fairly normal sort of bracket. Notice that the main 'thrust' of the bracket occurs towards – that is, closest to – the serif itself. Note also that there are no extra drawing points needed for the bracket in this case: ***very frequently no extra points are needed: this contributes to the economy of the design***.

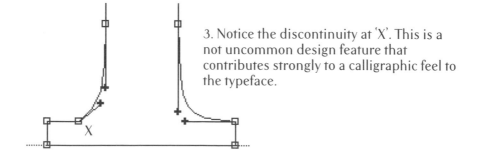

3. Notice the discontinuity at 'X'. This is a not uncommon design feature that contributes strongly to a calligraphic feel to the typeface.

17. _The size and shape of the serif._ Serifs come in many Serifs, cupping
different kinds: Look at the section that deals with serifs to see a Ascenders,
    descenders
small selection of them. You might want to keep a collection of serif x-height
shapes to which you can refer when you are putting together a new
typeface.

Another issue here is the cupping of serifs. This is part of
the larger and more general issue of _flex_ in Type 1 fonts, and may
apply either to horizontal or vertical strokes. The purpose of flex is to
simplify a slightly curved stroke so that, at low size and resolution,
the stroke is made straight, which in turn makes it look cleaner. The
qualifications for flex were outlined earlier. When you form the cup,
the middle of the cup—the highest point for a baseline serif, the
lowest point for a cap height or ascender height serif—should be
on the baseline or at the cap height or ascender height, respectively.
Cupping is a relatively common design feature, and the care needed
to incorporate that design element (and invoke flex) leads me to
suggest that you should start a collection of carefully drawn serifs.

18. _Ascender and descender dimensions._ Notice that Fontographer refers to ascender and descender in the Font Characteristics
dialog box. For a 1000-unit em-square (800 units ascender, 200
units descender) this might seem to imply that the ascenders should
be 800 units in height: they usually are not. You should leave approximately 150 to 200 units of ascender available for diacritical marks.
Descenders, however, are frequently drawn to the full descender
dimension.

19. _x-height._ This important dimension exerts a crucial influence
on the 'color' of the type. In addition, a large x-height often requires
extra Leading. A relatively large x-height assists in the legibility
of a typeface. Typefaces intended for high legibility invariably have
large x-heights, for example newspaper types such as Ionic, Imperial,

Summary of
shape info

Design pro-
cess: one
possible
method

Corona, and even Times. When reading, the eye skims along the tops of lines looking for patterns of shapes it recognizes as words; notice that the tops of letters have more varied and distinctive forms than their bottoms. A generous x-height, therefore, allows the letters without ascenders to participate more actively in the process of reading. Too great an x-height lends a kind of blandness to the look of a typeface, and can actually be distracting. The critical issue is not so much the ratio of the x-height to the em-square, but rather the ratio of the x-height to the cap height (typically 50% to 80%).

20. A summary of the numbers.   The following table summarizes the essential information that we have discussed thus far. The numbers in the table are suggestions only, and not imperatives.

Stroke	Size for 1000-unit em-square
Uppercase thick stroke	100
Uppercase thin stroke	45
Serif	20
Lowercase thick stroke	85
Cap height	670
x-height	300–500

21. The design process.   We now embark on the process of actually drawing the letters. We begin by drawing a few critical characters whose strokes and structure recur in other characters. When we are satisfied with the look of these initial characters, we use them as the basis for drawing other characters. By using the basic structure of certain characters in the formation of new ones, we ensure uniformity of design. We also reduce considerably the amount of time and effort needed to draw the typeface.

You might also begin by drawing a portion of the alphabet and using a sample word containing the letters you've drawn to judge the effect of your work. An article by Allan Haley in *U&lc* (see Bibliography) says that many type designers use the word "Hamburgerfonts" (I have also seen 'Hamburgerfontsiv') for this purpose. Set the word as 'Hamburgerfonts,' 'HAMBURGERFONTS,' and 'hamburgerfonts.' This approach would probably catch mistakes and bad design judgments before they adversely affected the entire typeface. Use this technique both for the drawing of new typefaces and the revival of old ones. The use of 'Hamburgerfonts' is one of the steps in submitting a typeface to the International Typeface Corporation (see Chapter 8).

Hamburgerfonts

ITC submissions: see Chapter 8.

22. A stroke and serif 'bank'. When you have drawn a particularly good serif, or stem or bowl or tail or whatever, make a copy of it and store it away. Store it in the first 32 characters of the typeface (0–31), for use within the typeface. Make a general collection of nothing but serifs, stems, bowls, etc., in a separate file. This saves considerable amounts of time both when you are drawing a particular typeface, and when you are starting on the design of a typeface.

23. A sample procedure. The following annotated table sets forth a step-by-step procedure for the uppercase font. Included in the table is a summary of the matters we have discussed thus far. It is merely a suggestion. It is largely aimed at the creation of a mainstream serif typeface, but the principles used here could form the basis for drawing virtually any kind of face. The basic principle to remember is this: Identify and create the basic drawing units you will need (e.g., stems, serifs, ascenders, descenders, bowls and counters, etc.) and use those to build up the resulting typeface. This ensures consistency and an efficient use of your time.

Letters Comments

I This letter will form the basis of any number of other characters (e.g., *E, F, L, H,* etc.). This is an excellent opportunity to establish the balance between the size/shape of the serifs and the principle thick vertical stroke. The *I* itself is frequently slightly thicker than similar strokes found in other letters.

V Uses both thick and thin strokes; evaluate the serif structure. The proper formation of these stems is critical: They must have the appearance of structures that can bear weight. Too thick and they are merely clumsy, too thin and they are brittle and weak. Also, the angle should not be too small as it will tend to fill up with toner, ink, etc. Bear in mind, too, that slanted strokes are usually a little wider than their unslanted counterparts so as to maintain optical uniformity. Typical size of the angle lies somewhere between 38° and 55°.

O This will determine the shape of characters such as Q, C, and G.

!!! Notice that *O* always thins at the top and bottom of the letter, even for a sans-serif which may look as if the stroke does not vary.

P Begin with *I*, opening up the right-hand side of the top serif. Continue the opening into a bowl. See above at *V* for comments about stems. The bowl of the *P* is usually (though not always) larger than the bowl of the *R* and *B*. In many examples the bowl does not close completely. The angle that the bottom of the bowl makes with the stem also varies with height.

!!!   *Do not go beyond this point until you are satisfied with every aspect of the design of these first four letters.*

W   Use two *V*s. For more, see *M* below.

D   Use *I* for the vertical, and merge the right-hand half of the *O* with it.

J   Use *I* and reshape the bottom accordingly.

H   Two *I*s with a crossbar, the placement of which is crucial because it will determine the middle strokes of letters like *B* and *E*. Judge the width carefully; compare it with the *O*. The width is generally on the order of 65% to 85% of the height (the width measured as the horizontal distance between the centers of the two vertical strokes), but this is a matter of taste, so judge for yourself.

K   Use *I* for the vertical. The short slanted strokes can be taken from *V* and *A*; note that they meet approximately where the crossbar of the *H* is and have about the same width. This means that they will be more inclined than the strokes from their parent letters. Note, too, that the arms are often at about a 90° angle to each other.

U   Place two *I*s as for *H* and alter the bottom of each to create *U*.

L E F   Using *I*, attach the appropriate horizontal strokes. The middle strokes often — but not always — occur where you put the crossbar on the *H*.

B Use the *P* as the basis for this letter, but see comments at *P* above.

Q This one is easy: just add the appropriate tail to the *O*.

C G First fashion the *C* using *O* as the basis; use the resulting *C* to make the *G*, possibly using the upper part of the *I* for the vertical stroke.

A Rotate the *V* and attach a crossbar. Note that this does *not* have to be in the same place that the crossbar for the *H* was placed; indeed, it is usually lower so that the upper space will not look too small in relation to the bottom space.

T Use the *I* as a basis, and draw the crossbeam at the top.

M Start with a *V*, rotate it 180°, duplicate it; the right stroke of the left *V* will be joined with the left stroke of the right *V*. *M* is usually one of the two widest letters — the other is *W*, which is usually the widest. Observe that *M* and *W* are not merely upside-down versions of each other. The two outer apex angles of the *M* are smaller than the middle angle, whereas the angles between the strokes of the *W* tend to be more nearly equal, which is why the *W* is often wider than the *M*.

N Start with a *V*, rotate it 180°, make the left-hand (thin) stroke vertical and move the bottom of the right-hand stroke (thick) so that the character will be about as wide as the *H*. Duplicate the thin stroke, rotate the duplicate (180 degrees) and merge the thin end with the thick stroke. It may be necessary to thicken the diagonal stroke slightly.

R Take the *P* and add a tail, but see comments at *P* above.

X An excellent approach was suggested by Richard Beatty: Copy the serifs of the *V* and once in place paste again and rotate 180°; now connect the top left and the bottom-right serifs; connect the other serifs; remove overlap. Voilà. You might want to move the top serifs closer together and/or the bottom serifs further apart: the intersection of the two diagonals is usually slightly above the mathematical center of the character.

Y Merge a *V* with an *I* (from which the top serif has been removed). This will mean scaling the *V* or repositioning the base: in either case, be sure to check the width of the diagonal strokes. Alternatively, take the top of the *X* and merge it with an *I*.

Z Use a thick stroke (from *V*); copy the bottom stroke of the *L* and the top stroke of the *E* (reflecting it across the vertical axis); merge the two horizontal strokes with the diagonal (thick) stroke. The letter will be about the width of an *H*.

S Possibly the most difficult letter to form, particularly as there are no patterns to follow in the preparatory work you have done. Notice that the optical center of the letter is higher than the geometric center, making the upper part look smaller than the bottom.

John Woodcock groups the uppercase in an interesting way:

Round Circular	Rectangular Diagonal	Half-Width
O	H	B
Q	U	P
C	N	R
G	T	S
D	Z	E
		F
		L

Triangular	Multiple Shapes	Intermediate Widths	Thin
A	M	K	I
V	W	Y	J
X			

In a similar way, it is possible to approach the creation of a lowercase alphabet. The following "genealogy" of letters indicates the process. Be careful that the counters are not too small or they will be finicky to reproduce (i.e., they will fill up with toner or ink): Pay particular attention to the *e* and *a*. Notice that the entire lowercase is based upon four letters — o, h, p and v (notice that the uppercase is based on the same four letters):

o   h   p   v

c   n l   b q d   y w

e   u m r i f   g a   x z

            j t   s   k

John Woodcock groups the lowercase in an interesting way:

Round	Note 1	Note 2	Triangular
o	d	a	v
c	b	h	x
e	p	u	y
	q		z

Medium Wide	Compound	Note 3
f	m	g
t	w	
k		
s		
r		
i		
j		
l		

Note 1   These letters are closely related by their shape and may be compared with the uppercase *D*.

Note 2   These letters have a circular part, but are slightly narrower than the *o*.

Note 3   The lowercase *g* is a difficult letter to judge. The upper bowl sits above the baseline, and the lower bowl sits below; for reasons of balance, the upper bowl is smaller than the lower and smaller than the lowercase *o*; at the very least, the lower counter is wider than the upper bowl. The upper shape might be circular, but if the bottom is circular as well, it will probably be too big: that is why the lower counter is almost always oval in shape.

24. An interesting check.   When you have completed drawing and spacing your typeface, try viewing it in reverse, i.e., white on black:

hamburgerfonts

hamburgerfonts

 This is an excellent way of checking consistency of stroke weight. Even small imbalances can be easily spotted and corrected. Try turning the type sample upside down so as to unhook the letters from their linguistic significance.

25. Hyphens and dashes.   As a rule, hyphens and dashes are placed at about half the x-height above the baseline. Sometimes dashes are placed slightly higher, say, two-thirds to three-quarters of the x-height above the baseline. Hyphens are occasionally angled upward slightly, but their center is usually at half the x-height above the baseline. The width of the hyphen is approximately that of the lowercase *i* (or slightly less) so that it will disturb as little as possible the right margin when hyphenating a word at the end of a line in justified text. The en-dash is about twice as long as the hyphen — maybe a tad more; and the em-dash is about a third longer than the en-dash. Some typographers prefer the ¾-em-dash, set with a thin space on either side, to the em-dash. The thickness of the hyphen and dashes lies somewhere between the prevailing thick stroke and thin stroke. They should never be so heavy as to call attention to themselves.

26. Fonts for borders.   Let's turn our attention to something quite different, but still very typographic: the fabrication and use of typefaces for borders. There is nothing particularly difficult or demanding about this, as long as you have certain objectives very clearly in mind at the outset. The 'characters' of a border font have one important characteristic: They usually connect seamlessly with the elements around them. This means that they must extend precisely to the boundaries of their em-squares. Likewise, this implies that the software that uses them to make borders must be able to set lines of type 'solid', that is, with no extra space between lines.

27. The em-square for border characters.   The most convenient placement of the character is such that the em-square is entirely above the baseline, i.e., there is no descent. A suitable dimension for such an em-square would be 1000-by-1000 units.

28. Making the parts connect.   Particularly in the case of complex interconnected parts of complex border elements, everything has to fit together perfectly. The best way to ensure this is to place guides in the Guide Layer that will control the uniform placement of design elements from character to character.

29. BorderMaker from Monotype.   Monotype's BorderMaker program automates the creation of borders. For the program to work properly, the characters must be named correctly. Each character name has three parts:

BorderpartidentFrameidentPartident

where Borderpartident identifies which type of border part the character is:

corner
straight
flower
space

A straight element connects corner elements, while a flower is a single independent element that does not necessarily have a part in a frame. The Frameident element identifies which frame to which the piece belongs. The Monotype frames are often numbered: Remember that a PostScript name can have numbers. The Partident element refers to the specific place in the frame that the character occupies, and is indicated by:

BL   Bottom left corner
TL   Top left corner
TR   Top right corner
BR   Bottom right corner
T   Top
TL   Top left
TR   Top right
B   Bottom
BL   Bottom left
BR   Bottom right
L   Left
LT   Left top
LB   Left bottom
R   Right
RT   Right top
RB   Right bottom

A complete frame would then look like this:

TL TL T TR TR
LT   RT
 L   R
LB   RB
BL BL B BR BR

The distinction between, for example, the first two elements of the top row, both called TL, is that the name of the first is 'cornerBlablaTL' while the next element is named 'straightBlablaTL.' Permissable names might be:

straightdwigginsR	A straight from Dwiggins for the right side
corner212TL	A corner piece from 212 for the top left
flowerFourier	A flower called Fourier

Character names in Fontographer are assigned in the Selection Info (Command-I) dialog box. Simply enter the appropriate name into the box labelled 'Character name.' Be sure to choose convenient locations for the border elements; they should be assigned to keys that have approximately the same relation to each other as the border elements have to each other.

Figure 2.6 shows some examples of borders done in Adobe Illustrator, and offers some advice on how to proceed.

Figure 2.6   On Borders

Monotype's BorderMaker is a tremendous convenience in that it automates the creation of borders. Any piece of layout or drawing software which allows sufficient control of font size and leading can be used to create borders. In this case I used Adobe Illustrator with Richard Beatty's Borders M set.

Because you want the characters to fit together perfectly, you will have to tell your drawing or layout software how to accomplish this. Horizontal fit must be exact: All automatic letterspacing should be turned off. Lines must fit snugly together, that is, set solid: In some cases this means specifying no leading, or (in Illustrator, for example) specifying that the leading is the same as the type size.

I purposely chose simple borders for this example (using no more than four characters) to show just how rich an effect is possible with a minimum of raw materials. This is yet another form of typographic solitaire (see Figure 7.4), and can provide endless hours of entertainment. Bruce Rogers was an enthusiastic and expert practitioner of this art; see Figure 7.6.

N ENORMOUS AMOUNT of study has been devoted to this topic. The main thrust of the research has been aimed at finding algorithms that will aid both computers and human beings to arrive at good letterspacing relatively automatically. To this end, application has been made to the physical sciences to gain insights into the shape and construction of letterforms, and how this might influence letterspacing.

Many of the newer letterspacing models are based on what are perceived to be similar physical — electrostatic, inertial, mechanical, optical — phenomena. This allows the math that governs those phenomena to be applied to letterspacing, in turn allowing the process of letterspacing to be automated. For example, some models are based on the premise that a letterform might be spun around its vertical axis. The various moments would be a true indication of the real axis of the letterform. Some models are based on the assumption that letterforms might represent shapes that are electrostatically charged and either attract or repel other similarly charged letterforms. Still other approaches examine letterforms as optical entities and subject them to interference gratings or filtering to ascertain where the greatest effective weight of the character lies.

All this reminds me of a remark I heard from Sherman Lee (formerly curator of the East Asian Collection at the Cleveland Museum of Art). He was talking about appropriate and inappropriate design, and cited an example of the latter by postulating a very stylish-looking eggbeater that was aerodynamically designed to fly through the air at 500 miles per hour. The problem is, he pointed out, that eggbeaters don't fly through the air, much less at 500mph. Letterforms are neither spun, nor electrostatically charged, nor again are they individual entities that react individually with light and dark. Their appropriate spacing is a matter of perception in the context in which they have their application, that is, on the printed page.

The principles on which letterspacing is based are relatively simple to state, even if they are challenging to apply.

1. Interior spaces are helpful in establishing the overall spacing of a typeface.
2. Exterior spaces are used to judge the spacing between two or more specific letterforms.
3. Principal shapes (such as stems) are used to judge letterspacing; serifs, when present, are used to *confirm* good letterspacing.
4. Spacing is both typeface-dependent and size-dependent.
5. The mathematical center of a letterform will rarely coincide with the optical center.

Most approaches to letterspacing begin by establishing the best spacing for the letters that have the most important interior spaces, *O* and *H* for example, and confirm this with a simple shape such as *I. O* and *H* (or *I*) are also interesting in that they establish, respectively, the smallest and largest sidebearings. It usually takes at least two passes to "get it right" with adjustments being made for difficult shapes — such as *S* and *L* — and for the size at which the type is to be used.

The result, in a way, ought to be analogous to the effect produced by a well-typeset page of text: You ought to be able to look at a page of text at arm's length — turn the page upside-down, possibly blurring your vision a little — and see a uniform area of gray where the text is. Likewise, you ought to be able to look at a string of correctly spaced letters and see a relatively uniform amount of black throughout the string of letters. In either case, gaps or holes are indicative of problems that should be fixed. Letterspacing is used to establish the overall spacing between letters. Individual problems are fixed with pair kerning, bearing in mind that optimal letterspacing minimizes pair kerning.

In the present context, because it is a very important aspect of a typeface design, you should establish the proper letterspacing for a typeface with your own hands and eyes. If, on the other hand, you must use automatic or algorithmic procedures for letterspacing, you should not accept the results uncritically, but be prepared to adjust the results for the best effect.

1. *Letterspacing: techniques.* There are no formulas here. The eye is the arbiter of the best spacing between letters. It is very important to remember that the object of good letterspacing — and kerning, for that matter — is not merely to see how closely letters can be placed together, but how rhythmically and gracefully they can be placed together. With experience, you will learn to recognize the cramped illegibility of letters placed too close together, and the disconnected illegibility of letters spaced too far apart.

There are two aspects of good letter fit. First, the letters must be placed so that the spaces between them are consistent. A common analogy here is to look upon the spaces between letters as a sort of volume that is filled with sand: you ought to be able to put about the same amount of sand between any pair of letters. Second, good letter fit is a function of the absolute amount of space between letters. In display work using type in large sizes, the relative amount of space between letters is reduced, sometimes to the point that the letters touch or even overlap. Type used at text sizes, say 9 to 12 pt, often has somewhat more generous letterspacing than display type. Let me put this another way. Let's say that we space a typeface so that it

Letterspacing

Letterspacing,
the
principles

looks good at 18 pt. At 60 pt we will have to remove space between the letters, and at 10 pt we will have to add a small amount of space between letters. All of this is to aid in the legibility of the type.

When setting caps and/or small caps, the amount of space between letters is increased for added legibility. Some typefaces look better when tightly letterspaced, others look better loose. The amount of space is a function of good taste, while consistency is a matter of skill. Both can be learned and/or developed.

The method described here is essentially that of Walter Tracy. Let's begin by reviewing the principles upon which this approach is based.

We distinguish essentially three kinds of characters: (1) characters with perfectly vertical sides, such as *H* or the right side of *d*; (2) characters with sloping sides, such as *W* or certain forms of *M*; and (3) characters with curved sides, such as *O* or the right side of *p*. To the extent that the side of a character is not perfectly vertical (that is, to the extent that it slopes or is curved), to that extent it seems to introduce empty space around it, which should be compensated for by placing the non-vertical side closer to its neighbor. Both *S* and *s* are problematical. The characters are rounded shapes but the internal spaces and the nature of the roundness vary with the design, as does optical fit.

Be very clear about this fact: When you are establishing the correct letterspacing for a serif typeface, remember that you are measuring horizontal space from stem to stem, not from serif to serif. Serifs are used to confirm and tweak letterspacing, not to establish it.

We begin with the letter H. In the Metrics window, type four of them, and space them so that they look right. Be aware that you are in the presence of an optical illusion: The horizontal crossbar of the H appears to draw the vertical strokes closer to each other, making the interior space look smaller. The distance between the Hs will be smaller, therefore, than the interior space of the H. (A bold font may have the letters spaced at a distance equal to the interior space.) The left and right sidebearings should be equal. Note the amount and write it down.

When the H has been satisfactorily adjusted, move on to the O. Clear the Metrics window and type HOHOH. Adjust the sidebearings of the O so that the letters look evenly spaced. The sidebearings of the O are usually somewhat less than those of the H. When the letters look evenly spaced, type HHOOHH in the Metrics window and see if they still do. You may have to refine the spacing of the H at this point: if you do, go back to the beginning and check to see that HHHH and HOHOH still look good. If no satisfactory balance can be struck (and you are designing the typeface from scratch) you may have to alter the shape of the letters for better fit. If you are tracing an existing typeface, you may be in the presence of a typeface with letterspacing problems.

With the O properly spaced, and taking care that the left and right sidebearings are equal, write down the amount of the sidebearings. If the resulting sidebearing amounts are:

1	=	The sidebearing of H
2	=	A little less than the sidebearing of H
3	=	Half the sidebearing of H
4	=	The minimum sidebearing
5	=	Same sidebearing as for 'O'
6	=	Spaced visually between standards

then a good first approximation for the sidebearings for the other letters is

$_4A_4$ $\quad$ $_1B_3$ $\quad$ $_5C_3$ $\quad$ $_1D_5$ $\quad$ $_1E_3$

$_1F_3$ $\quad$ $_5G_2$ $\quad$ $_1I_1$ $\quad$ $_4J_1$ $\quad$ $_1K_4$

$_1L_4$ $\quad$ $_2M_1$ $\quad$ $_2N_2$ $\quad$ $_1P_5$ $\quad$ $_5Q_5$

$_1R_4$ $\quad$ $_6S_6$ $\quad$ $_4T_4$ $\quad$ $_1U_2$ $\quad$ $_4V_4$

$_4W_4$ $\quad$ $_4X_4$ $\quad$ $_4Y_4$ $\quad$ $_3Z_3$

The lowercase proceeds in the same way, but the base letters are *n* and *o*. The horizontal interior space of the *n* is measured, and half that amount is used for the n's left sidebearing, and about 90% to 95% of that amount used for its right sidebearing (the curved stroke seems to add some space to the right side of the character). Then, in the Metrics window begin with nnnn.

When these characters look right, move on to the o in the following combinations nnonn, nnonon and nnoonn. Interestingly, in the case of fitting a sans serif typeface, there is a tendency to begin by fitting the letters too tightly at this point and they must be moved apart slightly to improve the fit. Again, make sure that the left and right sidebearings of the o are equal.

Write down the left and right sidebearings of the n, and the sidebearings of the o. With these sidebearings at hand we have:

1 $\quad$ = $\quad$ Left sidebearing of n
2 $\quad$ = $\quad$ Right sidebearing of n
3 $\quad$ = $\quad$ Slightly more than the left sidebearing of n
4 $\quad$ = $\quad$ Minimum sidebearing
5 $\quad$ = $\quad$ Same sidebearing as o
6 $\quad$ = $\quad$ Slightly smaller sidebearing than o
7 $\quad$ = $\quad$ Spaced visually between standards

The following guidelines give a good first approximation:

₇a₇	₁b₅	₅c₆	₅d₁	₅e₆
₇f₇	₇g₇	₃h₂	₃i₁	₁j₁
₃k₄	₃l₁	₁m₂	₃p₅	₅q₁
₁r₄	₇s₇	₇t₇	₂u₂	₄v₄
₄w₄	₄x₄	₄y₄	₇z₇	

2. Richard Beatty's method.   Let's assume that all characters are drawn. Open the Metrics window, and adjust it so that you can type six or seven characters. Fill all of the character slots with *l* (lowercase *L*): 'llllll'. You are going to begin by adjusting the space on the left and the right of the character — the left and right sidebearings. Move the character and the width line until you arrive at letters that are neither too close nor too far apart: you are looking for a balanced, even appearance. When you have this, go to the Character Edit window and center the character on its bounding box. That is, the space on the left of the character should be the same as that on the right of the character. Make a note of how much that is. Now return to the Metrics window and fill the character slots with *o*, and proceed as you did for *l.* Again, make a note of the sidebearings.

This first step — finding the sidebearings of the *l* and *o* — is critically important. These sidebearings are usually the largest and smallest, respectively, in a typeface. The *o* needs to be closer to its neighbors because of the added space at both sides of its circular shape; whereas the *l* must be somewhat further apart because it is vertical. All other letters fall somewhere between: The sloped shoulder of the *h* may call for a smaller sidebearing; the internal spaces of the *s* and *c* may call for some adjustment.

Having established the limits, you can confidently make a good first approximation for the proper sidebearings for the rest of the lowercase. Having done this, proceed in exactly the same way for the uppercase starting with *I* and *O*. Fine-tune the letterspacing by typing dll_llb (DII_IIO for the uppercase) in the Metrics window, placing each letter in turn in the center and checking for balance.

I have found an interesting cross-check. Using the pattern loo_ool — or IOO_OOI — I have often been able to fine-tune the spacing.

3. *Tips on letterspacing.*

1. Do not under any circumstances proceed to the creation of kerning pairs until you are completely happy with the letterspacing of your font.

2. Don't rely on random sets of letters: use lots of real words with which to test your letterspacing. The eye, after all, reads words (and groups of words), not individual letters.

3. Test your letterspacing (and letter forms themselves) in words with repeated letters and similar letter shapes. Letters that can be doubled such as bb, dd, ff, gg, ll, will frequently show that the character's sidebearings are too small the first time around. Also try words like 'minimum', 'homology', etc.

4. Resist the temptation to put punctuation into too narrow a space. Punctuation set too close to neighboring letters yields an unpleasant cramped look, if it does not get lost altogether. Walter Tracy suggests placing the period, comma, colon and semicolon in a space that is half that of the width of a numeral. The colon deserves extra care in its use: You should insert a small amount of space before it to set it off slightly from the word it follows.

5. The Metrics window, naturally, shows characters much enlarged. If you adjust the spacing between characters so that it looks tight in the Metrics Window, then the text will look *too tight* at text sizes — say, 10 pt or 12 pt. Therefore, when you are using the Metrics window to letterspace type for text use the type will look somewhat loose at first until you get used to it. If your typeface is destined for use at display sizes — around 18 pt or larger depending on the face — then you will letterspace somewhat tighter, and the type will look tighter in the Metrics window.

6. Auto-Space — This Fontographer 4.x function can be a time-saver if you use it carefully. Don't expect it to do all your work for you — think of it as an "assistant" whose work requires a lot of checking before you let it out the door. Auto-spacing requires a lot of experimentation. Much depends on the shapes of the letters — the same procedure applied to two different typefaces may produce acceptable results in one case and not the other.

7. Quotation marks should be handled with care. It is possible to play all sorts of games with the sidebearings of quotes, but they should probably all have the same sidebearings. There are problems, though, when two or more quotation marks occur together: "He said: 'She said: "I beg your pardon?"'" indicates the sort of problem that can come up. The answer to this problem (and in this I anticipate the next section on kerning) is to kern out pairs of quotation marks. The alternative is

Letterspacing text type in the Metrics Window

Auto-Space

Letterspacing quotation marks

to exercise care in typesetting them, and to be sure to insert thin spaces between pairs of quotation marks.

8. If you have the *fi* or *fl* ligature, you might begin your letterspacing procedure with it. Type several of the ligatures in the Metrics window and space them so that they contain approximately the same space between the ligatures as between the constituent letters of the ligature, *f* and *i*. Then type some *i*'s on either side of the ligature, and set the letterspacing of the *i* until it has about the same or perhaps a little more space around it as the *i* in the ligature. Then type iiooii and adjust the letterspacing of the *o* to accord with that of the *i*. I suggest this because a ligature is designed with the appropriate letterspacing "built in." This technique does not always work: in some typefaces the letters of the ligature are placed abnormally close together.

9 David Kindersley in (*Optical Letterspacing*, pages 12 and 19, see Bibliography) implies that letterforms can, within reason, have their spacing uniformly increased or decreased while maintaining a useful interletter relationship. What this would suggest is that the application of either positive and negative tracking would not jeopardize the utility of a typeface. This all assumes a typeface that has been correctly letterspaced in the first place; tracking an improperly letterspaced typeface quickly reveals any flaws in letterspacing.

4. *The space character.*   The size of the space character (ASCII 32) is crucial in the design of a typeface. If it is too big, words look disjointed and unconnected, making type that is ugly and hard to read. If it is too small, there will be insufficient space between words, again making for difficulties in reading.

Space character in a serif font

Space character in a sans-serif font

The space character: not too big, not too small

A good place to start, for a serif font, is to make the space character about the width of the lowercase *i*. Remember that the serifs do some of the work of spacing, so that the width of a serif would indeed be a good place to start in the search for the proper size of the space character.

For a sans-serif font, the width of the space seems to be dependent on the weight of the stroke. A survey of a number of sans-serif typefaces reveals that the space varies from the same as that for the *i* character for relatively heavy faces (e.g., Frutiger), to about 1.4 times the width of the *i* character for relatively light typefaces (e.g., Avant Garde Book). This implies that there exists the notion of a Constant Space (for a constant em-square), and that, as the *i* character grows wider, this Constant Space responds by being reduced in size to arrive at the space character — for sans-serif faces.

In any event, the space as formulated above may seem very narrow at first, but a surprisingly small amount of space is needed to show the breaks between words. The space should be just big enough to distinguish words quickly and easily, but no bigger. Avoid any sort of eccentric space character because most software, programmed with its own sense of what comprises correct spacing, will not give good results with it.

5. An interesting observation.   Kurt Weidemann makes an interesting point in an article he wrote in *URW Spectrum*, volume 7, no. 4. This remark is in the context of a discussion of the generally low quality of much DTP typography and of a program developed by Hermann Zapf and Peter Karow which attempts to automate fine typography:

...Photosetting had no material substance, no backbone. The type size was always determined from the linear enlargement or reduction of a single master drawing. A punch cutter had however cut freehand into steel for each point size. This was not only a genuine wonder of precision craftsmanship but also an absolute mastery of form: Small point sizes were wider and had thicker strokes; larger point sizes were correspondingly narrower and had thinner strokes... .

...Spacing is performed as a function of point-size: at 6 pt it's wider, at 72 pt narrower. Type sizes are adjusted according to the white space in the character image: for light weights, wider and broader spacing with thicker character stems; for heavier weights the opposite. This achieves what a master punch cutter with solid experience and expert capabilities understood as a matter of course: an appealing visual effect for each size... (pp. 22–23)

This passage raises the interesting notion that there is an active relationship between the elements of size, drawing and spacing of a character: These elements vary with each other, and cause each other to change when changed. Some have called into question the notion of optical scaling — altering the width of a character and its strokes depending upon the size — asserting that this is a mechanical necessity occasioned by the fact that thin strokes cast in metal would be structurally weak and would break down under the pressures of printing. Others, such as Weidemann, clearly believe that there is a design, and therefore optical, issue involved. It may be that optical and mechanical necessities converge on the same point (no pun intended) and reinforce each other.

6. *Kerning.* Once you have letterspaced your typeface to your satisfaction, it is time to consider kerning; letter-pairs that must have their natural separation (as dictated by their sidebearings) altered. The only reason to do this is to maintain the appearance of even spacing between the letters that would, in some cases, be otherwise impossible. Again, remember that the object of good kerning — and letterspacing — is not to see how closely letters can be placed together, but how rhythmically and gracefully they can be placed together. With experience, you will learn to recognize the cramped illegibility of letters placed too close together, and the disconnected illegibility of letters spaced too far apart.

Some combinations of letters are known to cause problems: 'Ty', 'Wa', 'rn' for instance. In the first two cases, the second letter should be kerned slightly to the first; the third case is interesting because it is a case where the two letters should be moved apart, or 'kerned out.'

Pay particular attention to the fact that type in the Metrics window is very large, and, when reduced to text size, will look tighter than it did in the Metrics window. Type, therefore, that looks correctly kerned in the Metrics window may be kerned too closely. You have to learn to anticipate and to compensate for this effect: At first, type may, indeed, look a little loose in the Metrics window, but will appear correct at text sizes. Display type usually has to be more tightly kerned.

Let's put that another way. Type used at text sizes — smaller than 18 pt — is not as sensitive to kerning as text used at larger sizes. Therefore, type at text sizes is more dependent upon correct letterspacing to look good, and type at display sizes is more dependent on kerning to look good. It almost makes you wish that there were a Multiple Master effect for kerning that would dynamically alter as the type got bigger.

There is an interesting sidelight to this. At display sizes, letters are either likely to appear as individual entities when there is no kerning or not enough, or as part of an illegible puzzle of white and black when kerned too closely together. Kerning display

Problem pairs

Proper kerning in the Metrics window

Kerning in display as opposed to text type.

TNT

Kerning
    method of
    Richard
    Beatty

Kerned vs. un-
    kerned type

type, therefore, is a process of watching letters suddenly spring off the screen at you as they become recognizable entities next to their neighbors, and likewise seeing words suddenly form as recognizable entities as their constituent letters are brought into the correct relation with each other — a really fascinating process to behold. TNT — Tight, Not Touching — is an extreme of spacing that brings letters as close together as possible, but not to the point that they touch — usually.

7. *Richard Beatty's kerning method.*   Richard Beatty's approach to letterspacing (outlined above) can be carried through to kerning. In the Metrics window, type the following: 'dlla_llb'. In the space, place each letter you want to kern with the 'a' and adjust the kerning accordingly. Replace the *a* with *b* ('dllb_llb) and run through the necessary pairs again. Then kern the uppercase to the lower case (e.g., Av), and the uppercase to the uppercase (e.g., AW).

8. *Kerning: how much, how many.*   There is a good deal of debate about whether or not text (or body) type should be kerned. As far as I am aware (and this is backed up by Walter Tracy's observations in *Letters of Credit*) there are no positive indications that kerned text is in any way necessarily superior (more readable or legible) to unkerned type. Where the matter does become important is in sizes large than 18 pt, i.e., in display type. Keep in mind too the observation that kerning is frequently overdone. The object is *not* how closely two letters can be placed together, but how best to maintain even and consistent spacing between letters.

　　To put the matter as generally and, I hope, as helpfully as possible, we will establish the following guidelines. First, we design a typeface carefully, adjusting the sidebearings so that the *unkerned* type is as even as possible: the test of this being that acceptability of the type at 9 to 12 pt. Second, where unavoidable gaps occur, they are filled up with kerning. Third, to the extent that the typeface might benefit from a tighter look, a larger number of letter pairs can be kerned. Fourth, where the number of kerning seems to be climbing into three digits, it might be better (given that the typeface is well designed and the sidebearings properly adjusted) to consider tracking — global kerning, as it were.

How many pairs?

Which pairs?

Additional kerning pairs

So, how do we answer the question: "How many kerning pairs does a typeface need?" That depends on the typeface, and it depends on the care with which the letters have been fitted into their individual spaces. It also depends on the purpose to which the type is to be put. One practical limit on the number of kerning pairs would be to refrain from kerning unlikely pairs, such as 'Tx'; to some extent this is dependent on the language in which the typeface will be used. Some typefaces need more kerning pairs simply because of the way in which the characters are drawn. A hundred kerning pairs or so seems minimal (Adobe Systems averages about 100–150), 200–500 (Bitstream's averages are in this range) good to excellent, 1000 or so is amazing, but over 1500–2000 begins to be excessive. There is an efficiency trade-off here: The more kerning pairs you have, the longer it takes the software to manage them.

The following are frequently used kerning pairs:

Av Aw Ay Ta Te To Tr Tu Tw Ty Ya Yo
Wa We Wo we yo AC AT AV AW AY FA LT LV LW LY OA OV OW OY
PA TA TO VA VO WA WO
YA YA YO

Here are additional pairs that are worth noting:

A' AG AO AQ AU BA BE BL BP BR BU BV BW BY CA CO CR DA DD
DE DI DL DM DN DO DP
DR DU DV DW DY EC EO F. F, FC FG FO GE GO GR GU HO IC IG
IO JA JO KO L' LC

LG LO LU MC MG MO NC NG NO OB OD OE OF OH OI OK OL OM ON OP OR OT OU OX P.

P, P; P: PE PL PO PP PU PY QU RC RG RY RT RU RV RW RY SI SM ST SU TC UA UC

UG UO US VC VG VS WC WG YC YS ZO

Ac Ad Ae Ag Ao Ap Aq At Au Bb Bi Bk Bl Br Bu By B. B, Ca Cr C. C, Da D. D,

Eu Ev Fa Fe Fi Fo Fr Ft Fu Fy F; F: Gu He Ho Hu Hy Ic Id Iq Io It Ja Je

Jo Ju J. J, Ke Ko Ku Lu Ly Ma Mc Md Me Mo Mu Na Ne Ni No Nu N. N, Oa Ob Oh

Ok Ol O. O, Pa Pe Po Rd Re Ro Rt Ru Si Sp Su S. S, Tc Ti Tr Ts Tu T. T, T; T: Ua Ug Um Un Up Us U. U, Va Ve Vi Vo Vr Vu V. V, V; V: Wd Wi Wm Wr Wt Wu

Wy W. W, W; W: Xa Xe Xo Xu Xy Yd Ye Yi Yp Yu Yv Y. Y, Y; Y:

ac ad ae ag ap af at au av aw ay ap bl br bu by b. b, ca ch ck da dc de dg

do dt du dv dw dy d. d, ea ei el em en ep er et eu ev ew ey e. e, fa fe ff

fi fl fo f. f, ga ge gh gl go gg g. g, hc hd he hg ho hp ht hu hv hw hy ic

id ie ig io ip it iu iv ja je jo ju j. j, ka kc kd ke kg ko la lc ld le lg

lo lp lq lf lu lv lw ly ma mc md me mg m n mo mp mt mu mv my nc nd ne ng no

np nt nu nv nw ny ob of oh oj ok ol om on op or ou ov ow ox oy o. o, pa ph pi

pl pp pu p. p, qu q. ra rd re rg rk rl r m r n ro rq rr rt rv ry r. r, sh

st su s. s, td ta te to t. t, ua uc ud ue ug uo up uq ut uv uw uy va vb vc

vd ve vg vo vv vy v. v, wa wc wd we wg wh wo w. w, xa xe xo y. y, ya yc yd ye yo

'A '. ', .' ,' 'S 's 't " " " " " " " " " , " , ,"

9. AutoKern.   Fontographer 4.x's AutoKern function can be of assistance when time is short. Like Auto-Space, it should be considered as a first approximation, and its results should be thoroughly checked before using the typeface. AutoKern works best, of course, when the letterspacing of the typeface has been perfected. For this reason, I recommend that you letterspace the letters manually and then apply AutoKern: There should be no question whatever that the letterspacing is absolutely perfect before the kerning is calculated.

❖ ❖   **10. *Blending and Multiple Masters.***   Just in case it crossed your mind, as it did mine, let me tell you about the relationship between sidebearings and kerning and Blend Fonts and Multiple Master fonts. Fontographer (from version 3.5) interpolates the sidebearings and the kerning for fonts that are being subjected to the Blend function. Likewise, Multiple Master technology interpolates the character widths and kerning between any of the "master designs."

❖ ❖   ***11. A novel Multiple Master application.***   Suppose for a moment that we consider the appropriate spacing and kerning of a typeface, but at different sizes: for example Times Roman at 12 pt and at 72 pt. The 12 pt font is obviously for text type, while the 72 pt font is equally obviously intended for display. The problem is that the spacing and kerning appropriate to 12 pt text type is not appropriate to 72 pt display type. The display type will usually be more tightly spaced and more extensively kerned. It may also be true that carefully spaced fonts intended for display might need very much less kerning than text type that has merely been enlarged (along with its spacing and kerning) to display size. What we need is a way to produce a typeface spacing and kerning appropriate to a specific size.

❖ ❖   Enter Multiple Masters. Let's begin by supposing that a proper titling face, as such, is not available to you, but that you want to be able to use the type that you do have at hand for careful display work. You could formulate one solution to this problem by using Multiple Masters. The principle is this: you begin with two copies of the same font. One you leave as it is: it is probably already optimized for text work. The other copy is subjected to extensive alterations in letterspacing and kerning, which alterations have as their

[margin notes:]

AutoKern

Blend, Multiple Masters, kerning and letterspacing

Multiple Masters for specialized kerning and letterspacing

Kerning, letterspacing in text vs. display

object making the font suitable for use as display type at, say, 72 pt, or whatever size you like.

❖ ❖ These two fonts now become your master designs. The usual problems that attend the creation of Multiple Master fonts disappear: the outlines of the characters in the two master designs are identical in every way — number of points, their location and the location of the First Point. The only things that do change are the letterspacing and kerning, and these — as was pointed out above — are interpolated between the master designs of a Multiple Master font.

❖ ❖ *12. The effects of H&J.*   Hyphenation and justification (H&J) will usually significantly alter the look of a typeface. The object of H&J is to arrive at acceptable spacing between words given the artificial requirements of justified text. To do this, especially in a narrow measure, software attempts one or more of several solutions: 1) to adjust the spaces between words in order to fill out a line; 2) programs will try to hyphenate the text into smaller and more flexible pieces; 3) programs will adjust spaces between letters in words if that would result in a lesser evil.

❖ ❖ Generalities are impossible to make about letterspacing — if that were not the case, letterspacing could be done entirely algorithmically, and it can't, at least not reliably. Bear in mind that the wordspace and the space between letters is built into the typeface and has a crucial role to play in how the type looks on the page. Spacing is just as much a part of the typeface as is x-height or cap height. The space between letters is adjusted by the type designer in response to the shapes of the characters, the amount of white space in the characters and the overall rhythm of strokes in the characters. The wordspace is adjusted so as to give individuality to words without letting them be so far apart that they look like unrelated, disjunct entities. Another way to put this is to say that the spacing is adjusted so as to optimize ease of reading.

❖ ❖ Word spaces tend to be about the width (or slightly less) of the lowercase *i* or approximately .25 em, or, for sans serif faces, about half the width of a lowercase *n*. Italic faces, often condensed to some extent, generally take a narrower space, about .2 em. Very dark and/or condensed typefaces may take a space of as little as .15 em. You will occasionally see some type that has a space character equal in width to half the figure width, assuming that the figures all have the same width. It is generally felt that this is not a sufficiently sensitive indicator of the appropriate word space. The amount of stretch usually allowed for word spaces is on the order of 75%–150% of the font's space character.

❖ ❖ So it is that wordspacing and — to an even greater extent — letterspacing are built into the typeface. They are as much a part of the typeface as x-height or cap height. Altering these characteristics without regard for the nature of the face itself is bound to produce unsatisfactory results. The eye will accept a relatively large variation in wordspace, and this is the principle on which justification rests. Letterspacing, that is *proper* letterspacing, is a matter of high precision, the acceptable tolerances being just a small fraction of those for word spacing.

❖ ❖ Having said all that, the practice of letterspacing the lowercase for justifying text may appropriately be called into question. While it may be possible to adjust the overall spacing of the letters, the line-by-line variation in setting text probably does not show the type off to its best advantage. Eric Gill and Geoffrey Dowding (to name only two) make very persuasive arguments for relatively tight word spacing — consistent typographic color, ease of reading, and so on. If we accept that, then the practice of altering letterspacing for justified text seems, at best, an irony. As a type designer, there is absolutely nothing you can do to anticipate the effects of ill-used H&J. The only thing you *can* do is to letterspace your typefaces to perfection, give them an appropriate wordspace, and hope that users have the good sense and good taste to use the type correctly.

13. Emil Ruder examples.

The problems associated with proper letterspacing are so important and yet so difficult to convey merely by the description of a method or formula, that I have included these interesting examples. Use these examples in conjunction with the methods outlined in here to gain an intuitive feel for just what makes for good letterspacing. Both of these example formats are based on those found in Emil Ruder's book *Typographie* (see Bibliography).

14. Triplets.

The first section consists of triplets of letters in the format a-b-a. The lines that separate the letters show the left and right sidebearings of the letters. Notice just how important serifs are in establishing letterspacing; notice how much more difficult and tenuous a thing it is, therefore, to space sans serifs type; notice how the difficult letter *f* is handled; and pay close attention to the handling of italics — isn't *that* interesting? Pay particular notice to the different approaches used to establish proper letterspacing in italics: Some faces have no left sidebearing, while others have equal left and right sidebearings, while yet others have no right sidebearing. In any event, pick your approach and be consistent.

Italian Oldstyle

lal	aaa	oao	vav
lbl	aba	obo	vbv
lcl	aca	oco	vcv
ldl	ada	odo	vdv
lel	aea	oeo	vev
lfl	afa	ofo	vfv
lkl	aka	oko	vkv
lll	ala	olo	vlv
lol	aoa	ooo	vov
lsl	asa	oso	vsv
lvl	ava	ovo	vvv
lpl	apa	opo	vpv
lql	aqa	oqo	vqv

Italian Oldstyle Italic

lal	aaa	oao	vav
lbl	aba	obo	vbv
lcl	aca	oco	vcv
ldl	ada	odo	vdv
lel	aea	oeo	vev
lfl	afa	ofo	vfv
lkl	aka	oko	vkv
lll	ala	olo	vlv
lol	aoa	ooo	vov
lsl	asa	oso	vsv
lvl	ava	ovo	vvv
lpl	apa	opo	vpv
lql	aqa	oqo	vqv

Livingston

lal	aaa	oao	vav
lbl	aba	obo	vbv
lcl	aca	oco	vcv
ldl	ada	odo	vdv
lel	aea	oeo	vev
lfl	afa	ofo	vfv
lkl	aka	oko	vkv
lll	ala	olo	vlv
lol	aoa	ooo	vov
lsl	asa	oso	vsv
lvl	ava	ovo	vvv
lpl	apa	opo	vpv
lql	aqa	oqo	vqv

Livingston Italic

lal	aaa	oao	vav
lbl	aba	obo	vbv
lcl	aca	oco	vcv
ldl	ada	odo	vdv
lel	aea	oeo	vev
lfl	afa	ofo	vfv
lkl	aka	oko	vkv
lll	ala	olo	vlv
lol	aoa	ooo	vov
lsl	asa	oso	vsv
lvl	ava	ovo	vvv
lpl	apa	opo	vpv
lql	aqa	oqo	vqv

15. *Typographic color.*   The second set of examples is based on a selection of words that, together, demonstrate problems in spacing. Here is what Ruder has to say:

> On the left [*of each pair of facing pages*] are words which are difficult to set because their letters (ktyvwfrz) leave awkward gaps of white when they are set against each other. On the right page are words comprised of letters which cause no trouble (lignchb). With correct set-width and well-cast characters the degree of greyness should be the same on the left and right pages. It is advisable to hold the two pages some distance away to judge this effect. Composition with spacing too narrow would give an area too light on the left page and one too dark on the right.

vertrag	crainte	screw
verwalter	croyant	science
verzicht	fratricide	sketchy
vorrede	frivolité	story
yankee	instruction	take
zwetschge	lyre	treaty
zypresse	navette	tricycle
fraktur	nocturne	typograph
kraft	pervertir	vanity
raffeln	presto	victory
reaktion	prévoyant	vivacity
rekord	priorité	wayward
revolte	proscrire	efficiency
tritt	raviver	without
trotzkopf	tactilité	through
tyrann	arrêt	known

Italian Oldstyle

bibel	malhabile	modo
biegen	peuple	punibile
blind	qualifier	quindi
damals	quelle	dinamica
china	quelque	analiso
schaden	salomon	macchina
schein	sellier	secondo
lager	sommier	singolo
legion	unique	possibile
mime	unanime	unico
mohn	usuel	legge
nagel	abonner	unione
puder	agir	punizione
quälen	aiglon	dunque
huldigen	allégir	quando
geduld	alliance	uomini

Italian Oldstyle

16. Line spacing.   Nothing shows the interconnectedness of the typographic elements of the page quite as clearly as the issue of leading: a term we use to mean the total distance between baselines. The principle is this: the distance between baselines — taking into account the descenders of one line and the ascenders of the next line — must be perceptibly greater than the space between words. This distance must then be adjusted to account for the overall color of the type, the x-height, and the line length, that is, the measure.

The goal is to create a body of type that is comfortable and easy to read, that places no impediments in the way of efficient reading. Such obstacles are, for example, type that is either too dark or too light, making it difficult to read; long line length uncompensated for by additional leading, causing the eye to have trouble finding the beginning of the next line; lines that are too close together causing the eye to jump to adjacent lines while trying to read one line. A large x-height appears to move lines closer together, and can contribute to this problem.

Adjustments can be made to counteract these problems, but we will start with two assumptions. First, most software defaults to a linespacing of 120% of the prevailing point size. Second, the optimum line length is about 2–3 lowercase alphabet widths in length. I would suggest that the 120% approach is too insensitive to the way in which type, as it were, fills up its point size: A more telling approach would be to baseline spacing on 120% of the height of ascenders plus the depth of descenders, plus a correction for x-height. This produces remarkably consistent results, but you need Fontographer or another font-production tool to get at the ascender and descender information. You could also get the information from the typeface's AFM (see below). As for line length, you should produce a sample of type with a width of from two and a half to three lowercase alphabets so that you can determine the optimal length.

The adjustments themselves consist of increasing or decreasing line spacing in response to various typographical factors discussed above. As type gets darker, as x-height increases, line length increases, as the sum of ascender height and descender depth increases — all these are cause to increase linespacing. Start with an increase of, say, 10% or so and check the results — *on paper, not merely on the screen.*

Algorithmic
determina-
tion of line
spacing

Line spacing
algorithm

17. A linespacing algorithm.   Take a look at Figures 3.1 and 3.2: Figure 3.1 shows text linespaced according to the algorithm I will develop below; Figure 3.2 shows the same examples, but all linespaced 14 pt. I have used the following typefaces in this order: Livingston, ITC Bookman, New Century Schoolbook, Palatino, Helvetica and Avant Garde. I used the following algorithm to determine the linespacing seen in Figure 3.1: I added the ascent and descent together and multiplied this by 1.2; I then determined if the x-height was greater than 57.5% of the ascent — if it was, I added twice the difference between the x-height and 57.5% of the ascent. Perhaps a bit of algebra will help: Let l be the leading, a the ascent, d the descent, x the x-height and c the correction for large x-height. Then: $l = 1.2(a + d) + c$ where c equals zero if x/a is less than 0.575; if x/a is greater than 0.575, $c = 2(x - 0.575a)$. The width of each paragraph is the width of 2.5 lowercase alphabets. The results are tabulated in the following table (all measurements are in points, and the samples are all in 12 pt type):

Typeface	Width	Ascent + Descent	x-Height Corr.	Leading
Livingston	360.54	11.35	0.88	14.06
ITC Bookman	424.80	11.34	2.05	15.02
Schoolbook	406.11	11.31	1.33	14.11
Palatino	399.63	12.02	1.24	15.33
Helvetica	381.78	11.38	2.51	16.00
Avant Garde	422.23	11.17	2.92	16.22

FIGURE 3.1   LINE SPACING: 1

We are going to examine some of the options with respect to line spacing. We will look at a variety of typefaces with a broad range of characteristics in order to demonstrate the interrelatedness of cause and effect with respect to line spacing. We are looking at several variables: the combined height and depth of the characters, the x-height, the color of the type, and line length.

We are going to examine some of the options with respect to line spacing. We will look at a variety of typefaces with a broad range of characteristics in order to demonstrate the interrelatedness of cause and effect with respect to line spacing. We are looking at several variables: the combined height and depth of the characters, the x-height, the color of the type, and line length.

We are going to examine some of the options with respect to line spacing. We will look at a variety of typefaces with a broad range of characteristics in order to demonstrate the interrelatedness of cause and effect with respect to line spacing. We are looking at several variables: the combined height and depth of the characters, the x-height, the color of the type, and line length.

We are going to examine some of the options with respect to line spacing. We will look at a variety of typefaces with a broad range of characteristics in order to demonstrate the interrelatedness of cause and effect with respect to line spacing. We are looking at several variables: the combined height and depth of the characters, the x-height, the color of the type, and line length.

We are going to examine some of the options with respect to line spacing. We will look at a variety of typefaces with a broad range of characteristics in order to demonstrate the interrelatedness of cause and effect with respect to line spacing. We are looking at several variables: the combined height and depth of the characters, the x-height, the color of the type, and line length.

We are going to examine some of the options with respect to line spacing. We will look at a variety of typefaces with a broad range of characteristics in order to demonstrate the interrelatedness of cause and effect with respect to line spacing. We are looking at several variables: the combined height and depth of the characters, the x-height, the color of the type, and line length.

FIGURE 3.2   LINE SPACING: 2

We are going to examine some of the options with respect to line spacing. We will look at a variety of typefaces with a broad range of characteristics in order to demonstrate the interrelatedness of cause and effect with respect to line spacing. We are looking at several variables: the combined height and depth of the characters, the x-height, the color of the type, and line length.

We are going to examine some of the options with respect to line spacing. We will look at a variety of typefaces with a broad range of characteristics in order to demonstrate the interrelatedness of cause and effect with respect to line spacing. We are looking at several variables: the combined height and depth of the characters, the x-height, the color of the type, and line length.

We are going to examine some of the options with respect to line spacing. We will look at a variety of typefaces with a broad range of characteristics in order to demonstrate the interrelatedness of cause and effect with respect to line spacing. We are looking at several variables: the combined height and depth of the characters, the x-height, the color of the type, and line length.

We are going to examine some of the options with respect to line spacing. We will look at a variety of typefaces with a broad range of characteristics in order to demonstrate the interrelatedness of cause and effect with respect to line spacing. We are looking at several variables: the combined height and depth of the characters, the x-height, the color of the type, and line length.

We are going to examine some of the options with respect to line spacing. We will look at a variety of typefaces with a broad range of characteristics in order to demonstrate the interrelatedness of cause and effect with respect to line spacing. We are looking at several variables: the combined height and depth of the characters, the x-height, the color of the type, and line length.

We are going to examine some of the options with respect to line spacing. We will look at a variety of typefaces with a broad range of characteristics in order to demonstrate the interrelatedness of cause and effect with respect to line spacing. We are looking at several variables: the combined height and depth of the characters, the x-height, the color of the type, and line length.

This fascinating demonstration shows, as indicated by the examples, how close we can come to an excellent first approximation to correct line spacing, and line width, by basing much of our judgment on the nature of the typeface itself. The visual consistency in the examples of very different typefaces shown in Figure 3.1 indicates that we can safely base our work on an algorithmic approach. Nor is this the only such approach: Dozens of others could be found; I'm simply showing you that it can be done. The only thing that we have not accounted for is stroke weight, but this might best be done by eye anyway. It also shows that a one-size-fits-all approach to linespacing cannot possibly do justice to all typefaces.

This demonstration is doubly pertinent in that it works, as it were, in reverse. If you are looking for a typeface — or creating a typeface — that is subject to certain constraints with respect to the way in which the type must fill a given space, then you might well begin by applying the lessons learned here. Most interesting is the enormous influence of the x-height in determining optimal line spacing.

❖ ❖ *18. TEX and the algorithm.*   This book was typeset using TEX, a superb environment for precise typographic control. One of the useful things about the way in which TEX works is that is has access to precise information about the bounding box for each character. I can, therefore measure the height, depth and width of any character and use that information in any way I choose. Indeed, the line spacing demonstration above would have been possible outside of TEX, but much more difficult, and it might not even have occurred to me to attempt it at all. I hope that the vendors of other layout packages are paying attention.

Samples confirm algorithm

Applying the algorithm to design

TEX and the algorithm

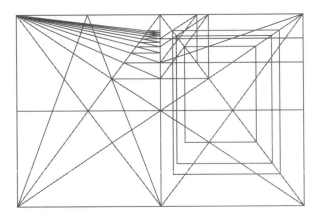

The Serif ❑ 4

SERIFS ARE THE SUBJECT of this chapter: an important but easily overlooked aspect of type design. The plan is to take a number of examples, and to look at them very close-up in order to examine their construction in detail. In the process, we will see some interesting and imaginative examples of PostScript typeface drawing. The lessons demonstrated in this chapter can be applied to a broad range of type design and PostScript drawing. On the principle that you learn by doing, this entire chapter —brief though meaty— consists entirely of annotated illustrations. Enjoy.

FIGURE 4.1   RELATIONSHIPS

The format of this chapter is different because I want to give you a practical, visual appreciation of the design of serifs, and I will do that exclusively by the use of examples taken directly from Fontographer.

We spoke of the relation between thick and thin strokes of a letter. We do so again because now we must relate that to the dimensions of the serif. Table 1 shows the results of measurements taken from three quite different typefaces.

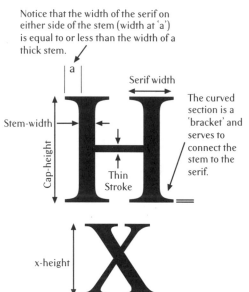

Notice that the width of the serif on either side of the stem (width at 'a') is equal to or less than the width of a thick stem.

Serif width

The curved section is a 'bracket' and serves to connect the stem to the serif.

Stem-width

Cap-height

Thin Stroke

x-height

Table 1

	Bookman	**Times**	**Bodoni**	**Palatino**	**Centaur**
Cap-height	100	100	100	100	100
x-height	71	68	59.3	66.6	57
Thick stroke	14.7	15.4	15.3	13.8	11
Thin stroke	6.2	6.7	3.7	7	5.4
Serif width	41.4	42	48.8	42.5	33
Serif height	4.4	2.9	3.7	4.3	2.37

Note: Lowercase serifs are generally about 90% of the width of uc serifs

The table establishes the cap-height as the dimension against which all of the others are measured, so that the various dimensions are expressed as a percentage of the cap-height for each font. Diagonal strokes frequently have to be somewhat wider than their vertical counterparts to maintain optical consistency.

FIGURE 4.2   SAMPLE SERIFS

Let's begin. We will use the bottom of an uppercase 'I' in each of the following typefaces.
  We begin with **Helvetica**. Hmm. Well, there's not much to say about that, I guess… so much for the sans-serif faces. In point of fact, this is what makes the sans serif so great a challenge to the type designer. Serifs, through their diversity of shape and size lend distinctiveness to a face. Their absence forces the designer to rely on more subtle means of creating individuality.

Again, not a serif typeface, as such, but with a swelling where serif would be. **Optima**, created by Hermann Zapf, also has the pro-portions of traditional roman letterforms.

Tiepolo, in a sense, continues the pattern begun by Optima in enlarging the ends of the stroke. Now we

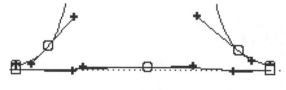

have something that definitely looks more like a serif. The shape of the formative bracket is controlled by curve points.

FIGURE 4.3 MORE SAMPLE SERIFS

At last, in **Times Roman**, we have fully formed brackets and serifs. Notice how the brackets are formed: by extending the handles (which *are* orthogonal

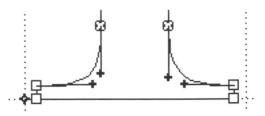

to ensure proper hinting) so that they almost touch each other.

Everything about this example from **Souvenir Demi** is of interest. The exclusive use of tangent points and curve points is fascinating. The tangent points

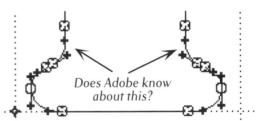

Does Adobe know about this?

have even been used to create a small straight line segment of the bracket/serif.

Clarendon simply continues the process. The serifs are bigger, though the brackets are relatively smaller. Again, note the construction of the brackets.

FIGURE 4.4   STILL MORE SAMPLE SERIFS

In **Bodoni** we can see the effects of no brackets at all. Note, too, how thin the serifs themselves are; this is 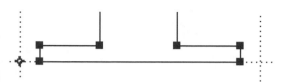 what gives Bodoni its characteristicly brittle look. Such types must be handled very carefully: the serifs tend to disappear or appear fuzzy if they are not printed with extreme care.

And now for something completely different: **Goudy Oldstyle**. At first glance, this looks all wrong. But it is actually quite clever. Notice that adjacent handles never cross each other (though 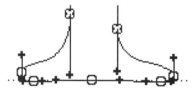 they do go beyond each other, so to speak) and that the shapes of the serifs and the brackets are handled together by a curve point and a tangent point.

The **Garamond** example is, in a sense, the opposite of the Goudy. Instead of controlling the shape of the serif with a curve point at the tip of the serif, curve points on either side of the serif determine its width and its shape. Notice that a curve point at the tip of 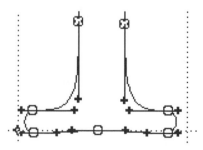 the serif is not necessary, although this is an exception to the rule we laid down about placing drawing points on curves when they are parallel to an axis.

FIGURE 4.5 SOMETHING FASCINATING...

One final, and surpassingly instructive example, this time from the typeface **ITC** 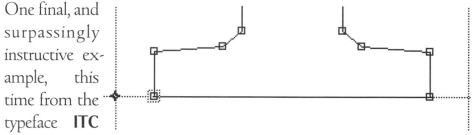 **Charter** of Matthew Carter, who also designed Galliard, among many others. Notice what has become of the brackets: They are now short, straight-line segments attaching the vertical stroke to the serif. At small type sizes, this looks like a smooth, curved—if very small—bracket. It is only at large sizes, such as here, that the true nature of the bracket is made clear. Notice that the serif itself is very mildly wedge shaped which helps to confirm the illusion established by the straight-line bracket, and at the same time makes a more interesting serif. The straight-line bracket also makes this face draw very quickly, and suitable to less than ideal printer resolution. This approach, using a straight line in place of a Bézier curve, is a useful technique and can be used whenever any kind of bevel is needed to join two strokes.

The Calligraphic Tools 5

**W**ITH THE RELEASE of version 3.5, Fontographer began an exciting new period of experimentation and utility. For the first time, we can use the movements of the human hand to create new typefaces, and new approaches to type design. This new tool is a freehand pen: You draw the curve directly, leaving Fontographer to place the drawing points, rather than laying down points which Fontographer then connects with a curve.

The tool has two forms: 1) *Calligraphic pen*—a pen with a nib the width and angle of which can be set by the user, and 2) *Pressure sensitive*—a pen the width of which varies in response to varying the pressure on the drawing stylus. The pressure-sensitive option is best suited to use with a pressure-sensitive tablet, but it is also possible to use this option with a mouse or non-pressure-sensitive drawing tablet. The two options can be used together to create myriad interesting and subtle calligrapic effects. The exciting news is that the Calligraphic pen option can be used with Expand Stroke: This allows you the option of drawing the characters as usual (for a Type 3 stroked font), but expanding the original uniform strokes into calligraphic ones.

There are three characteristics of the present form of the calligraphic tools of which you should be aware. First, these tools will perform most of the effects that can be executed with pen and ink. Second, while there are some things that Fontographer's calligraphic tools cannot do, very close approximations to these things can be obtained through the use of the pressure-sensitive tool. Finally, it is not at present possible to alter the angle of the pen through a

Various possible working formats

Hardware setup

Templates on the tablet

stroke, although this, too, can be simulated. In Fontographer 4.x the calligraphic tools have thickness.

The possible uses to which these new tools can be put depend on the hardware available to you:

1. *Mouse only, no tablet* — calligraphic flourishes, letters with quite a bit of practice and patience, pressure-sensitive effects only with much luck.

2. *Mouse and non-pressure-sensitive tablet* — calligraphic flourishes and alphabets with ease, pressure-sensitive effects only with luck and patience.

3. *Mouse and pressure-sensitive tablet* — an easily available full range of the calligraphic and pressure-sensitive effects.

1. Calligraphic work: the hardware.   This involves two things. First, you will decide on the orientation of the tablet. For instance, I have the 6-by-9 Wacom and in some cases it is easier to work in the 'portrait' mode rather than the more usual 'landscape' mode. Any drawing pad seems to work well: I have used both the Kurta IS/ADB and the small Acecat tablet. The Wacom is pressure sensitive, while the other two are not.

Second, you will want to create a template on which the characters are drawn. This template will show ascent and descent, x-height, cap height, width, etc. The sort of paper you use for this should be fairly *tough* as the pen might cause ripping; and thin and hard to provide no barrier to the signal coming from the pen, and so that the paper will not become 'ribbed' with previous strokes and cause trouble in forming character shapes. The importance of a template cannot be overstated. Once the characters are drawn, there is very little to be done in the way of scaling them to the correct size. This is because, when scaled, the stroke widths are scaled. Unless all characters are scaled by precisely the same amount, the stroke weights will not be consistent from character to character. Editing calligraphic-style characters to correct problems in stroke width is tedious work. It is much better to start off with consistently scaled characters when they are drawn.

Software setup

Getting used to pressure sensitivity

Char Info settings

Software tablet settings

I have found that some tablets (particularly the Kurta) have a surface that is too slippery. It is a little like trying to write on extremely hard, glossy paper with a very smooth ballpoint. Personally, I expect the paper to offer some resistance to the pen. So, you might try experimenting with attaching a piece of heavy paper to the tablet with some tape. I think this gives a better feel and is more like writing with pen and ink.

2. Calligraphic work: the software. There are several software decisions to be made. Double-clicking on the freehand tool brings up a dialog box in which the available effects can be chosen and specified. The decisions are straightforward, but important in that once made, and characters are drawn, they cannot be undone, and your only recourse (in case you change your mind about the look of the font you are working on) is to re-draw the font completely. If you have not used a pressure-sensitive tablet before, you will find that this takes a good deal of getting used to. At first, the tool seems unruly or willful; after some practice, you do develop a feel for it. In practicing with this tool, you will want to vary the maximum and minimum stroke width to appreciate what looks and works best under different circumstances. There are more software choices to be made under *Character info*, and these have an important influence on the way Fontographer expands the stroke.

Finally, be sure that all of the software settings for the tablet are correct. Most important is the scale: You will want there to be a 1-to-1 relationship between motion on the tablet and strokes drawn on the screen. Avoid mapping the entire width of the tablet to the

The choice:
automatic
or man-
ual stroke
expansion

Watchpoints

entire width of the screen because this will create distorted strokes, unless, of course, that is the effect you want. A good place to start, then, is with the following setup:

- Pen angle, 45°, although if you want to achieve a contrast between horizontal and vertical strokes, you might try 20°–30°.
- Pen width, 5% to 10% of the em-square.
- Pressure sensitive, minimum and maximum set between 4% and 10% of the em-square.
- Draw with an italic angle of between 6° and 12°.

3. Summing-up.   Let's review the options and possibilities in a general sort of way. Our purpose is to create strokes of a calligraphic sort, i.e., varying in width with pressure and/or direction of movement. We have two options: 1) We can use the freehand tool and draw the stroke directly, leaving Fontographer to expand the stroke automatically using the settings that we have established for the freehand tool; or 2) we can use the standard drawing tools (Corner, Curve, Tangent and Pen) to create a path, which we can then explicitly expand with the *Expand stroke* command.

The freehand tool is the one to use when the goal isn't absolute consistency, and you want your work to have a spontaneous feel to it: things like calligraphic flourishes or a logo using calligraphic elements. Expand Stroke is useful when you do need absolute consistency (in a roman alphabet, for instance): You can draw the basic strokes (putting them in a safe place for future use) and expand them precisely, thus ensuring consistency throughout your work.

4. Some possibilities and pitfalls.   What follows is a moderately random collection of thoughts and suggestions that have emerged out of my own experience with these new tools.

❡ In doing freehand work, keep your eyes on the screen, not on the tablet. Don't worry, you will gain a sense of connection between what you see on the screen and what your hand is doing.

–Look at the screen, not the tablet

❡ The guideline layer in Fontographer probably needs more information in it. In addition to cap height, ascender height, x-height, and descender depth, you will want to indicate the "italic angle" for the typeface. In addition, when the letters are intended to connect to each other, you will want to indicate the height at which this occurs (see Figure 5.1).

–Additional Guideline layer info

FIGURE 5.1   THE CALLIGRAPHIC WINDOW

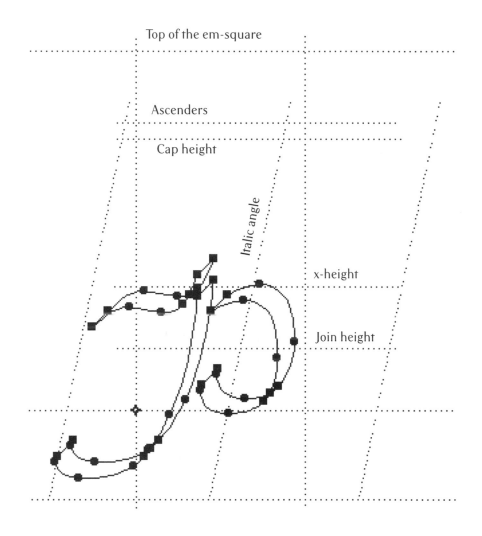

❡ Having placed this information in the Guideline layer, you might consider transferring it to a piece of heavy paper and taping the paper to the drawing tablet.

–Guideline layer info to paper template on tablet

❡ An as-yet-untested-idea: You could attach a child's "erase-a-sketch" to your tablet for immediate feedback about the character's shape. This could be useful in judging the fit of letters and their constituent parts prior to editing them in Fontographer.

–Erase-a-sketch on tablet

❡ The points placed by Fontographer are not etched in stone: they can be, and frequently ought to be, edited. Look upon Fontographer's suggested path as a conservative suggestion for the way in which the stroke should be formed. As pointed out before, there are some limitations in the way that Fontographer fleshes out a freehand stroke. See Figures 5.2 to 5.4 for some ideas. Figure 5.5 examines some of the consequences of the angle of the pen.

Figure 5.2 Calligraphic Techniques: 1

Notice the flat spots at 'y'. There are two things you might consider here. 1) If you want to keep the straight line effect, you should probably convert the corner points on both ends to tangent points. This will preserve the line, and also preserve the smooth motion of the curve into the line. 2) If, instead, you want the straight-line to be curved, convert both of the corner points into curved points.

Fontographer assumes a pen with a width that you set, but that has a minimal thickness. At the points marked 'x', therefore, (where the curve is changing direction and the motion of the pen is parallel to the thin edge) there may be too little width to the stroke: simply move the points a bit in the indicated direction.

Notice that the suggestions made above have been carried out here. Expect to have to edit the handles and BCPs, especially when you move drawing points. Converting the corner points to either tangent or curve points usually requires little in the way of further editing.

This corner point could also be converted to a curve point.

To tangent points

Two curve points, which could be merged.

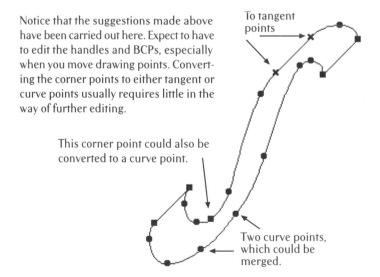

FIGURE 5.3   CALLIGRAPHIC TECHNIQUES: 2

A calligrapher may vary the width of a stroke in one of two ways: the pen can be rotated while drawing a stroke, thus changing the angle of the pen and therefore the width of the stroke; or pressure can be put on the pen making the tip spread out, thus widening the stroke. The two techniques are frequently used together for subtle and intricate calligraphic effects. The following illustrations show some of the possibilities.

Begin with a line. I am using Expand Stroke... for this example, but you might have used the freehand tools directly. Either way, the principle is the same.

Expand the stroke. I used a width of 75 units and an angle of 35°. Place two curve drawing points on the two vertical lines: they are usually a little above the geometrical middle of the character. Move them in slightly towards each other: I moved the left by 8 and the right by 6 units. A pen would do this by varying the pressure slightly, or by rotating the pen counterclockwise.

You can finish off the character by cupping the ends. Simply place curve points as shown and move them for the best effect. Notice at the bottom of the stroke, the curve point at the top of the cup is on the baseline, and the corner points have been moved so that the character sits better on the line.

FIGURE 5.4   CALLIGRAPHIC TECHNIQUES: 3

A horizontal stroke (for an *E* for example) could be made in this way:

1

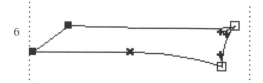

Again, begin with a line (1) and expand it (2).

Place a tangent point on the lower line and an optional curve point on the right diagonal (3).

2

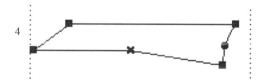

Move the lower-right corner point down and to the right: remember the pen is being rotated counterclockwise so the angle is steeper (4).

Draw out a BCP from the tangent point by using Option-Drag (5).

3

At this point you could call the stroke finished. Or you could add further calligraphic touches by pulling out some of the BCPs from the other corner points to give the stroke further elasticity (6).

Notice that I merged the curve point: I could do without it by using the BCPs from the corner points.

4

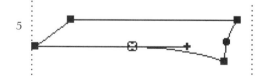

5

6

FIGURE 5.5   CALLIGRAPHIC TECHNIQUES: 4

Observe the effect of changing the pen angle:

70°   Horizontal is thicker than vertical.

20°   Vertical is thicker than horizontal.

45°   Vertical and horizontal are equal.

Consistent stroke widths with italic angles

Suppose, though, that we are creating an italic font with an italic angle (admittedly quite large) of 13°. If we let the pen angle remain at 45° we observe the situation in *A* below: The inclined stroke is clearly thinner than the horizontal; indeed, too thin. We would like both the horizontal strokes and those following the italic angle to be about the same width. We accomplish this by changing the pen angle to ***45° minus the italic angle***. In this case, that gives us an angle of 45°-13° = 32°. We set the pen angle to 32°, expand the stroke and obtain *B* below: The strokes are now equal in width. You could further weight the inclined strokes by reducing the angle still more. If the resulting strokes are too thin, increase the width of the pen as at *C*.

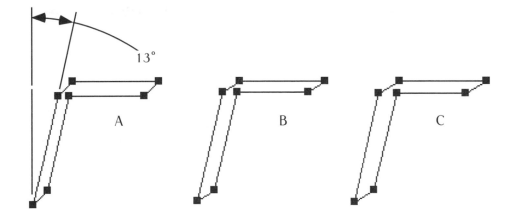

13°

A   B   C

5. *Create a resource file of shapes.* When you create a typeface using the drawing tools, you should make a collection of commonly used parts — stems, serifs, diagonal strokes, bowls, etc. — so as to ensure consistency and to reduce the amount of time necessary to draw a typeface. The same thing is true for calligraphic typefaces. Make a collection of calligraphic elements — Andrew Meit calls them "backbones" — that can be assembled to produce calligraphic characters. This is a venerable practice suggested by the great Renaissance writing masters: Palatino and his "three strokes"; Augustino likewise dissected characters into a few constituent strokes; Madariaga's scalene triangle; Mercator's four elements; and Tagliente's more general approach of describing the formation of each character in terms of simpler characters containing basic strokes.

One last word about the base or "backbone" or constituent shapes that you create: Make sure that you are entirely satisfied with them. The few extra minutes that you spend making sure that all is in order will save you from having to edit an entire font.

Look at Figures 5.6–5.8. These illustrations of the letter *O* demonstrate the interesting and interconnected use of the tools in Fontographer, and how the calligraphic strokes can be modified by the other tools. Any of these shapes could be used as backbones in the creation of any number of other characters, or an entire typeface.

Figure 5.6   The Letter O

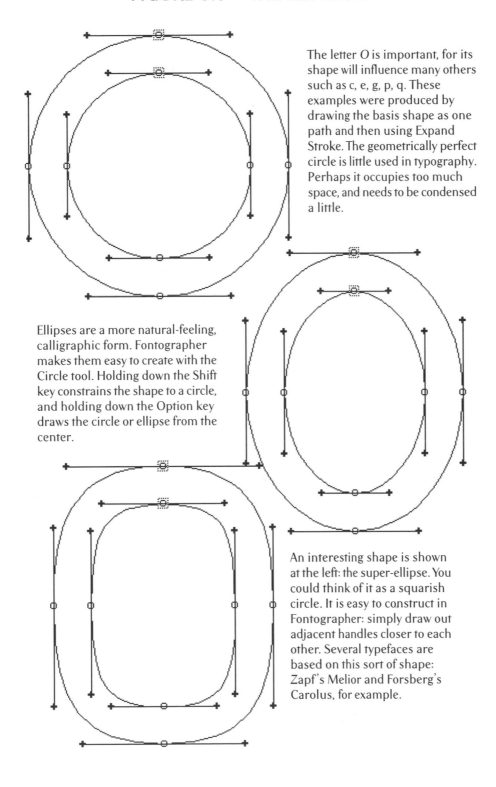

The letter *O* is important, for its shape will influence many others such as c, e, g, p, q. These examples were produced by drawing the basis shape as one path and then using Expand Stroke. The geometrically perfect circle is little used in typography. Perhaps it occupies too much space, and needs to be condensed a little.

Ellipses are a more natural-feeling, calligraphic form. Fontographer makes them easy to create with the Circle tool. Holding down the Shift key constrains the shape to a circle, and holding down the Option key draws the circle or ellipse from the center.

An interesting shape is shown at the left: the super-ellipse. You could think of it as a squarish circle. It is easy to construct in Fontographer: simply draw out adjacent handles closer to each other. Several typefaces are based on this sort of shape: Zapf's Melior and Forsberg's Carolus, for example.

FIGURE 5.7   THE CALLIGRAPHIC O

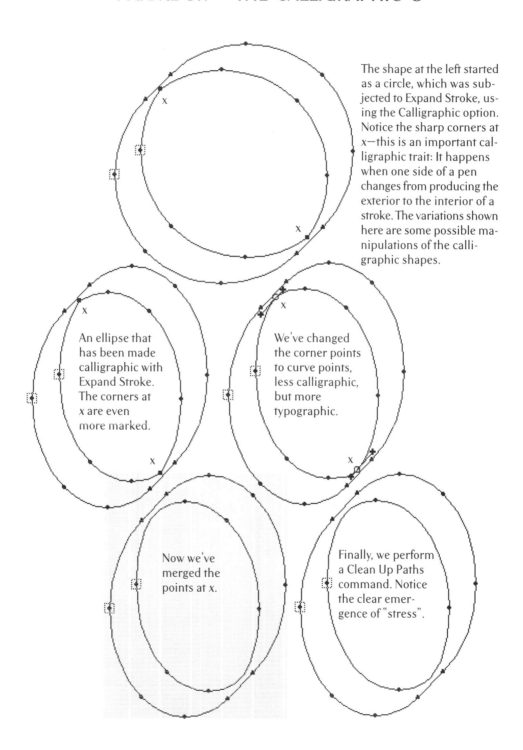

The shape at the left started as a circle, which was subjected to Expand Stroke, using the Calligraphic option. Notice the sharp corners at x—this is an important calligraphic trait: It happens when one side of a pen changes from producing the exterior to the interior of a stroke. The variations shown here are some possible manipulations of the calligraphic shapes.

An ellipse that has been made calligraphic with Expand Stroke. The corners at x are even more marked.

We've changed the corner points to curve points, less calligraphic, but more typographic.

Now we've merged the points at x.

Finally, we perform a Clean Up Paths command. Notice the clear emergence of "stress".

FIGURE 5.8   THE CALLIGRAPHIC SUPER-O

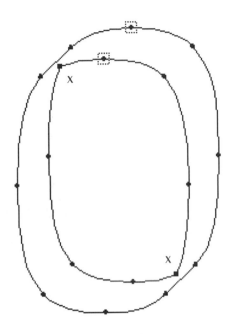

The same kind of operations shown in the previous illustration can be worked on the super-ellipse, with results that are equally interesting. Actually, the shape at the left is very beautiful, and requires no alteration. Still, if you wanted to soften the effect, you could again convert the corner points at x to curve points, the result of which is shown at the lower left. And again, if you choose, you could merge the points at x, shown below at the right.

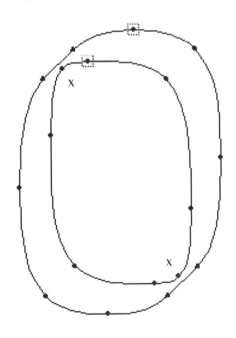

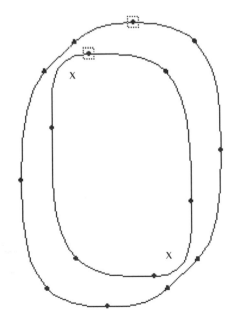

6. *Pen techniques.* Varying the pressure on the pen and rotating the pen point are techniques used in traditional calligraphy to bring a certain 'life' and elasticity to the letterform. These techniques can be obtained in Fontographer. The pressure-sensitive tool is extremely useful in this regard. Rotating the pen, however, is something that Fontographer cannot do at present. Take a look at Figure 5.3 for some suggestions for these techniques.

7. *An interesting use for templates.* Heretofore, we have used templates as the basis for tracing the outlines of a character. But there is another, and very familiar, use to which they can be put. I am old enough to remember having a penmanship teacher. I caused that cantankerous lady much grief because I was left-handed. Well, in order to atone for this failing, I was made to trace the Palmer Penmanship letters, at first directly with a pencil, and then with ink on tracing paper.

You, fortunately, do not have a Miss Forrester standing over you with a look on her face that could savage an Old Testament prophet. You can simply scan in a template calligraphic character, and trace it: use either the freehand, or the drawing tools and expand the resulting line. You will trace the median line, the center of the template stroke. If you have used the freehand tools, try various settings and combinations of pressure-sensitive and calligraphic. If you are using the point tools (i.e., Curve, Corner and Tangent), expand the stroke using various widths and pen-angles. The object is to achieve an acceptable level of agreement between what you have drawn and your template.

Strategies in Type Design ❏ 6

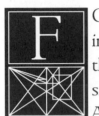**F**ONTOGRAPHER IS A VALUABLE TOOL Example: x-height nums in the solution of a wide variety of problems. Among these are the creation of x-height (or old style) numerals, small caps and supplying missing or alternate characters. A number of other projects such as altering the weight of a font, or its descent or ascent or x-height, and the problem of extended or condensed type — all can be conveniently tackled with Fontographer.

1. x-height numerals. This is one of the most impressive feats, yet in many ways the simplest, in which Fontographer plays an important part. Before we begin, you might want to compare a typeface (such as Palatino) that has both lining (cap height) numerals and x-height numerals. Often there are not many numbers on a page, but they frequently occur in important places and have important functions; for example, page numbers. X-height numerals seem to fit better with text.

By the way, the method discussed here is *not* to be confused with the actual design of x-height numerals. This little demonstration has two purposes: First, it demonstrates that the raw materials of type are at your disposal to do with as your good taste and good judgment dictate; second, it shows you how to derive useful results from pre-existing material, particularly in an emergency.

Let's begin by taking a close look at the nomenclature of numerals. Historically, most numeral designs up to the late eighteenth century were on the x-height model. The new cap height numerals came to be known as "modern numerals" with the original

131

x-height numerals being called old style in comparison. This implied slur that somehow the x-height numerals weren't modern and up-to-date probably helped modern numerals take over, virtually to the exclusion of old style numerals. The term *old style numeral* is not usefully descriptive. Much better is the term x-height or lowercase or text (because they match lowercase text) or *hanging* (because they hang off and below the baseline) numerals — in contrast to uppercase or cap height or ranging or lining (because they range, or line up with caps or other numerals) or titling (again because they match the cap height) numerals. These terms are more descriptive, and indicate their appropriate use: Use uppercase numerals with uppercase letters, and lowercase numerals with lowercase letters. You will frequently see reference to "lining numerals": This makes reference to the fact that cap height numerals are 'monospaced' — they all have the same character width — so that they will 'line up' in columns of figures.

Notice that the numbers are frequently very similar except:

- 3, 4, 5, 7 and 9 have been lowered until their tops align with the x-height. You may find that the top of the *4* is too high and must be lowered: be sure that the stroke widths are the same as the original. In addition, the serif at the foot of the uppercase *4* is usually removed in the lowercase form.

- 6 and 8 are untouched.

> 1 has had its top drawing points moved vertically down so that the top of the 1 aligns with the x-height. Be sure to refer to a typeface reference to make sure about this number. In many cases, the lower-case *1* looks like an upper-case *1*. In this case, simply copy the baseline serif, paste it, flip it across the horizontal axis; move the pasted serif up (using the Shift key to constrain movement to vertical); cut the top of the *1*; move the serif-piece down, and connect the dots: voilà. See Figure 6.1.

1: the procedure

FIGURE 6.1   MAKING A TEXT-HEIGHT 1

We are going to make this 1 into an x-height numeral.

Select the bottom serif: we are going to use it for the top of the new numeral.

Copy and Paste the selected portion. Use Flip... (through the vertical axis) and Move... (some large vertical amount).

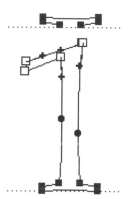

Select the top section of the character...

...and delete it.

Alternatively, simply lower the top of the 1, and the drawing points of the stem appropriately. It all depends on which kind of 1 you want.

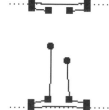

Using the Shift key (to constrain movement) move the new top serif down to the x-height.

Simply connect the dots, and you're done! You will want to make sure that the width is correct and that the handles are still correctly placed.

⌐ This leaves 2, which must have the curved section moved 2: the procedure vertically down so that the top aligns with the x-height; this involves some editing of the control handles to maintain the basic shape of the original figure; you may also have to shorten the horizontal stroke slightly for balance. Maintaining uniformity and consistency can be most easily done by pasting a copy of the *2* in the Background layer for comparison. See Figure 6.2.

FIGURE 6.2 MAKING A TEXT-HEIGHT 2

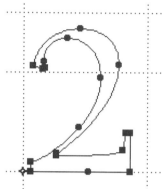

Select all the points, and Copy the numeral into the background layer so that you can compare the old numeral with the new: this comes under the heading of 'major surgery.'

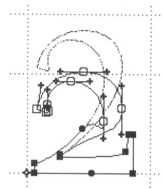

Select the upper points of the numeral and drag them down to the x-height using the shift key (or use the Move... dialog box). Make allowance for x- height overshoot. The result will look awful.

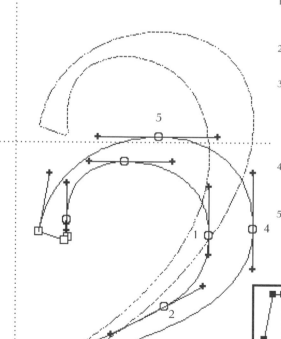

1. Begin by moving point 1 up, so that it is approximately at the vertical center of the curve. Shorten the bottom handle of point 1 (i.e., move it up).
2. Move point 2 down, and shorten the right-hand handle: the curve should start to look normal.
3. The join between the two sections is probably much too thin: correct this by moving the points at 3 to the right. Keep checking with the original in the background to make sure that you are being consistent. The handles at 3 will also have to be adjusted.
4. Move point 4 (usually by not too much), and shorten the bottom handle to get the right shape for the outer segment of the curve.
5. Notice the x-height overshoot at point 5. 6. You might have to move the points contained in the rectangle at 6 slightly to the left, in order to make the character as a whole look like it is 'sitting' properly.

Notice that this leaves the numerals monospaced (cap height numerals are always monospaced). Be sure to consult typeface specimens when possible so as to check your work against the original.

Paste original into template before altering it

Fractions

2. *Important note.* Whenever you make important changes to a character, it is vital that you paste a copy of the original into the Template layer. This ensures that the alterations you make are fully in keeping with the spirit of the original. It also preserves a copy of the original to paste back into the Outline layer in case you mess up beyond the power of Undo to restore the original.

3. *Fractions.* Fractions are a snap with Fontographer. You simply have to decide how you want to do them. They come in two flavors: diagonal and vertical. Both types can be created as composed fractions, wherein one character would represent an entire fraction. Diagonal fractions have the advantage in that they can also be created on the keyboard; that is, you can type the numerator, then the slash, and finally the denominator. Vertical fractions must be composed in their entirety, as there is generally no way to create them by keystrokes.

You begin by taking the numerals for the font in question and scaling to 50%–60%. There is the potential problem here that when you scale the numbers that much, they will look too light when placed with the original font. Two answers to this problem suggest themselves: first try scaling the numbers from the bold font of the typeface. For instance, suppose that you are making fractions for Times. Copy the numbers for Times Bold, paste them where you want them in your fraction font, scale them to, say, 50% and use these as the fractions to accompany Times Roman. The other possibility (particularly where there is no bold font in the typeface with which you are working) is simply to add weight to the scaled characters so that they are visually compatible with the font with which they are being used: see Figure 6.3.

Your next problem will be to decide how you want to approach a fraction font. You have two options. First, you could have a font of numerator- and denominator-position numbers so that you could create any fraction you liked. This is the approach taken by Sumner Stone in his typeface Stone Print, in which he has created an all-purpose number font: the number keys have cap height numerals, the Shift-key has numerator numbers; the Option-key has the denominator numbers, and Shift-Option has the x-height numerals. Second, you could compose a font of specific fractions. Or you could have an omnibus fraction font and have both possibilities in the font. Actually, the best approach would be to have both numerator and denominator numbers in the font: they could be referenced by the composed fractions that you create. There is, by the way, no reason why the numbers used for diagonal fractions should be monospaced, as they are not being used for columns of numbers.

4. *Aligning the elements.* Positioning the numbers for the numerator and denominator is the next order of business. For diagonal fractions, I think that everyone is agreed that the top of the numerator should coincide with the cap- or ascender-height: occasionally the denominator rises slightly above the cap height for optimal reasons. Most authorities are agreed that the denominator should sit on the baseline, although a few (Donald Knuth for instance) show the denominator going below the baseline by some 25% of the x-height of the basic font. Vertical fractions are going to be bigger vertically simply because the numbers have to sit on top of each other, and because there has to be sufficient room for the divider. The numerator will very likely rise somewhat above the cap or ascender height, and the denominator will very likely extend below the baseline. The trick is to center vertical fractions on the horizontal line of text of which they are a part. See Figure 6.3 for a summary of the process.

FIGURE 6.3 MAKING FRACTIONS

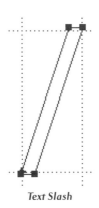

As a general rule, a text slash is about 70% of the width of the main stroke of an uppercase *I* and is inclined from the vertical at about 20°. The fraction slash, on the other hand, is only about 45% to 50% of the width of the main stroke of an uppercase *I* and is inclined at a somewhat greater angle of about 30° to 35° from the vertical. Notice the large negative sidebearings in the fraction slash.

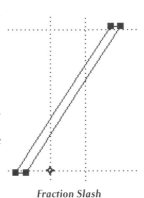

Text Slash

Fraction Slash

Numbers for Fractions

Simply scaling the numbers to, say, 50% is not enough. They will look too light when placed beside text or other numbers from the principal font. You have two options. You can scale the numbers from a bold font for fractions for a roman font, or you can scale the roman numbers and add weight to them.

The fraction on the left was created by simply scaling a *3* and a *4* to 50% and positioning them accordingly. The numbers are too light and do not match the *1* to which they are attached. The fraction on the right was made by scaling a *3* and a *4* from Times Bold to 50%. Now we have a more consistent, uniform look.

An interesting lesson emerges from this. We begin by noting that the principal stroke of the number *1* in Times Roman is 86 em-units. The width of *1* in Times Bold is 148 em-units, which when scaled to 50% would be 74 em-units. The bold *1*, therefore, when scaled 50% is some 86–74=12 em-units lighter than the roman *1* at full size: This indicates an acceptable agreement between the weights of the full-sized and reduced parts of the fraction. The reduced numbers could even be a little lighter. Indeed, acceptable results can be obtained when the principal vertical stroke of the scaled *1* is some 75% to 85% of the unscaled *1*. Use this information when you have to add weight to numbers: scale the numbers and then Add Weight so that the scaled *1* is about 80% of the unscaled *1* – you might have to work this in reverse if you scale bold numbers and need to remove some weight from them.

Notice how the numbers of a diagonal fraction fit together. The numerator and denominator tuck into the fraction slash. The numerator aligns with the top of the full-sized numeral, and the denominator aligns with the baseline.

The slash used to create diagonal fractions is not the same as the slash that is used for text, nor is the line that is used in vertical fractions the same as the hyphen. Both lines are lighter. The slash is also inclined at a greater angle from the vertical. The slash also has significant negative left and right sidebearings, so that the numbers will tuck neatly into the slash.

Algorithmic variations

Changing weight vs. scaling

Weights

5. Algorithmic variations.   A number of the changes that we are going to make on fonts in the material that follows come under the heading of "algorithmic." That is, we are using well-defined — indeed, mathematically defined — operations on the elements of the font. Algorithmic approaches have a number of advantages over instinctive, manual approaches. First, they can be broken down into a series of ordered steps and processes, each step clearly understood and its effect observable. Second, arising from this, variations of the basic algorithms can be easily and precisely made by altering any of their constituent parts. Third, the elements of a digital algorithm can be precisely specified. Fourth, algorithms can be applied repeatedly to a wide variety of materials with a relatively high level of confidence that they will produce the desired effect.

A number of the algorithmic variations take advantage of the fact that, in Fontographer, changes in *weight* are *absolute* — they are performed using a given number of em-units of change, while *scaling* changes are *relative*, done as a percent of the em-square. That means that we can add or subtract as much as a relatively large amount of thickness to a stroke — relative to the original stroke weight — but maintain the overall size of the character by small scaling amounts because the added weight is relatively small *relative to the em-square.*

6. The useful Change Weight command.   It is possible now to have Fontographer perform a weight-changing operation on selected

Change Weight
caution

Change Weight
to make
outline fonts

characters. Carefully used, this is a fabulously useful function. An example will show what I mean. Not long ago I recreated an interesting typeface that had been used in the first Bible printed in France (1476). The source was D. B. Updike's *History of Printing Types.* The example he gave contained no numerals and no ampersand. I found numerals in the Adobe's *Font & Function* for Winter 1992, and I found an ampersand in Goudy's study of ampersands in *A Half-Century of Type Design and Typography, 1895–1945.* Combined with a little judicious re-drawing and the Change Weight command, I was able to create characters that harmonized perfectly with the original typeface. This function might be very useful indeed in creating a credible set of small caps (see below).

Be careful: do not use this function indiscriminately. A small change (1% or so of the em) will probably not warrant great caution. Larger changes, however, might create overlapping paths, which, in turn, will produce a typeface that will not print.

7. *Outline fonts using Change Weight.* It is possible to use the Change Weight… command to produce an excellent outline font. The principle is that you copy the base character, change the weight of the character (making it bolder, letting the vertical and horizontal dimensions change), and finally paste the original character back. The difference between the two versions is what produces the outline version. Make sure that you select Correct Direction from the Path menu before you preview and generate the typeface (see Figure 6.4).

Figure 6.4   Making Outline Fonts

1. Start with an outline; select it and copy it.

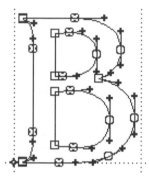

2. Change the weight of the outline. You will want both the horizontal and vertical size to change, unless you want a special effect. Be sure to check that Change Weight... has not created overlapping paths in the process.

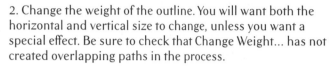

3. Paste the original copy back into the now heavier character. De-select all of the paths and, under Path, select Correct Direction.

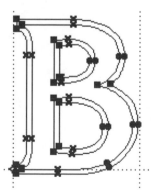

4. Voilà.

Weight
changes

Alternate font
weights by
hand or
by Change
Weight
command

8. *Creating different weights.* There are two approaches to this problem. The first is to let Fontographer do most of the work through the Change Weight command. This is useful but has its own drawbacks, pointed out earlier. The other method is the old-fashioned one of drawing the new weight by hand. This is not quite as difficult as it sounds. The light (or standard) weight is used as the basis, and by applying some simple principles (and some patience) a heavier weight can be produced relatively easily. A useful application of the techniques discussed here is found in Figure 6.5.

Figure 6.5   The Baking Soda Inquiry

One morning, not long ago, in the midst of my daily refurbishment of the outer man, I chanced to notice the most recent tube of toothpaste. It declares itself, now the fashionable thing, to contain baking soda. All well and good, but it does it in the following interesting way:

 Notice the difference in stroke weight.

What leapt out at me was not the words "Baking Soda" but the letters *BS*, not, literally or figuratively, an entirely agreeable association of ideas. The problem is that the designer used, or tried to use, small caps for the sans serif—Helvetica in this case—but the *B* and *S* are a great deal heavier than the software-generated small caps that accompany them. The small caps were scaled to about 70% of the cap-height. The really fascinating thing here is that there are few small caps for sans serif fonts, even for those patently based on roman models such as Optima. So I began to wonder if a better solution could be created by creating a more or less genuine set of sans serif small caps.

I began with Helvetica Bold Oblique, and opened the PostScript file in Fontographer. I copied the upper case letters and pasted them into the lower case positions. I scaled the lower case letters to 70%, relative to the character origin. The problem next was to determine how much weight to add. A normal vertical stem (I measured the upper case *I*) has a width of about 153 em-units; the scaled lower case stem has, therefore, a width of about 107 em-units. Simply adding 46 em-units would have been too much: the characters would have looked bloated. I decided to add 70% of [153−107=46], or 32 em-units—this turns out to be a good rule of thumb. I added the weight—allowing both horizontal and vertical changes in character size and moved all of the characters up by 16 em-units (i.e., half of the 32 em-units of added weight) to preserve the correct baseline. Had I continued, I would have corrected the letterspacing, kerning, and composite characters. In any event, the final product looked like this:

 Much better.

Several things to note. First, I didn't scale the weighted small caps to accord with the x-height, mainly because they are not x-height. Second, I managed to create the text I needed without ever leaving Fontographer—I simply exported the text I needed as encapsulated PostScript files. Finally, I don't seem to be any closer to answering the question of why small caps for sans serif faces are so rare. Maybe they are felt to be unnecessary or not idiomatic. Idiomatic or not, the present example shows that they might, on occasion, be quite necessary.

In creating a bold font, the operative principles are as follows:

⚐ Thick strokes usually get thicker faster than thin strokes get thicker. Thus bold fonts generally show greater contrast in stroke width. Some typefaces (e.g., New Caledonia and Bodoni) hardly seem to change the thin strokes at all, while others (e.g., Palatino) seem to show more change of the thin stroke. The principle seems to be that typefaces that (in the light weight) show large stroke-width contrast tend to increase that contrast in the heavier weights, while typefaces that show relatively uniform stroke width in the light weight preserve that uniformity in the heavier weights.

⚐ The important measures of the typeface — cap- and x-height, ascent and descent — may change slightly. The x-height is often somewhat higher (to accommodate the thicker strokes) and the descent might be a little smaller to counteract the optical effects of the thickening.

⚐ Serifs become thicker by about the same amount thin strokes become thicker. They do not usually change appreciably in width, so that the wider stems to which they are attached make them appear narrower, or stubbier.

⚐ The additional width of a vertical or inclined stroke is added symmetrically around an imaginary line running down the middle of the stroke.

⚐ The addition of a horizontal stroke (usually thin) is added in such a way that the cap height and x-height, ascent and descent are not altered.

 9. *Changing weight with constraints.* In this case, we want to change the weight of a font, but to retain the original cap height and x-height. The steps and reasoning behind them are as follows. Begin by selecting the characters you are going to alter — if you are weighting an entire font, select all of the characters *except the composite characters, e.g., accented characters if they are composites.* Composites will be altered automatically because their constituent parts are being altered. Select the Change Weight command and enter the appropriate value. Be sure that the Check Path Direction check box is checked, and that the other two check boxes having to do with altering the vertical and horizontal dimensions of the character are unchecked. One other thing to remember is that Change Weight command will occasionally add drawing points to a path when redrawing it with added weight. This probably won't make any difference to you most of the time, but it is something to be aware of.

❖ Notice that the characters no longer sit on the baseline, and that they extend above the x-height and cap height — or, if you are taking weight away from the face, the characters are sitting above the baseline, and do not meet the x-height or the cap height. So the next step is to move the characters *up* (if you are adding weight, *down* if you are subtracting weight) by half the amount you entered in the Change Weight dialog box: Change Weight works by taking half the change weight amount and adding it on both sides of the path. This takes care of putting everything back into its proper relation to the baseline.

❖ Now you must scale the characters so that they are in the proper relation to the x-height or cap height. It would probably be best to determine the scaling amount by taking the original cap height, and dividing that by the new cap height. This is simple because if the original cap height is, say, 600 em-units before adding 12 em-units of weight, it will be 612 em-units after being weighted (and moved): The appropriate scaling factor in this case would be 98.04% (=600/612). This will mean that the x-height of the weighted characters will be ever so slightly higher than the unweighted characters, which is probably not such a bad thing, as x-height often does increase with weight.

❖ Let's summarize the process. Select the appropriate characters; if you are weighting an entire font, select all of the characters except composite characters (characters made up of references to other characters). Select Change Weight, enter the appropriate amount; make sure that Correct Path Direction is checked, and that the other two options relating to keeping the dimensions unaltered are *unchecked.* With the characters still selected, move the characters

Change Weight can add drawing points

Adjustment relative to the baseline

Adjustment relative to the x-height

Adding weight summary: Change Weight, Move, Scale

vertically by *half* the amount entered in the Change Weight dialog box. Again with the characters still selected, scale the characters to bring them back to the correct (or original) cap height or x-height, whichever is appropriate. If you have added more that about 20% of the prevailing original stroke weight or weight of the widest stroke, you might want to check that you have not created overlapping paths: if so, you will have to simplify them. See Figures 6.6 through 6.8.

FIGURE 6.6   PUTTING ON AND TAKING OFF WEIGHT: 1

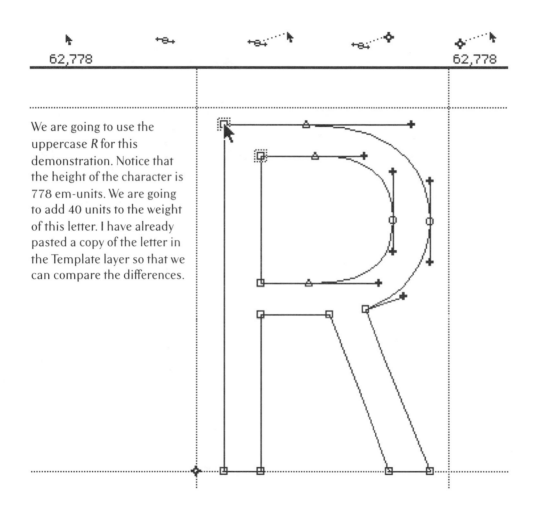

62,778   62,778

We are going to use the uppercase *R* for this demonstration. Notice that the height of the character is 778 em-units. We are going to add 40 units to the weight of this letter. I have already pasted a copy of the letter in the Template layer so that we can compare the differences.

FIGURE 6.7   PUTTING ON AND TAKING OFF WEIGHT: 2

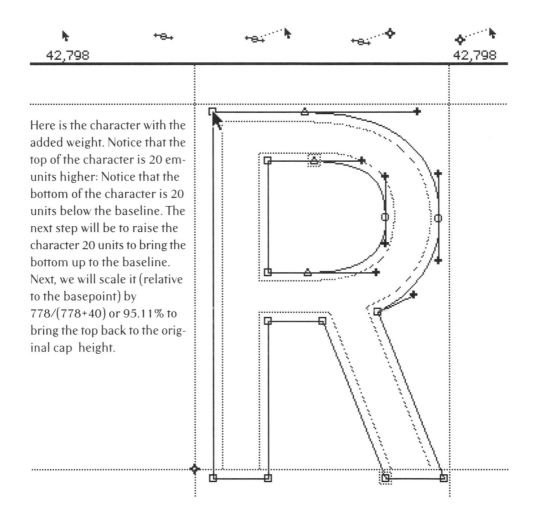

42,798

42,798

Here is the character with the added weight. Notice that the top of the character is 20 em-units higher: Notice that the bottom of the character is 20 units below the baseline. The next step will be to raise the character 20 units to bring the bottom up to the baseline. Next, we will scale it (relative to the basepoint) by 778/(778+40) or 95.11% to bring the top back to the original cap height.

FIGURE 6.8   PUTTING ON AND TAKING OFF WEIGHT: 3

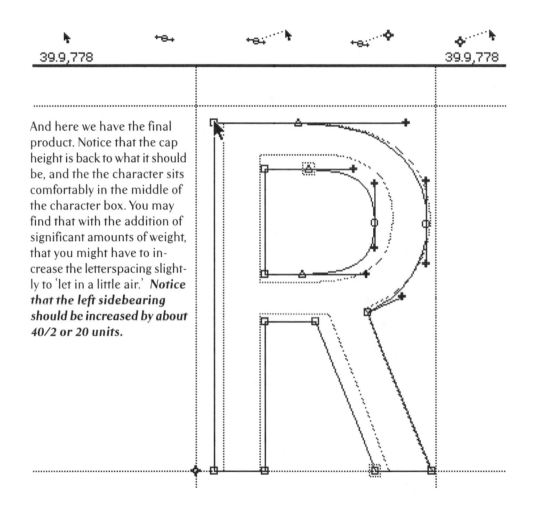

39.9,778   39.9,778

And here we have the final product. Notice that the cap height is back to what it should be, and the the character sits comfortably in the middle of the character box. You may find that with the addition of significant amounts of weight, that you might have to increase the letterspacing slightly to 'let in a little air.' **Notice that the left sidebearing should be increased by about 40/2 or 20 units.**

❖ ❖ Attentive readers will have noticed that the process described here adds weight which is then scaled, so that the originally requested weighting amount is altered. Actually, this turns out not to be very significant. If we let the original height of a character be H, the original amount entered in the Change Weight dialog d, and let b equal the subsequent value of d after scaling to return the weighted character bach to a height of H, then $b = Hd/(H+d)$. In the example above where H=600 em-units and $d = 12$ em-units, b would be 11.76 em-units after scaling: a mere quarter of an em-unit in difference. If you knew that you wanted b to equal, say 35 em-units (where, again, $H = 600$), you could use the equation $d = bH/(H-b)$ to find that d (the amount you would enter into the Change Weight dialog box) would have to be 37.17 em-units *before* in order to arrive at a weight change of 35 em-units *after* scaling.

❖ ❖ **10. An interesting observation.** In doing a project that required adding a small amount of weight to a font, I discovered an interesting thing. If you take a plain font and its companion italic or oblique and add the same amount of weight using Change Weight, the change is far more visible in the italic than in the roman. Indeed, If you want to retain the typographic color of the fonts relative to each other, you will add slightly less weight to the italic or slightly more to the roman.

❖ ❖ There is yet another possibility. You could use the Blend Fonts function to create an intermediate weight, provided you have the the two weights needed for blending: say, a light and a bold. There are, however, some problems with this approach. You must be sure that the two base fonts lend themselves to this process. The characters should be similar and drawn similarly in the two extreme weights; there should be the same number of drawing points (or nearly so) in the characters; and the First Point should be at the same location in each pair of characters used for blending.

❖ ❖ **11. Nonuniform change of weight.** There are times when we would like to change the weight of, say, vertical stems, but would like to leave horizontal elements — serifs, or the thin bits at the top and bottom of the letter 'o', for example — largely untouched. A serif face, for instance, can be emboldened effectively using the technique I am about to describe.

❖ ❖ The principle is simple. You scale a character by some very large horizontal or vertical amount, add the amount of weight needed, and then scale the character back — again, horizontally or vertically by an amount nearly reciprocal to the first scaling — so that it has the correct height. What has happened? Let's take an example. Suppose that you want to widen the vertical stems of a character. You begin by scaling the character *vertically* by some very large amount, say, 5000%. What this does is to make all of the horizontal strokes 50 times the height they were, while the vertical strokes are unchanged. You then add the weight you want, say, 30 em-units. A vertical stroke 100 em-units wide is now 130 em-units; a horizontal stroke that was originally 40 em-units high, is now (40 × 50) + 30 or 2030 em-units. Re-scaling back vertically by 2% (the reciprocal of 5000%), again leaves the vertical stroke untouched, while the original 40 em-unit horizontal stroke is now only 40.6 em-units. So we have changed the weight of the vertical strokes while leaving the horizontal strokes virtually unchanged. This technique is used to produce a bold weight of a *Font Chameleon*-derived typeface: see below.

❖   ***12. Expanding & condensing type.***   Simply scaling a typeface horizontally in order to expand or condense type is mostly doomed to failure. Significant amounts of scaling will cause the thick and thin strokes of a character to fall out of harmony with each other. Think about it: Horizontal scaling will cause the *vertical* strokes to become thicker, while the horizontal strokes (like serifs) will become wider; all of the vertical strokes — the heights of the serifs and the thin bits at the top and bottom of an 'O' for instance — will remain the same. In some cases — particularly sans-serif fonts with one major stroke width — a stroke weight contrast is created where there was none, and *vice versa*. Serif fonts will generally have serifs that become too wide. See Figures 6.9 through 6.11.

FIGURE 6.9   EXPANDING & CONDENSING TYPE: 1

The problem here is to avoid the change in the width of vertical strokes when type is expanded or condensed. The principle we use to solve this problem is this: (1) expand or condense the type as you desire; (2) scale the character vertically by a very large amount (8000%); (3) add the weight lost in condensing (or subtract the weight lost in expanding) the type – note that typefaces that show a significant contrast in stroke width (this would include most serif faces) may need less adjustment in weight, perhaps little or none at all; (4) scale the type by the reciprocal of 80 (=8000%) or .0125 or 1.25%. This also brings the type back to *very nearly* its original vertical dimensions—for very precise work you will have to adjust the final results by a very small amount, usually 1% or less.

The character at the left, below, is Helvetica Bold, uppercase *O* which we are going to condense to 80% as indicated in the Transform... dialog box shown below.

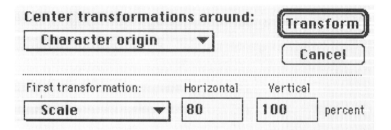

At the right is the result: now you can see the problem. The vertical width (120) is now less than the horizontal width which remains 127: horizontal scaling changes vertical strokes and leave horizontal strokes unchanged. This makes for a lighter and at the same time ungainly typeface – nasty. This is what you get when you condense type in all layout packages, and why it should be avoided. We want to preserve the color of the type by making the vertical width remain the same that it was in the original character, i.e., 150. Very important: notice that the scaling is done relative to the character origin – this preserves the original sidebearings.

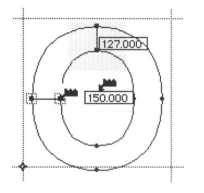 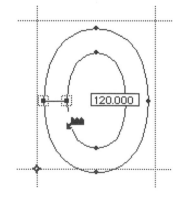

FIGURE 6.10   EXPANDING & CONDENSING TYPE: 2

We are going to begin with the original character and scale it horizontally by the desired amount. We are scaling vertically by a very large amount: remember that vertical scaling leaves vertical widths unchanged while it alters horizontal widths. We are making the horizontal widths huge so that when we add or subtract weight, the amount of weight change, relative to the now huge horizontal widths, will be negligible.

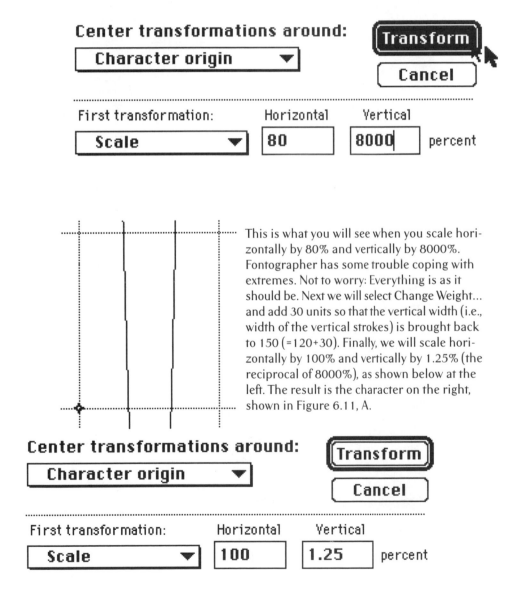

Center transformations around:

| Character origin ▼ |

Transform

Cancel

First transformation: Horizontal   Vertical

| Scale ▼ | **80**   **8000**   percent

This is what you will see when you scale horizontally by 80% and vertically by 8000%. Fontographer has some trouble coping with extremes. Not to worry: Everything is as it should be. Next we will select Change Weight... and add 30 units so that the vertical width (i.e., width of the vertical strokes) is brought back to 150 (=120+30). Finally, we will scale horizontally by 100% and vertically by 1.25% (the reciprocal of 8000%), as shown below at the left. The result is the character on the right, shown in Figure 6.11, A.

Center transformations around:

| Character origin ▼ |

Transform

Cancel

First transformation: Horizontal   Vertical

| Scale ▼ | **100**   **1.25**   percent

FIGURE 6.11   EXPANDING & CONDENSING TYPE: 3

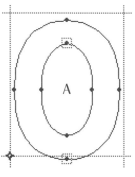

At the left, then, we have the three versions of the character. At the top (A) is the correctly condensed letter. Below it (B) is the letter that has simply been condensed without taking account of the resulting narrowing of vertical strokes. At the bottom (C) is the original character. We use the letter *O* because it has, as it were, stroke width in all possible directions.

Notice how dissimilar B is either to A or C: B is lighter and spindly looking, almost as if it were from a different (and inferior) typeface. Vertical strokes are usually thicker than horizontal ones—they certainly are in Helvetica, but in B this relationship has been destroyed. Notice that the correctly scaled character at A has virtually the same height as the original C.

This technique has numerous applications. You can vary the amount of vertical scaling and weight change to achieve various effects. Below is the letter *O extended* by 120%: on the top (D) is the result of simple horizontal scaling; on the bottom (E) the vertical stroke width has been preserved. All the numbers were the same except for Change Weight..., which was -30. units.

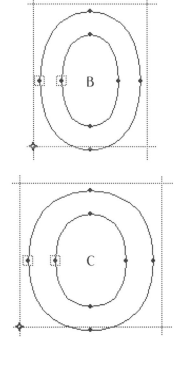

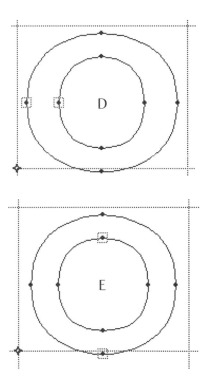

Serif typefaces and/or typefaces that show significant contrast between thick and thin strokes may not need as much adjustment with Change Weight..., perhaps even little or no adjustment at all.

❖   I think that I have arrived at a reasonable algorithmic solution to the problem, though one that does not relieve you of all responsibility for the final product, you might have to touch up a few things and on guard against a few others. The object will be to expand or condense a character without badly disturbing the relationships between its various elements.

❖   The method is simple. We start with a character, alter its weight so that the scaling process will not distort the character in an undesirable way, and then we will scale the character to achieve both the needed expansion or condensing, and the necessary adjustment for the change in weight we carried out. Finally we will reverse the weight change we made at the start of the process. Extending a typeface to 125% of the original — or condensing it to 80% of the original — is actually rather a lot, and should be considered a reasonable limit. Anyway, the more you expand or condense a font, the more trouble you have to go to get it to "look right."

❖   The following table summarizes the process. There are six things to bear in mind. First, the value of the necessary weight change — x in the table — will vary with the amount of extension or contraction you desire. One approach would be to start with the width of a vertical thick stem and note its width; multiply that width by the percentage by which you are going to extend or condense the face; subtract the smaller from the larger figure and use that difference to start with. Second, the Change Weight command has two constraints: not altering the width, and not altering the height of a character. The first step requires these to be *unchecked*, while the fifth step requires them to be *checked*. Third, be prepared to experiment until you arrive at a pleasing result. Fourth — and not for the first or last time — bear in mind that this is not necessarily the best or only way to arrive at an extended or condensed font: It is one way, one you might want for the sake of convenience, to amuse yourself, or as an alternative in a time-constrained situation. Fifth, be prepared to do some touch-up work on the horizontal serifs since they will still probably be somewhat too wide. Finally, condensing a typeface has its own perils. If you are using the 1000-unit em-square, you may find that the horizontal scaling to condense the font has merged some points. You might want to consider quadrupling the scale of the font for more precision when you are working on it.

To extend a font	To condense a font
1. Remove weight from the character, using neither constraint, call it x units.	Add weight to the character, using neither constraint, call it x units.
2. Move the character horizontally and vertically by $-x/2$ units.	Move the character horizontally and vertically by $x/2$ units.
3. Scale the character vertically to bring it back to the height of the original character: the amount will be greater than 100.%	Scale the character vertically to bring it back to the height of the original character: the amount will be less than 100%.
4. Scale the character horizontally to extend it.	Scale the character horizontally to contract it.
5. Change the weight by $.8x$ to x, using both constraints.	Change the weight by $-.8x$ to $-x$, using both constraints.

❖ ❖ Alternatively, the problem of expanding and condensing type could be thought of as an example of nonuniform change of weight. Expanding a character might add 30 units of weight to vertical strokes. This vertical weight could be removed by the method outlined earlier.

❖ **13. Altering major font characteristics.** This amounts to altering the cap height, ascender height, x-height or descender depth — or any combination of these — of a font. Actually, there are several typefaces available in versions with long and short descenders simply depending on the sort of use to which the face will be put, and how necessary it is to get as much text on the page as possible. As for altering the other characteristics, well, to each their own. Note that changing the cap and descender height and changing the x-height are but different sides of the same coin.

You may be wondering: Why anyone would want to alter the characteristics of a typeface? Why shorten a descender or enlarge an x-height? Shortened descenders are usually made available in order to facilitate fitting more copy onto a page. Increased x-height might help to make a typeface more legible, particularly at small sizes. Or you might want a particular look for a particular job, but can't find one typeface that fulfills all of the requirements: These

transformations might allow you to transform a typeface already in
your collection. Ideally, it would be best to redesign the type from
scratch, but the quick algorithmic variations given here will save
some time in an emergency.

❖   Lengthening ascenders and descenders is relatively straightforward. Most
         characters are formed in such a way that by moving the upper points of
an ascender — or the lower points of a descender — the change can be simply
made. The only exception to this is the lowercase letter *g* because its descender
must be treated separately: Scale the descender vertically ("Center of Selection")
by itself so that it has the proper depth; lighten the horizontal strokes, which will
have become heavier through *vertical* scaling, to their original width. You might
have to detach the descender of the *g* to perform the necessary changes, and then
re-attach the descender when you are finished. As always, it helps to have pasted
a copy of the original in the template layer for comparison. Notice also that the
g often does not have a descender as long as the *p, j, q* or *y*: this relationship
should be preserved when altering the *g*.

❖ ❖ *14. Using blend fonts.*   This is an interesting and useful tool. While
             you can use it to make a blend between Palatino and Helvetica — an
enterprise of doubtful utility — you can use it to produce intermediate weights
of fonts. My purpose here is to give you an approach to the tool and to point out
a few potential problems. See also Figures 6.12 through 6.14.

FIGURE 6.12   BLENDING FONTS — 1

I'm going to demonstrate the Blend function using News Gothic, largely because it is very consistent between the plain and bold weights. Even here, though, there are some problems, as the lowercase *f* will demonstrate. Notice that I have opened both weights and have placed their outline windows next to each other so that I can directly compare the letters. What you can't see is that I have also opened a new, untitled font.

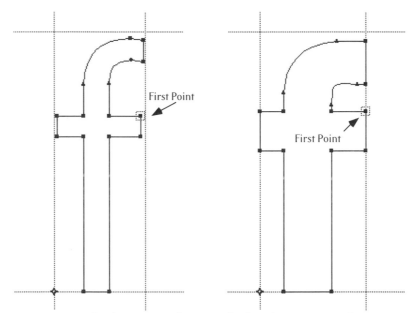

Interestingly, when Fontographer opens this font, the First Point in the two characters is at the same relative location: as well, both characters have the same number of points, and they are all in the same relative positions. A perfect candidate for blending, as the next figure shows.

FIGURE 6.13   BLENDING FONTS — 2

And here we have a perfectly blended *f* with no problems whatsoever.

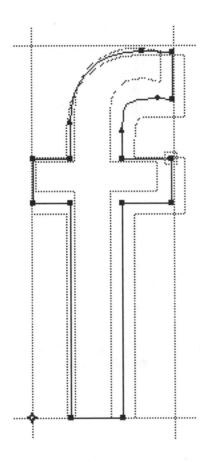

There are problems, however, when you let Fontographer correct path directions on its own, before it performs the blending. See Figure 6.14.

FIGURE 6.14   BLENDING FONTS — 3

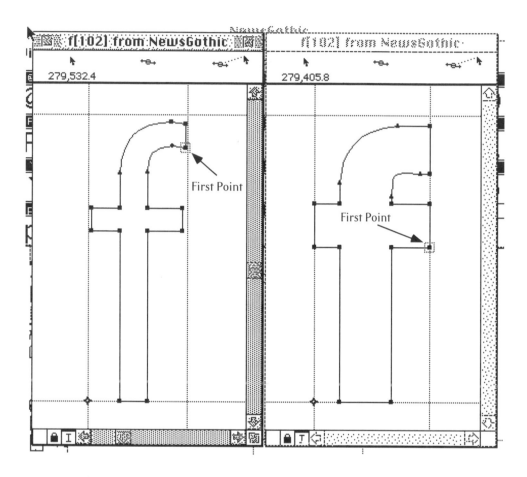

Notice that the First Point is no longer in the same relative position in the two characters. Left to its own devices, Fontographer fixes the First Point as the lowest and rightmost point, as the characters above demonstrate. If we were to blend these characters (in which Fontographer has automatically calculated the position of the First Point) we would arrive at the following mess:

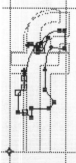

This is not Fontographer's fault, but is a direct consequence of the mathematics of blending two outlines, and of the fact that the lowest, rightmost point changes in the two characters. It also indicates that you are better off to work on a character-by-character basis to establish that both base characters have the same number of points, that they are in the same relative positions, and that the First Point is in the same relative position.

❖ ❖ The ideal is to blend between two characters that have the same number of drawing points in the same relative positions; the First Point must also be in the same relative location in the two characters to be blended. Under most circumstances — and here I am referring principally to two weights of the same typeface — these conditions hold true: Where they do not hold true, you would be better advised to work on a character-by-character basis in generating a blended font. You could blend an entire font — Select All, Blend — but there are bound to be problems, problems that could be avoided by stepping through the characters of the base fonts individually before blending.

Candidates for blending

Blending caveats and work method

❖ ❖ Begin, therefore, by opening the two base fonts, and then by opening a new, untitled, font. Be sure that you have given Fontographer an ample amount of RAM to use, at least 4mb and preferably more: each font you open consumes at least 200K. Then open character outline windows from the two base fonts and place them side-by-side to compare the characters. You are looking for the same number of points in both base characters, those points should be in same relative positions, and the First Point is in the same relative position in the two characters. Select the character you have inspected in the base fonts, and select Blend.

❖ ❖ The resulting dialog box will show you the names of the base fonts and the name of the destination font; it will also ask if you want to blend "All existing source characters" or "Selected destination characters": make sure that "Selected destination characters" is checked. Finally there are the Settings, in which you tell Fontographer how much to blend and the steps it is to take in blending. As you are working on a character-by-character basis, you might — or might not, depending on how aggressive you have been about regularizing the base font outlines — want to check the "Insert points to force a match" option. You do *not* want the "Correct path directions first" option to be checked — you have already taken care of this. Finally, click on 'OK' and await developments.

15. *From roman to italic.*   The pairing of a roman to an italic is a thorny issue. Sometimes you discover, as Bruce Rogers did, that the roman (his Centaur) is perfectly matched by an already-existing italic (in this case Frederic Warde's Arrighi). In other cases, a design is made from scratch based on the best italic models. In still other cases (which will be our object here) italic design elements are

introduced into an already-existing roman. Type design is never easy, and designing companion faces is one of the greater challenges of the art.

Begin by taking your original roman and creating an oblique version of it. You will use skew; special-skew-vertical 0° to 25° (Fontographer 3.x); element-transform-skew-HORIZONTAL 0° to -25° (Fontographer 4.x). The more you slant the face, the less readable it becomes, so don't overdo. When the characters are slanted, the handles attached to the drawing points are also slanted, i.e., they are no longer orthogonal. In Fontographer 4.x, therefore, you will want to select all the characters and subject them to Clean Up Paths (setting 1) to correct this problem.

Most italic typefaces are narrower than their companion romans. The next step might be, then, to condense the typeface (i.e., scale it horizontally) by something between 5% and 25%: again, don't overdo. You might find that the type has become a little spindly looking. If so, use Change Weight… (under Special menu in Fontographer 3.5, and Element in Fontographer 4.x) to add a few units of weight to make up for the condensing.

Remember that the end result of this effort is not an italic, but rather a sloped, or oblique roman. A real italic has elements of the italic hand, i.e., calligraphy, and these can either be grafted on to your sloped roman, or you can start from scratch by designing an italic face using design elements (serifs, for instance) from the roman. One of the first candidates for change would be the lowercase *a,* which has a recognizably italic form. From there you could work on the *e, g,* and *y* which also have distinctively italic forms.

16. *Small caps.* Small caps on the desktop are a bit of a problem. If we let the software create them, they are inevitably too light for the surrounding type. This happens because software-produced small caps are simply normal caps scaled down. True small caps are a little wider and have had their strokes widened slightly after scaling, thus preserving the color of the type. If you do not wish to redraw the uppercase to produce small caps (a lot of work!), then the careful use of the scaling and/or Change Weight functions will produce remarkably good results.

Small caps in Fontographer:

- Scale caps

- Horizontal scaling: caution

- Change Weight ...

The approach you use will vary from typeface to typeface. What I will do here is present you with a structured setting-forth of the possibilities and note along the way some of the things to watch for or avoid.

- ⁊ You begin by uniformly (i.e., both horizontally and vertically) scaling the characters. Normally, small caps are slightly larger than the lowercase. How much you scale the characters at the outset will depend upon what you do next. Print a sample of the caps, small caps, and lowercase together to see how much alteration is necessary.

- ⁊ You might try scaling the characters horizontally by a relatively small amount, 5% or so. Do not overdo!! This will thicken the vertical strokes somewhat, but the horizontal strokes will stay the same, thus altering the character of the typeface. Some typefaces are more sensitive to this than others. If the results look sufficiently promising, you could alter the widths of the horizontal strokes by a suitable amount to create a consistent appearance.

- ⁊ You might also try the Change Weight... command. This approach suggested to me the observation that, in the absence of real small caps, I could substitute type in a bold font at a smaller size for them. For instance, I would use caps in Times Bold at 7 pt for small caps with 12 pt text type. This in turn suggests that you could apply a weight change of, say, 0.5% to 1% of the em to the scaled-down upper case to arrive at small caps. If you have scaled the original caps down to exactly the x-height, then be sure that "Don't change vertical size" and "Don't change horizontal size" are *unchecked*: We want the small caps to be slightly larger than the x-height, and slightly wider than simple scaling would make them. With "Don't change vertical size" *unchecked*, the bottoms of the characters will end up below the baseline.

▸ Subject the results of these transformations to severe scrutiny: The eye is the final arbiter in these matters. If you find anything amiss, go back and change it. In particular, small caps should never detract from the flow of reading: The instant you are consciously aware of seeing a different typeface, or there is a change in type color, you can be sure that something needs correction.

17. *Missing or alternate characters.* Some case histories from my own experience may indicate what I mean. Not long ago Adobe Systems released Rudolf Koch's Wilhelm Klingspor Gotisch, a magnificent and distinctive blackletter. I was pleased that the type had been released, but not so pleased that some of the ornamental characters (a vine leaf and a cross) were missing, and that the paragraph sign (also called the pilcrow: "❡") was not the one originally designed by Koch, but rather a bland all-purpose example of the character. Fortunately, I knew of an article in the fifth volume of *The Fleuron* (1926, see Bibliography) that contained the original form of the pilcrow as well as the other ornaments. It was the work of an instant to enlarge the original, create a TIFF file, import the TIFF files into Fontographer as templates, trace the templates, and thus restore the typeface to something closer to the original.

Not long after I received a version of Eric Gill's *Perpetua*, I chanced to see an interesting advertisement done in letterpress for a book. Looking closely at the really magnificent presswork, I noticed that the typeface was *Perpetua*, but the lowercase *y* had a straight back. Hmm. I went to my reference sources (among them *Anatomy of a Typeface* by Lawson) and discovered that, indeed, Gill had designed a straight-back *y*, which he intended to be used *inside* a word, while the standard *y* with the curved tail was to be used at the end of a word. In this case, though, I could not find a suitable original that could be enlarged and scanned for a TIFF file. Instead I opened the type-1 file in Fontographer, took the original *y* from the PostScript file, and altered it appropriately until I was satisfied with the new character.

18. The *f*-ligatures.   The lowercase letter *f* is a tough one — the top of the character often extends considerably to the right, thus requiring either a negative right-sidebearing, or kerning with the next character, or often a combination of both. Most typefaces have tackled some of the more difficult f-pairs by making them into ligatures, i.e., two letters joined into one character.

   Almost all PostScript typefaces have two f-ligatures: *fi* and *fl*. Notice that the dot over the *i* often disappears, the top of the *f* being extended slightly to make up for the disappearance of the dot. The reason is simple: the dot *and* the top of the *f* tend to bump into each other, thereby creating a distracting visual jumble. Likewise, if you place the *l* far enough away from the *f* so that the two do not bump into each other, the distance between the two letters will be too great; put them at the correct distance and they will bump into each other. The solution is to form the *f* and the *l* artfully into a ligature.

19. The *t* ligatures.   There are some ligatures with *t* as their connected element. Most common are the *ct* and *st* ligatures seen, for example, in this paragraph.

20. *A basic font for a quick project.* You should own the *Adobe Collector's Edition.* It contains both a serif and sans serif typeface. These can be used for any number of purposes: make swash characters or fancy drop caps of them or use them as a basis for a typeface.

21. *From handwriting to font.* This is a particularly interesting problem because it requires us to create a typeface — with all of the structure and limitations that implies) that mimics handwriting, which is notorious for lacking much in the way of structure.

Depending on the writing instrument that created the original, you will proceed in one of two directions. If the original was done in pencil or ballpoint pen, you might consider creating a *stroked* font: Simply follow the curves of the original with a single line; select a stroke width that looks natural in the Metrics window; and select the appropriate *end caps* and *line joins.* Finally, expand the strokes into outlines, check for proper path direction, and remove any overlap (some of which may have to be done by hand if an outline crosses itself).

If, on the other hand, the original was executed with a calligrapher's pen with a fairly wide point, then you will want to treat it as an outline font from the start.

In such work, the guideline layer should contain some more information. First it should indicate where letters join, that is, the height above the baseline that the connecting strokes actually connect; this will help to ensure consistency. Second, there should be some indication of the angle at which the strokes connect, also for the sake of consistency.

22. *PC font conversions.* There are zillions of PC typefaces available both in Type 1 and TrueType formats. The trick is to get them into the Mac format. Fontographer makes this easy:

▸ If the original PC file is compressed (that is, it has a .zip suffix) then you will need to use Stuffit or UnZip to decompress the file.

▸ PC files all have suffixes. You are looking for the following: .PFB—Type 1 outlines; .AFM—Adobe Font Metrics data; .TTF—TrueType outline

▸ If the PC files are on a 3.5-inch disk, run them through Apple File Exchange and put the resulting files on your hard disk.

▸ Make sure that the resulting files (for .PFB and .TTF files) have the TYPE 'BINA' (notice the uppercase letters) and the MAKER 'mdos' (notice the lowercase letters). If necessary, use a file utility such as FileTyper to accomplish this.

▸ For the AFM files, use the Text translation facility of AFE to convert CR/LF (carriage-returns/linefeeds) to CR; file TYPE must be TEXT; MAKER can be anything. This sort of conversion could also be done with a utility/text-editor like McSink.

- Uncompress PC font

- Locate .PFB, .AFM, or .TTF

- Optional AFE

- Check file TYPE and MAKER

- PC AFMs

Fontographer 4.x & PC fonts from CD

TrueType to PostScript

TrueType has more drawing points

Fontographer will now open the files, and the AFMs can be read for correct character spacing. By the way, Fontographer 4.x will open PC fonts directly from PC font CDs, such as the Bitstream 500 font CD. You must have the appropriate extensions loaded from the installation of the CD software for this to work. Fontographer 4.x knows about file extensions and will open the PostScript automatically. It also imports the metrics (including kerning) from TrueType automatically.

23. *TrueType to PostScript conversion.* When you convert True-Type to PostScript format, you may be in for a surprise—all those drawing points! TrueType is drawn using quadratic splines as opposed to the Bézier curves used by PostScript. Without going into all the math, the bottom line is this: TrueType needs more drawing points

Quadratic
splines of
TrueType
vs. Bézier
curves of
PostScript

than does PostScript, about twice as many. This makes characters *much* harder to edit. Indeed, if it is your purpose to edit a TrueType typeface by converting it to PostScript, it might be worth your while to find a PostScript original to work with and save yourself some aggravation. Indeed, I believe that it will always be easier to develop TrueType from PostScript rather than doing it directly: the quadratic splines of TrueType are ornery critters that are very difficult to control, whereas the supple Bézier curves are very well behaved and easy to control. See Figure 6.15 for an example.

FIGURE 6.15   FROM TRUETYPE TO POSTSCRIPT

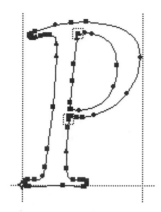

By way of example, we're going to use the letter *P* from a typeface designed by Arthur Baker called Oxford. This shows the TrueType character as it was opened in Fontographer. I have already copied the letter and pasted it into the Template layer so that we can compare the results of Clean Up Paths. ***There is a total of 60 drawing points.***

Clean Up Paths

☒ **Inserts points at extrema (recommended)**

☒ **Simplify paths**

How much to simplify:

⬅ ▥ ▨▨▨▨▨▨▨▨▨▨▨ ➡ | 1 |

Less   **More**

| **OK** |

| Cancel |

Notice how little simplification it takes to get the job done.

Sometimes the serifs are not true to the original after 'Clean Up', so check them.

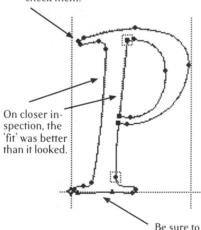

On closer in-spection, the 'fit' was better than it looked.

Be sure to check things like cupped serifs to make sure the program 'caught' them.

Wow – only 22 points! All of the usual clutter of TrueType points is gone, and all we are left with is (pretty much) the basic shape we need using only a third as many points. There is still a little touchup work we need to do, particularly on the vertical stem and the serif at the top. Still, for all practical purposes, we're done. The interesting thing to note here is that as long as Clean Up Paths has enough information about the path (i.e., has enough points on the path), Clean Up Paths can maintain the shape of the path with a very high degree of reliability.

TrueType to
Type 1
pitfalls

Clean Up
Paths ...
in Fonto-
grapher 4.x

Clean Up
not to be
applied
successively

Warning! There are some things to keep in mind when you convert TrueType to Type 1. First, there is almost inevitably an alteration of the outline: You will want to check to see that this is not serious, and be prepared to do some hand editing. Second, it is perfectly possible (in some cases even likely) that the resulting Type 1 font will crash the PostScript interpreter. This can happen for two reasons: Either there are too many points in the character, or the number of 'turn points' has been exceeded — or both. In either case, you might try Clean Up Paths to solve the problem.

24. Clean up paths.   It is possible to convert virtually any curve to conforming Type 1 curves using the Clean Up Paths command in Fontographer version 4.x. There are two parts to Clean Up Paths. First, the command can place drawing points at extrema and orthogonalize those handles. Second, the command can simplify the path, i.e., reduce the number of points on the path. The command's dialog box offers both options and, under most circumstances, you will want both. The "How much to simplify" slider bar has values from 1 to 5, and determines how aggressively Fontographer attempts to remove extra points. Bear in mind that point removal is done often at the expense of the accuracy with which the remaining points conform to the original shape. Experiment with the settings. I have found that a setting of 1 or 2 is entirely satisfactory; higher settings might remove a few more points, but at the cost of more hand editing later.

The more points there are in the original path(s), the better a job Clean Up Paths will be able to do in maintaining the original shape(s). With this in mind, then, there is an important point to be made. Successive simplifications are not the same as simplification with a higher simplification index — successive simplifications are carried out on fewer and fewer points, so the resulting shape cannot remain faithful to the original. So, if I simplify a path twice with Simplification set at 1, the results will not be the same as one Simplification at an index of 2. If the results of a given Clean Up Paths command are not satisfactory to you, *be sure first to undo the original Clean Up before applying the next.* In addition, for very careful work, paste a copy of the original into the Template layer for before-and-after comparison and final hand-editing.

An example will show you the power of this command, and possibly suggest other uses to you: see Figure 6.15. Notice that the operation is not completely foolproof and that there is almost always a little manual clean-up to be done. Still, the resulting shapes will be much easier to edit and/or alter. You might even do the entire TT font over into a Type 1: that would depend on the type of type, so to speak. In any case, your best bet would be to proceed character-by-character, first putting a copy of the TrueType outline in the Template layer to compare with the 'cleaned-up' character. The more meticulous you are, the more hand-editing you can expect to do.

In fact, the Clean Up Paths command is very powerful indeed and can do a lot of messy odd-jobs very quickly and easily. If you are given a piece of artwork done in Illustrator or FreeHand — but not drawn using standard Type 1 techniques — you can quickly make it conform to Type 1 rules by using Clean Up Paths. Or if you are working on a very tricky or involved outline and/or are in a big hurry, you can place more drawing points than you need (letting Automatic Curvature take care of the shape of the curve for the present) and then apply Clean Up Paths.

25. *From artwork to font.* This is an interesting problem. How do you take a graphic executed in MacDraw, MacPaint or Canvas and port it to Fontographer for use as a logo font? Much depends

Format
translation

Option-Copy
from Illus-
trator or
Freehand to
Fontographer

Check im-
ported
paths

Improve orig-
inals in
Photoshop

upon the nature of the graphic. Type 1 and TrueType formats do not admit the use of grayscales and bitmaps. A bitmap or TIFF graphic must therefore be pasted into Fontographer and traced.

PICT and object-oriented graphics present a few complications, but nothing that can't be overcome fairly easily. The trick here is to *translate* the graphic into a format that can easily be understood by Fontographer, while losing as little information as possible. My experience is that Canvas is a useful translation program. It can open a wide variety of files, which it can then save to Illustrator format (either 1.1 or 88). Use can also be made of the DrawOver utility (which comes with Adobe Illustrator) which converts PICT format files into Illustrator files. That done, it is then a piece of cake to open the Illustrator file in either FreeHand or Illustrator, Option-Copy the graphic to the clipboard (thus preserving the Bézier curve information), and finally paste the graphic directly into Fontographer as an outline character. The Option-Copy technique does not work directly from Canvas.

You're not quite done. First, make sure the path direction is correct. Second, if the character is very complex, you may have to break it up into sections. Or you may be able to simplify the graphic. Third, check that there are no overlapping paths. Finally, especially if this is intended for a Type 1 font, make sure that the handles conform to the rules set out in the Chapter 1: failure to do this could result in a font that will not print, or which could crash the PostScript interpreter. (See above for the use of Clean Up Paths in Fontographer 4.)

If you are copying a TIFF, PICT or bitmap file into Fontographer for tracing, you might consider cleaning up the file in a program like Photoshop first. This is particularly useful if the template is dirty or is a bitmap at a mere 72 dpi.

26. *Breaking up complex paths.* Complex paths with a large number of drawing points often won't print as characters in a font. The PostScript interpreter is strict about enforcing the number of points that can be in any given character. Also the turn point restriction will be encountered. For these reasons, it is better to break up a complex character into two or more parts. See Figures 6.16 and 6.17 for an interesting approach to this problem, brought to my attention by Richard Beatty. This same approach can be used to break up any graphic, no matter how simple or complex, that would be best assembled by the user: a frame, for instance. A frame would require the application of the method shown here not only to the horizontal dimension, but to the vertical dimension as well. Note: If the path is really complex, and/or has been imported from an illustration program, run Clean Up Paths before applying Remove Overlap.

Figure 6.16   Divide & Conquer: 1

We are going to take a complex character and chop it up
into two smaller pieces, so that we will not over-burden the
PostScript interpreter. To do this we are going to exploit the
nature of clockwise and counterclockwise path directions.

The dividing
rectangle (selected)

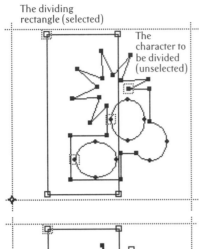

The
character to
be divided
(unselected)

The illustration at the left shows a complex character
that we are going to cut into two parts. We are going
to use a rectangle to act as a convenient dividing
shape. *The rectangle must be given a counterclockwise path direction: select this in the Element menu.* Fontographer assumes that an external
path is clockwise when drawn. Changing the direction of an external path to *counterclockwise* makes
that path act like cookie cutter, cutting out whatever
lies inside it.

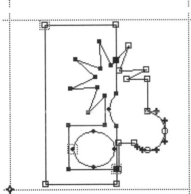

Deselect everything and select Remove Overlap
from the Element menu: the results are shown at
the left. Notice that everything inside the rectangle
has been retained, while only the outer path remains outside the rectangle. I double- clicked on
the outermost path to select and show it. Now I'm
going to delete it...

Voilà. Now we have the left-hand side of the character, which I have taken the liberty of showing in
Preview. Now select all, copy and paste into a convenient character slot. Return to the original character and hit Undo until you have the original shapes
back to where they were just before you performed
Remove Overlap.

FIGURE 6.17   DIVIDE & CONQUER: 2

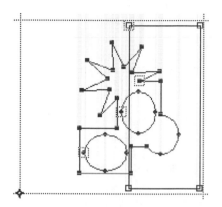

Notice that the division rectangle has been moved to the right; we want the left side of the moved rectangle to coincide exactly with what used to be the right side: make sure that Snap to Points is "on"; select the rectangle; holding down the Shift key (to constrain movement), take hold of the lower-left-hand corner point and move it until it snaps to the lower-right-hand corner point.

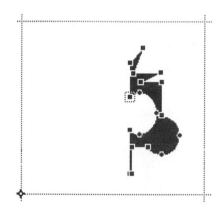

Once again, use Remove Overlap (making sure that the division rectangle still has a counterclockwise path direction), delete the resulting path that contains the remains of the rectangle, and you should have something like the illustration shown at the left (again shown in preview).

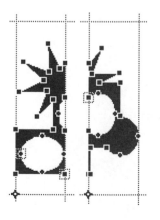

All that remains is to make the right side of the left-hand character coincident with its right sidebearing (i.e., give it a 0-unit right sidebearing), and to make the left side of the right-hand character coincident with its left sidebearing (i.e., give it a 0-unit left sidebearing): this will make the characters match up perfectly giving the illusion of being one character. Use Set Metrics in the Metrics menu.

27. *Combinations of typefaces.*   Italic upper-case letters were not devised until the middle of the 16th century. Up to that time, people who wrote in the italic hand used standard roman upper-case letters. The effect is striking and beautiful in the extreme, and worthy to be used again. Fontographer can assist: create a new file; copy the roman upper-case and the italic lower-case to the new file; if possible, copy the *lowercase numerals* to the new file, or create them as we discussed above. This could be done with virtually any typeface, but gives the best effect when the italics are based firmly on Renaissance models: Palatino, Garamond (any), or Perpetua, for example.

28. *Swash characters.*   There are a number of typefaces which have effective swash characters that are not currently (or readily) available in PostScript — Bookman, Weiss, and Post Medieval, for example. This would be an excellent source of material to work on, particularly as the work would go fairly quickly, and there would be a relatively large return for comparatively little work.

29. Font Chameleon.   This program from Ares Software repre- sents an interesting departure from the usual font-design technology. The system works by taking basic letter-shapes, a template typeface if you like, and altering the templates algorithmically to produce other typefaces. Thus the same template could give rise to a variety of Bodoni-like or Helvetica-like fonts. If, further, you carefully create the templates in such a way that they are mutually compatible, as it were — that is, any given character has the same number of drawing points in the same relative position as the same character in the other templates — then you can interpolate between any two template typefaces to produce yet a third typeface. See Figures 6.18 and 6.19 for an example.

FIGURE 6.18   FONT CHAMELEON & BLENDING TYPE: 1

In the next illustration (Figure 6.19) you will see the progression of materials that led to the creation of the typeface "Felice" through the use of Font Chameleon from Ares Software.

Samples 1 and 2 are ITC Berkeley (based on a Goudy typeface) and Melior (designed by Hermann Zapf), respectively. Sample 3 is the unedited result of blending those two typefaces 50/50. Not bad, there are just a few points to be cleared up. The 'Q' has a hairline, vestigial stroke at the bottom left, and the top of the '7' is a bit coarse. The ligatures, too, are a bit unhappy. The only consistent problem was some kinking in the areas of the serifs. Still, the result is not bad at all, and certainly a good place to start for a new typeface. It is interesting to note that Melior is clearly the dominant face.

The roman shows some alterations due to personal taste: The 'M' has serifs at the top, the 'e' has a lip, and the 'y' has been made to be rather more like the Berkeley character. The text you are now reading is shown in sample 4.

All of the derivative fonts (*oblique,* **bold**, and ***bold-oblique***) were created in Fontographer using the roman. I altered a few characters (a, e, and f) to give some individuality to the oblique. The bold and bold-oblique were made using the techniques of Chapter 6. I scaled the characters vertically by 1000% relative to the basepoint, added 40 em-units, and then scaled the characters vertically relative to the basepoint by 9.9693%, which brought them back to their original vertical size. This had the effect of adding weight to the vertical strokes, but only very slightly to the horizontal strokes, thus increasing the stroke-weight ratio, and preventing the faces from becoming too dark. Some of the thin vertical, or near-vertical, strokes, such as in the A, M, W, and X, had to be made thinner by hand to preserve the desired stroke-weight ratio.

FIGURE 6.19   FONT CHAMELEON & BLENDING TYPE: 2

ABCDEFGHIJKLMNOPQRSTUVWXYZ   1
abcdefghijklmnopqrstuvwxyz
1234567890&fifl

ABCDEFGHIJKLMNOPQRSTUVWXYZ   2
abcdefghijklmnopqrstuvwxyz
1234567890&fifl

ABCDEFGHIJKLMNOPQRSTUVWXYZ   3
abcdefghijklmnopqrstuvwxyz
1234567890&fifl

ABCDEFGHIJKLMNOPQRSTUVWXYZ   4
abcdefghijklmnopqrstuvwxyz
1234567890&fifl

ABCDEFGHIJKLMNOPQRSTUVWXYZ   5
abcdefghijklmnopqrstuvwxyz
1234567890&fifl

ABCDEFGHIJKLMNOPQRSTUVWXYZ   6
abcdefghijklmnopqrstuvwxyz
1234567890&fifl

ABCDEFGHIJKLMNOPQRSTUVWXYZ   7
abcdefghijklmnopqrstuvwxyz
1234567890&fifl

There has been some criticism of the fidelity of the letterforms produced by the base fonts in Font Chameleon. I think this misses the point. If you absolutely need genuine Palatino, for instance, you should acquire it without hesitation and not rely on an approximation. If, however, the work at hand is conveniently done by what Font Chameleon thinks of as Palatino, all well and good.

30. Blending typefaces.   In the early 1980s, Donald Knuth devised a program for drawing typefaces called Metafont. The idea was that you could describe a letterform by, in turn, describing the path of a pen drawing the letterform* and the description, finally, was in the form of a computer program of sorts that told the pen what to do and when. The advantage is that that you can then change a few variables in the 'program' and produce a very different typeface, without having to redraw the whole typeface character-by-character. So, in 1982 Knuth wrote: "The idea of Metafont should now be clear. But what good is it? The ability to manipulate lots of parameters may be interesting and fun, but does anybody really need a 6½-point font that is one fourth of the way between Baskerville and Helvetica?"

❖   As an aside, you might be wondering: If Metafont is so clever and flexible, why not use it? There are a variety of reasons. First, the learning curve associated with Metafont is absolutely monumental. Second, I do not have the necessary temperament and skills to manipulate it well: You have to be a good mathematician, computer programmer, *and* have the necessary skill in drawing typefaces.

With Font Chameleon, Knuth's "font that is one-fourth of the way between Baskerville and Helvetica" is now a practical possibility. In a way, using Font Chameleon to blend typefaces is

---

*   The "pen" in Metafont is considerably more sophisticated than anything currently available. It can have any shape. It can change shape in the course of a stroke, and it can change direction and width in the course of a stroke.

a very good reason to own Fontographer — among many other reasons, of course. Even the best blends can use a bit of refinement, and Font Chameleon has a few problems that can best be remedied by bringing Fontographer to bear on the finished product. The key thing to remember is this: weird in, weird out; you can try to blend ITC Kabel and Bodoni, if you insist, but don't expect a masterpiece of typographic design and good taste to be the result. Blending, at its best, should happen between two reasonably compatible typefaces, say, Melior and ITC Berkeley, as shown in Figures 6.18 and 6.19.

Blending typefaces

FC: No kerning pairs...

...but too many drawing points

31. *Fonts directly from FC.* There are a few points you will want to watch out for when you generate typefaces from Font Chameleon. First, they have no kerning pairs. If you are using a pure font, you could try to import a similar AFM that has kerning pairs. For blended fonts, this is problematic as there may be no premade AFM that will work. Fortunately, you use Fontographer and can get it both to adjust letterspacing and to create kerning pairs. Yet another alternative would be to use a utility like URW's Kernus.

Second, most characters have too many drawing points, particularly those that have been produced from blending. The best thing to do is to open the Font Chameleon-produced typeface in Fontographer, select all the characters and perform a global "Clean up characters" with a setting of 1 or 2. This will produce both font files that are smaller and typefaces that are easier to edit.

Finally, some blended characters don't work out very well. The *fi* ligature, for example, can look a little peculiar with the dot from the *i* partly merged with the overhang from the *f.* Again, Fontographer, or, for that matter Ares' own FontMonger, can be helpful in working out the rough spots. There were also some problems with kinks at the brackets that connect serifs to strokes. All of these had to be remedied before the derivative faces were created.

Drop shadows

Concept of the envelope

The Expand Stroke method

32. FC typefaces as a starting point. You might be better off looking on the output from Font Chameleon as a starting point for your own further designs. In the example given here, I began with a blend of Melior and Berkeley. I then decided that the *fi* and *fl* ligatures needed work. I also decided to create text (or x-height) numerals. I also decided that I wanted a full set of f-ligatures. Finally, I wanted to reshape the tail of the lowercase *y* into something that appealed to me more. Incidentally, I reduced the final x-height somewhat and had to condense the face very slightly as a result in order to preserve the proportions of the x-height portions of the lowercase characters. Further work produced a full family of fonts (or even an italic face with still more work), and will eventually produce a small caps font. See Figure 6.18 for more details.

33. Drop shadows. This is an effect that I see rarely in actual use, but about which a great deal has been written. It is an effect of limited utility, though in the right circumstances it can be very interesting. All approaches aim at the creation of an envelope shape that will contain the original character shape; part of the envelope shows the character outline, while the other part of the envelope shows the shadow.

The method detailed in the ReadMe file that accompanies Fontographer begins by expanding, via Expand Stroke, the existing character outlines, and then moving the outer part of the resulting shape diagonally to create a shadow effect. This is a useful approach in some instances, but has the failing that it is not algorithmic (except for the use of Expand Stroke): Each character must be created and adjusted by hand. It also has the limitation that the original character shape is distorted.

I have devised a method which is entirely algorithmic except for a few minor clean-up operations, and preserves the original shape of the character. These are the steps:

1. To begin, copy the original character to the clipboard — you'll need it later. *Tip:* You can paste characters into the Template layer as a convenient holding area — make the Template layer invisible if you have to.

2. Next, clone the character and move the clone diagonally in the direction of the desired shadow, by the distance that will give you the desired size of the shadow.

3. Deselect everything and use Remove Overlap.

4. Add weight by the amount that you want the outline portion to have. At this point there might be some artifacts of the Add Weight command — delete them.

5. Paste the copy from the Clibpoard.

6. Correct path directions. In Preview, you should now see a character with a shadow.

Alternatively, and for greater flexibility, you could proceed as follows:

1. Copy the original character to the clipboard. Let's call the character in the window Copy1.

2. Clone Copy1 to create Copy2.

3. Move Copy2 in the direction and by the distance you need for the shadow.

4. Add weight to Copy1 for the desired amount of outline.

5. Add weight to Copy2 — *not necessarily the same amount of weight you added to Copy1, indeed, it may not be necessary to add any weight to Copy2 at all* — to adjust the shadow segments.

6. Remove Overlap.

7. Paste the character from the clipboard.

8. Correct path directions.

In either case, you may have to do a little touching up by hand, but the nature of the touchups makes them predictable and simple. See Figures 6.20 and 6.21 for examples.

34. *Calligraphic inline.* The inline shape does not have to be uniform in width. You can use the Calligraphy tool to create a more interesting inline letter. Figure 6.22 has the details.

FIGURE 6.20   CASTING SHADOWS — 1

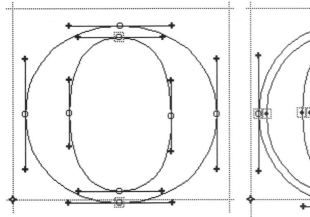

1. Begin by selecting all the points.

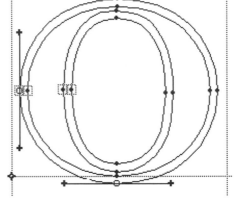

2. Expand Stroke—in this case 30 units.

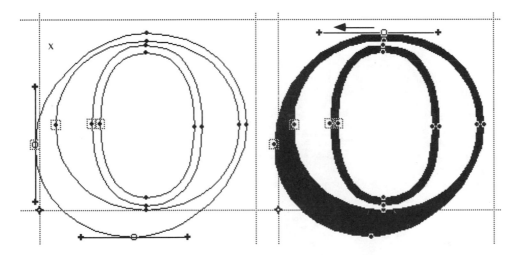

3. Select the left- and bottom-most points and move them diagonally—in this case -50 units horizontally, and -75 units vertically. Notice a thinning of the stroke at 'x'.

4. The final character as shown in Preview. The left handle of the selected point is moved to the left to counteract the thinning effect.

FIGURE 6.21 CASTING SHADOWS – 2

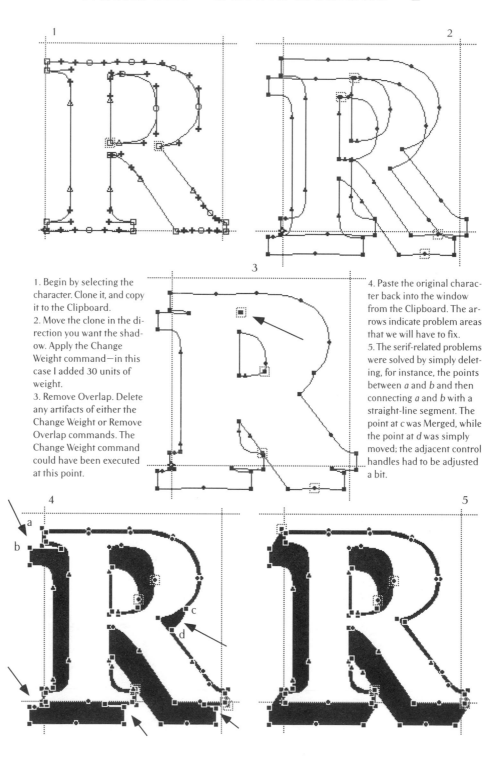

1. Begin by selecting the character. Clone it, and copy it to the Clipboard.

2. Move the clone in the direction you want the shadow. Apply the Change Weight command—in this case I added 30 units of weight.

3. Remove Overlap. Delete any artifacts of either the Change Weight or Remove Overlap commands. The Change Weight command could have been executed at this point.

4. Paste the original character back into the window from the Clipboard. The arrows indicate problem areas that we will have to fix.

5. The serif-related problems were solved by simply deleting, for instance, the points between *a* and *b* and then connecting *a* and *b* with a straight-line segment. The point at *c* was Merged, while the point at *d* was simply moved; the adjacent control handles had to be adjusted a bit.

FIGURE 6.22   CALLIGRAPHIC INLINE

Normally, you would select a character, clone it,
expand strokes, and correct path directions to obtain
an inline character. Try using the Calligraphic Pen
option instead:

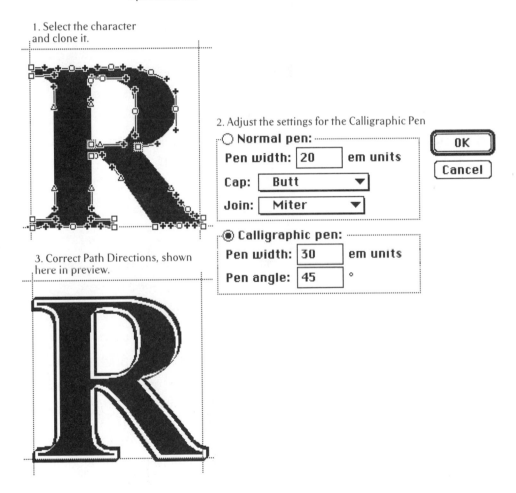

1. Select the character and clone it.

2. Adjust the settings for the Calligraphic Pen

○ **Normal pen:**

Pen width: 20   em units

Cap: Butt ▼

Join: Miter ▼

◉ **Calligraphic pen:**

Pen width: 30   em units

Pen angle: 45   °

OK

Cancel

3. Correct Path Directions, shown here in preview.

35. *Using other programs.* Fontographer is a specialized Post-Script illustration program very much like Illustrator or FreeHand. Illustrator and FreeHand — and all other programs that can read, write and edit PostScript artwork — have capabilities that Fontographer may not have. Don't overlook the possibility of exporting a character from Fontographer, re-working it in another program, and finally re-importing the finished character back into Fontographer. Programs that come to mind, in addition to Illustrator and FreeHand, are Canvas and Intellidraw.

And if you can *edit* type in other programs, you could also *create* type in those same programs. For typefaces consisting of alphabetic characters, I think that Fontographer cannot be bettered. But you might want to draw, say, dingbats, or symbols for specialized work (electronics, for example), or to create some printer's flowers. All of this could be done on other programs that have unique and specialized drawing tools.

Exporting is easy. Select Export in the File menu — the resulting dialog box allows you either to export selected characters or to specify the characters there. The character(s) will then be exported as an Illustrator 1.1 document. Open that document in your editing software, perform the necessary operations, and finally re-export the file to Illustrator format. Alternatively, and very conveniently, you can option-copy the character in Illustrator or Freehand and Paste it into the appropriate character window in Fontographer. You will have to scale the result.*

---

* You might be wondering if the option-copy technique works when going from Fontographer to Illustrator or FreeHand. It doesn't work going to Illustrator. For Freehand (version 5) the short answer is: almost, but not quite. The outlines are distorted when pasted into Freehand in a way that is difficult to predict and not worth the time to fix.

What sort of editing would you do? Well, you might use Illustrator's Punk or Scribble or Calligraphy filters, or FreeHand's Fisheye filter. Further afield, if you have access to it, you could try Ikarus-M's Antique effect for a rough appearance.

Remember that any characters drawn or edited in other programs may not conform to basic PostScript standards for fonts — drawing points placed at local maxima and minima, orthogonal drawing handles, and a relatively small number of drawing points. To be on the safe side, perform a Clean Up Paths operation on any outline imported into Fontographer. You may be tempted to use the Simplify function in FreeHand (version 5). Resist this temptation. FreeHand's Simplify works very differently from Fontographer's. FreeHand does not place drawing points at maxima/minima, does not orthogonalize handles, but does perform absolutely ruthless simplification, sometimes to the point of subtly altering the shape.

36. Grunge, etc.   Another program that you might use to interact with Fontographer is Adobe Photoshop or Fractal Design Painter. These programs can distort type in ways that would otherwise be difficult or impossible. You might, for instance, subject type to any of the effects contained in Adobe Gallery Effects; or you could simply blur the typeface using Gaussian blur; and/or you could apply the wave effect, or twirl, or zigzag or whatever; use an interesting map; spherize; break the type into tiles; subject the type to a wind effect; etc. Your purpose is to stylize and/or distort and/or decompose the type in an interesting and suggestive way.

The next step is to save your Photoshop work in TIFF format, and to import that into Adobe Streamline. Streamline knows all about grayscale (and color) TIFFs. By adjusting the Streamline settings suitably, you can have the program trace your Photoshop-altered type. If you tell Streamline to look for several shades of gray, then you will be presented with several lettershapes from which you can choose the best one.

Finally, you have two options. You can simply place the derived outlines in Fontographer. Or you could take them into Illustrator or FreeHand for further manipulation (simplifying the paths in FreeHand, for instance) and then into Fontographer. If any of the resulting paths has more than 256 points (not out of the question, even after simplification) you will have to save the resulting face in Type 3 format. In any event, the subject of hinting is largely open to question in the case of highly distorted and irregular type.

Type Specimens ❑ 7

OW THAT YOU HAVE CREATED, or re-created, or modified the typeface of your choice, it is time to show it off in all its glory. This is done — in fact, has been done traditionally from the beginning of printing — by means of the type specimen. Indeed, the type specimen has served two important purposes: First, it is an essential step in the creation of a typeface: It allows the designer to observe, at important points in the design process, a quantity of type on a page and to judge its effect accordingly. Second, it has always been used as an advertisement for a finished typeface: Frequently virtuoso performances of typesetting have been employed to show off not only the beauties of the type, but the indubitable talent of the typographer as well.

There are several kinds of specimens, and you will choose the one that accomplishes what you need to do. You might choose a line-listing, in which various typefaces are sampled on a page in a simple abcdarium. Or you can create an analytic specimen, in which one typeface is shown at a variety of sizes and in several uses. Finally, there is the literary specimen, in which the chosen typeface is used to perfection to typeset a given text. The following pages show a number of possibilities that you might want to consider.

1. *Latin in specimens.* Many typographic specimens use Latin for their demonstration text. Why? For those accustomed to the act of reading, it is so natural an act, it verges upon the involuntary. Instantly, we are transported beyond the physical fact of the type itself, and into the mind of the author. Most of us, alas, are not fluent in Latin, so reading the text for meaning, or reading through the text into the information it contains, cannot happen. So, we are more likely to look at the type itself and to judge its effect. Why not use nonsense syllables or random letters? Even though the text cannot be read, it must neither tease us by looking as if it might contain meaning by being too familiar (i.e., containing words that can be recognized); nor must it be so bizarre or random that the purpose of text — conveying information — is denied. Latin fills the bill perfectly: It gives the impression of being language, without the temptation to read it as language.

2. A *few well-chosen letters*. If you want to spotlight a few letters, generally at a very large size (say, 24 pt or more), you should choose the letters carefully. Some letters are more prone than others to reveal the essential and/or interesting characteristics of the face. In the uppercase, the G and Q are generally very distinctive. For the lowercase, the g is likewise a good choice. The ampersand $\mathscr{E}$ is a character on which type designers usually lavish a good deal of inventiveness and often no little wit. Show the vowels: they are among the most common letters. Numbers are also important, no so much because they are used a lost, but because they are very often used in very important places: folios, chapter numbers, footnote numbers, dates, etc. Always show an unusual character, such as an e with a slanting crossbar (like this one), or a y with a florid descender, or an R with a particularly long tail, for example.

FIGURE 7.1   A LINE LISTING

TYPEFACES USED FOR
Fontographer: Type by Design

ITALIAN OLD STYLE
ABCDEFGHIJKLMNOPQRSTUVWXYZ
abcdefghijklmnopqrstuvwxyz
1234567890&

ITALIAN OLD STYLE ITALIC
*ABCDEFGHIJKLMNOPQRSTUVWXYZ
abcdefghijklmnopqrstuvwxyz
1234567890&*

LIVINGSTON
ABCDEFGHIJKLMNOPQRSTUVWXYZ
abcdefghijklmnopqrstuvwxyz
1234567890&

LIVINGSTON ITALIC
*ABCDEFGHIJKLMNOPQRSTUVWXYZ
abcdefghijklmnopqrstuvwxyz
1234567890&*

LIVINGSTON BOLD
**ABCDEFGHIJKLMNOPQRSTUVWXYZ
abcdefghijklmnopqrstuvwxyz
1234567890&**

LIVINGSTON TITLING
ABCDEFGHIJKLMNOPQRSTUVWXYZ
ABCDEFGHIJKLMNOPQRSTUVWXYZ
1234567890&

Figure 7.1 is a simple but effective line listing. Its purpose is simply to show the required faces, perhaps as an aide memoire, or to suggest to a client the possible faces that might be used for a project.

FIGURE 7.2   AN ANALYTICAL LISTING

Livingston Roman

AGQMstaefgpy1234?!&

AGQMstaefgpy1234?!&

AGQMstaefgpy1234?!&

AGQMstaefgpy1234?!&

AGQMstaefgpy1234?!&

AGQMstaefgpy1234?!&

Inches   1   2   3   4   5   6
1234567890$%&?(" ")
abcdefghijklmnopqrstuvwxyzabcdefghijklmnopqrstuvwxyzabcdefghijklmnopqrstuvwxyz
ABCDEFGHIJKLMNOPQRSTUVWXYZ

Picas   5   10   15   20   25   30   35

Typography may be defined as both an art and a craft. It is an art in
that what it does, it does for its own sake, according to its own internal
sense of what is beautiful and right. It is a craft in that what it does, it
does for a purpose outside itself: it provides a means of storing, shaping
and conveying information. Typography is, therefore, a selfless art – a
contradiction in terms, perhaps – and is at its best when it is least perceived
to be doing anything, indeed when there is no active awareness of perceiving
it, directly, at all, but rather perceiving, through it, the knowledge which
animates the type on the page. Quality in typography results from an
effortless perfection of conception and execution in the creation of a balance
between beauty & utility: compromising neither, calling attention to neither,
yet achieving both.

Livingston Roman: display lines are 48pt 40pt 33pt 26pt 19pt 12pt; text
block type is 10pt; distance between baselines is 11.3pt. The height of the
type block is 1.86in, and the width is 24pc9pt or 4.14in. The ratio of text
width to leading is 26.4. Typefactor is approximately 27.19. Designed by
Richard Beatty.

The purpose of the specimen displayed in Figure 7.2 is to show as much as possible about the face. A variety of sizes as well as some text is shown. Notice that the block of text is 2.5 lowercase alphabets wide. At the bottom are various statistics about the face.

FIGURE 7.3   AN HISTORICAL MODEL

A SPECIMEN

Produced by The Studio of Providence, Rhode Island
Livingston typeface designed & digitized by Richard Beatty

Roman   Italick

ABCD

ABCDE

ABCDEFG

ABCDEFGHI

ABCDEFGHIJK

ABCDEFGHIJKLMN

ABCDEFGHIJKLMNOPQ

ABCDEFGHIJKLMNOPQRST

14/16

Quousque tandem abutere, Catilina, patientia nostra? Quamdiu nos etiam furor iste tuus

14/16

Quousque tandem abutere, Catilina, patientia nostra? Quamdiu nos etiam furor iste tuus

Bold

Quousque tandem abutere, Catilina, patientia nostra? Quamdiu nos etiam furor iste tuus eludet? quem ad finem sese effrenata jactibit audicia? nihilne te nocturnum præsidium

12/14

Quousque tandem abutere, Catilina, patientia nostra? Quamdiu nos etiam furor iste tuus eludet? quem ad

12/14

Quousque tandem abutere, Catilina, patientia nostra? Quamdiu nos etiam furor iste tuus eludet? quem ad

Quosque

tandem

Quosque

tandem

Q u o s q u e

t a n d e m

Q u o s q u e

t a n d e m

Q u o s q u e
t a n d e m

Q u o s q u e
t a n d e m

Quosque tandem

Quosque tandem

Quosque tandem

Quosque tandem

QUOSQUE TANDEM

10/12

Quousque tandem abutere, Catilina, patientia nostra? Quamdiu nos etiam furor iste tuus eludet? quem ad finem sese effrenata jactibit audicia? nihilne te noctur-

9/10

Quousque tandem abutere, Catilina, patientia nostra? Quamdiu nos etiam furor iste tuus eludet? quem ad finem sese effrenata jactibit audi-cia? nihilne te nocturnum præsidium palatii, nihil urbis vigilæ. nihil

10/12

Quousque tandem abutere, Catilina, patientia nostra? Quamdiu nos etiam furor iste tuus eludet? quem ad finem sese effrenata jactibit audicia? nihilne te noc-

9/10

Quousque tandem abutere, Catilina, patientia nostra? Quamdiu nos etiam furor iste tuus eludet? quem ad finem sese effrenata jactibit audi-cia? nihilne te nocturnum præsidi-um palatii, nihil urbis vigilæ. nihil

Bold-Italick

Quousque tandem abutere, Catilina, patientia nostra? Quamdiu nos etiam furor iste tuus eludet? quem ad finem sese effrenata jactibit audicia? nihilne te nocturnum præsidium

Quousque tandem abutere, Catilina, patientia nostra? Quamdiu nos etiam furor iste tuus eludet? quem ad finem sese effrenata jactibit

Figure 7.3 is in the style of the early specimens of the Caslon Foundry. It certainly does pack a lot of visual information in the page. It is surprisingly time-consuming to prepare. I prepared this example in FreeHand version 5.

FIGURE 7.4   FONTFLAKES

Bored? Well, Figure 7.4 demonstrates a little game of typographic solitaire that will keep you out of trouble for a while. The principle is simple. Take a character, copy and rotate it by some angle that divides into 360 degrees an whole number of times: 10, 20, 25, 30 for example. Or use two or more characters, as in the lower-right example—which is Helvetica and shows that the font does not have to be ornate. The lower-left example is a variation. Take some type, reflect it, and then copy and rotate it. Not a specimen, as such, but more fun. I suppose that "FontFlake" could also be used as a synonym for "TypeNerd."

FIGURE 7.5   TYPE AS ARTWORK

OREM IPSUM DOLOR SIT amet, consectetuer adipiscing elit, sed diam nonummy nibh euismod tincidunt ut laoreet dolore magna aliquam erat volutpat. Ut wisi enim ad minim veniam, quis nostrud exerci tation ullamcorper suscipit lobortis nisl ut aliquip ex ea commodo consequat. Duis autem vel eum iriure dolor in hendrerit in vulputate velit esse molestie consequat, vel illum dolore eu feugiat nulla facilisis at vero eros et accumsan et iusto odio dignissim

Frederic Goudy's Italian Oldstyle from Richard Beatty

Here we pull out as many stops as we like. In Figure 7.5 I have used a drop cap from Goudy's extremely beautiful Cloister Initials: these are available from Giampa Textware. Notice, too that the punctuation hangs into the margin, so as not to disturb the line. Also pay attention to the fact that the caps following the drop cap align with the top of the drop cap. Chapter 8 will have much to say about the setting of display type to its best advantage.

I spoke earlier about pulling out the stops: consider Figure 7.6 on the opposite page as *full organ.* In 1924 Goudy designed, and Lanston Monotype released, Italian Oldstyle — the typeface you are now reading. At that time Bruce Rogers had an association with Lanston: he had designed some of Lanston's publications and specimens. In 1923 he designed a brochure displaying Goudy's Garamont, and in the next year was again asked to design a specimen, this time for Italian Oldstyle.

Clearly, Rogers enjoyed the typeface. The resulting sixteen-page specimen is an exciting and witty virtuoso performance of typography. Rogers thought that the type worked well in narrow measures, so you will notice the extremely narrow measure of some of the text. The delightful and ornamental drop cap was made entirely from pre-existing Monotype ornaments: This was something at which Rogers excelled. He could take a handful of ordinary-looking ornaments and manipulate them into intricate and beautiful designs.

This re-creation of that specimen was crafted by Richard Beatty, who digitized Italian Oldstyle as well as the ornaments. A rich variety of ornaments and borders is available from Beatty: see the Ergalography. Beatty also notes that he has substituted the Chap Book pilcrow used by Rogers with the pilcrow from Italian Oldstyle.

As reproduced on the page opposite, the figure has been somewhat reduced. The original text area measured about 8.95 inches by 5.625 inches.

FIGURE 7.6   A BRAVURA PERFORMANCE

EARLY PRINTERS
IN THE CITY OF
VENICE

From Dibdin's Bibliographical Decameron

THE FOURTH DAY

¶ SPEAKERS:

Lysander.
Philomen.
Lisardo.
Almansa.

¶ COMMENTS:

John de Spira, parent of the Venetian press.] This point, I submit, is now triumphantly established by the existing privilege of the Senate of Venice, granted to John de Spira, of the date of September the 18th, 1469. A copy of this privilege was transmitted to Denis, by the Abbé Morelli, & appears in the *Suffragium pro Johanne de Spira Primo Uenetiarum Typographo, Uiennæ,* 1794, 8vo. of the former.[1] It is too important not to occupy some twenty lines in this present note. Le voici! '1469, *Die 18 Septembris.* Inducta est in hanc nostram inclytam civitatem ars imprimendi libros, in diesque magis celebrior et frequentior fiet, per operam studium et ingenium Magistri Ionnais de Spira, qui ceteris aliis urbibus hanc nostram præelegit,

LYSANDER

T IS now really time to notice the rise & early progress of the typographical art in one other great Italian city: and you will perhaps readily give a guess in what other city this may be?

PHILEMON
LISARDO } Venice !

LYSANDER

¶ Twice accurately spoken! 'The nurse (as Philemon the other day not inaptly expressed it) of ten thousand useful & elegant arts, the central mart of European commerce, the city both of Jenson and of Titian, it was reserved for Venice to give a different turn, and to adopt a purer style, in the productions of its first printers.' All hail to thee, JOHN DE SPIRA, parent of the Venetian press! ⚐ I see thee yonder, in

ubi curn coniuge liberis et familiâ totâ suâ inhabitaret, exerceretque dictam artem librorum imprimendorum: iamque summâ omnium commendatione impressit *Epistolas Ciceronis,* et nobile opus *Plinii de Naturali Historia* in maximo numero, et pulcherrima litterarum forma, pergitque quotidie alia præclara volumina imprimere; adeo ut industria et virtute huius hominis, multisque praeclarisque voluminibus, et quidem pervili pretio, locupletabitur. Et quoniam tale inventum ætatis nostræ peculiare et proprium, priscis illis omnio incognitum, omni favore et ope augendum atque fovendum est, eidemque Magistro Joanni, qui magno urgetur sumptu familiæ, et artificum mercede, præstanda sit materia, ut alacrius perseveret, artemque suam imprimendi potius celbriorem reddere, quam desinere, habeat; quemadmodum in aliis exercitiis sustentadis, et

FIGURE 7.7 TYPE AND WIT

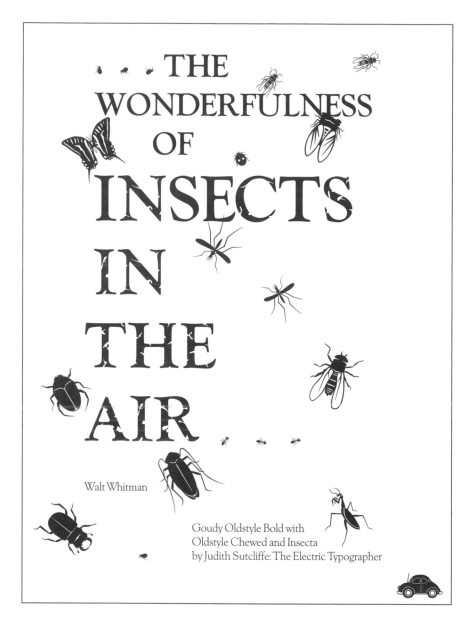

In Figure 7.7 I would draw your attention to the possibilities for playfulness in this type specimen from Judith Sutcliffe. It takes the right sort of type, and an appropriate text, but the rewards are worth the trouble.

Type in Context   8

YOU HAVE CRAFTED your typeface in exactly the way you wish. Now, you will want to use it in a way that best shows it off. This chapter is devoted to an examination of the problems of the use of type. This includes such matters as margins, line length, leading, and reproduction and printing possibilities (possibly reflecting back on the design of the type). There is an interesting relationship between type and its use on the page, and we will begin with that relationship. While you are in the process of creating a typeface, you may very well find that some of the matters reflect back upon the design.

Design synergy

Interaction of type and page

1. Typographic synergy. There is an active and complex synergistic relationship between type and its use. The choices of typeface, mastering process, printing process and paper all interact with each other in myriad and often unexpected ways.

Bruce Rogers in his interesting monograph *Report on the Typography of the Cambridge University Press,* points out two such instances:

> The principle of the matter is that the proportions of the average small letter should be approximately that of the page itself, a broad round letter for a square page and a narrower letter for a long and narrow page… (page 8)

> In other words, the paper for a book should not be arbitrarily chosen, but should be selected with due regard to the size and number of pages of the proposed volume, and especially as to the type that will be used. Both the size and the character of the typeface should be considered. Were it not a matter of almost daily disregard amongst printers, it would seem superfluous to

say that a small type should require a thinnish and comparatively smooth paper and a large type a correspondingly heavier and rougher one, though in no case should the heaviness and the roughness be extreme. The matter of selecting papers of varying surfaces for old face, old style and modern types calls for more discrimination, but we all realize and admit certain fitnesses without, perhaps, formulating any rules of procedure. (page 26)

The interaction of type, ink and paper is complex. Paper, generally speaking, comes in two kinds: coated and uncoated. Coated paper is impervious to ink, while uncoated paper will absorb ink, spreading the ink slightly in the process. The ink itself will also spread slightly as the type is pressed into the paper. Many typefaces, particularly those intended for use with letterpress, were designed for printing onto uncoated paper, and so, in turn, were designed with ink spread in mind. Most PostScript translations of these typefaces, however, do not take account of the roles of ink and paper in modifying letterforms. In addition, today's imagesetters output at very high resolutions directly to film, and little accuracy is lost when the type is transferred to plate. Further, there is now much greater use of coated stock — often glossy and dazzlingly white — which will reproduce the type virtually as the imagesetter created it. The end result is often thin, anemic and spindly type. This can even give rise to an optical effect called "sparkle" in which the lighter, thinner parts of letters seem to disappear, leaving only the serifs and thick strokes visible.

Let's take a hypothetical example to show the problems and suggest solutions. We are told that a given publication is going to use Bruce Roger's Centaur at 12 pt. The original will be mastered at 2540 dpi, and printed by lithography on a bright white paper with high gloss. We have a sneaking hunch that the glare of the paper will compete, successfully, with the delicate type for our attention. So we cast about for alternatives.

Structure of the page

Single-page vs. recto & verso

First we suggest a larger type size, say 14pt. No, we are told, that will not do: a large amount of text needs to be put into a limited space. We might suggest adding some weight to the face, on the order of 0.5% of the em-square. This technique has proved successful in a wide variety of applications. Typefaces in small sizes — both serif and sans serif — for example, have been rendered more legible for use in newspaper work by this technique. Some care is needed in performing this transformation. The finished typeface must have the same character widths as the original so as to preserve line-endings; in other words, the transformation must change only the weight, not the width, of the characters. This process is discussed in some detail in Chapter 7.

We might also suggest a different paper. Traditional typefaces, those intended for letterpress, tend to look best on the papers associated with letterpress printing. Such papers are off-white with little or no glare, and they have some measure of texture.

2. The page.   There are two approaches open to you: you can design the page as a single visual entity; or you can design the left and right (verso and recto) as a visual unit. The aspect of the book lying open and flat is called the opening. The first approach is appropriate to a great body of material for which the layout of the opening would not significantly increase the appreciation of the subject matter: scientific texts, newsletters which must use every square inch of space available. The second approach is appropriate to those projects in which the aspect of the page is expected to play a key part in the appreciation of the text: poetry, works of fiction, and any work of a visually distinctive typographic nature.

3. *The paragraph.* Having established that the ideal width of the paragraph is some two to three lowercase alphabets, there is another issue that deserves mention: rag-right vs. justified alignment. Justified text aligns both the left and right sides of the text; this is facilitated by altering the spaces between words, and often by altering the spaces between letters as well. Rag-right text aligns the left side, but keeps word spaces constant so that the right side is uneven.

The issue is not a trivial one: After having taken great care over the construction of the letterforms, after judging the fit of the letters to a nicety, and after arriving by careful judgment at the size of the word space — after all that, do you want to see the wordspacing varied from line to line of a paragraph simply to achieve justified type?

Some would say no. Two interesting trends lead to the preference by some for rag-right type. In 1931 Eric Gill wrote a delightful and infuriating little work entitled *An Essay on Typography* (see Bibliography). Among other things, he argued persuasively against justified setting (calling it the "Procrustean Bed") and for relatively tight wordspacing. At the same time, there was a movement in Germany called "die neue Typographie." Its most articulate spokesman was a young Jan Tschichold. The thrust of his argument is that it is type and its own inherent look and structure, that should determine how it is to be placed on the page; certainly, it should not simply be poured like concrete into an arbitrary mold. Tschichold even eschewed centered type (as in a title page). He later modified his views somewhat and determined that the old and the new typography could live harmoniously in the same world. In any event, the two works appearing when they did from two distinguished typographic designers combined to make their common view fairly influential.

It is almost as difficult to achieve a good rag as it is to produce well-justified type. The rag must not be too great, or it is visually disturbing and prevents efficient reading. Nor must it be too mild, or it will simply look like poorly justified type. There is a prevalent misconception that ragged setting means that type does not have to be hyphenated: this is incorrect.

You, of course, will want to make your own judgment. I am simply giving you a few things to think about. Either is a satisfying and valid form when done carefully. I was once told that rag-right is easier to read only when the typography is otherwise bad. I'm not sure I know what that means, except the questionable belief that the only good typography is justified typography. There is an undeniable charm about a gently ragged right margin, and the time is past (hopefully) when rag-right setting is considered merely a counsel of despair when the real thing (justified type) cannot be obtained.

There is also a long tradition of justified type: Medieval manuscripts are full of justified calligraphy, a style that was copied when movable type came into use. But much of the justification in medieval manuscripts is made possible by techniques not available to us today: altering spelling, or the employment of ligatures and abbreviations at will in order to get words to fit properly on the line.

In any event, to achieve perfectly justified type (with no rivers of white) or rag-right with a gentle rag, you must be prepared to do several things. First, you must be willing to hyphenate. There are still some who think the practice is objectionable, and that is a pity because even typographic color is often not possible without it. Second, you must, on some rare occasions, be willing (with the author's permission) to rewrite the text in order to alleviate problem spacing in a line. Third, letterspacing lowercase type for the purposes of justification should be avoided, except in those instances where the alternative would be even worse. Roger Black quotes Goudy to

Extent of rag

Neither justified nor right-rag inherently better

Justification in calligraphy

Justification: hyphenation

Justification: letter-spacing

the effect that a man who would letterspace lowercase letters would steal sheep.

Finally, in really critical work, you must train your eyes to spot the flaws in automatically justified or ragged type. Justified type (particularly from word processors) invariably looks terrible. There are two reasons for this: Tightly set lines are allowed to be placed directly above or below very loosely set lines creating the effect of alternately light- and dark-gray banding across the page; huge spaces occur between words because the word processor is more willing to increase word spacing than it is to hyphenate (some of that antihyphenation bias again). Ragged type is no less susceptible to problems with hyphenation: The amount of rag should be moderate with only a modest variation in line length.

4. Serif vs. sans serif.   I had originally promised myself that I would not enter into this debate. I find, however, that having written now somewhat extensively on the subject of type, I have something to say. Let's distinguish between legibility and readability. Legibility is an optical measure of the visual clarity of a character and the efficiency with which it can be recognized. Readability is a subjective measure of the ease and comfort with which a typeface is read, and may have as much to do with habit and custom as with the inherent characteristics of a typeface. Legibility can be quantified, whereas readability cannot. Legibility is often applied to letters in isolation, whereas readability applies to the act of reading a body of type.

It is possible to show, under some circumstances, that a sans serif face is more legible than a serif face. Indeed, this has been the argument since the 1930s. There was also a philosophical argument that the simpler and cleaner shapes of sans serif type were more properly expressive of the modern age. It would be an error to over-generalize from this and to assume that sans serif type is always and necessarily more legible in every case and under all circumstances. Legibility tests at best inconclusive And it would be a very great error indeed to go on to insist, as some have, that sans serif faces are more readable. This has never been Uses of sans demonstrated to anyone's complete satisfaction.

Caps & small caps

Nevertheless, and despite the contentious and conflicting results of legibility and readability tests, serif type continues to be the type of choice for virtually all printed communication that deals in large quantities of type for extended reading. This is simply not open to debate: visit a bookstore or look at any newspaper to confirm this fact. The shape and structure of the lowercase letters and their serifs have been refined and improved over a period of more than 500 years, to the point that they are tools that perfectly fulfill their function in assisting the eye in the effortless act of reading.

It is possible to use sans serif type effectively. It can be used to excellent effect as display type. With care and moderation it can complement a serif type, or serve to create an interesting contrast. Used with the greatest possible care, it can even be used for a limited amount of body text. The point is this: Serif type and sans serif type are distinct tools, each with their own purpose and most appropriate use.

5. *Caps and small caps.* If you are working with a typeface that has real small caps (that is, you are employing small caps in a typographic project or putting together a font of small caps) then you should be aware of their proper use. All too often caps and small caps are used incorrectly in that they are not correctly letterspaced, that is, they are not letterspaced at all. They need space inserted between them if they are to be conveniently read. You might even go so far as to provide for proper letterspacing in preparing a font of caps and small caps.

The amount of letterspacing will vary according to the typeface and the work at hand. Typically, a good place to start is on the order of 10%–15%. This is a tradition of great age: From Roman inscriptions, through Renaissance calligraphy to the best examples of present-day lettering art, there has always been a realization that roman caps look best when generously spaced.

6. *Letterspacing lowercase type.* This is a vexed issue. It has historical roots in Jan Tschichold's exhortations to German typesetters not to letterspace lowercase roman letters as they did fraktur, usually to indicate emphasis or other special purpose. With the coming of computers to typography, the question has taken on a new significance. It is now possible to specify some letterspacing of text in order to achieve justification. Indeed, some programs (like Microsoft Word) do this whether you want them to or not. This is thought a useful procedure particularly in the case of narrow columns when the alternative would be to have very large spaces between words.

Let me state my views unequivocally at the outset: lowercase type should *never* be letterspaced under any circumstances. One of a typeface's chief characteristics is the rhythm of line and stroke that is established by the proper orientation of the letters with respect to each other as specified by the type designer. It is this rhythm which is at the heart of fine type and fine typesetting. It is infinitely preferable to endure the occasional awkward spaces between words. Having said all that, however, I am willing to concede the fact that very narrow column widths often necessitate the use of letterspaced lowercase, because the alternative — an excessively large number of awkward spaces between words — would be even worse. See Chapter 3 for more discussion of these issues.

7. *Drop caps.* Drop caps are the large letters, or versals, that are cut, or mortised, into paragraphs that typically begin a section or chapter. Correctly executed, they are extremely attractive; poorly done, they lend an inescapably amateurish air to the page — much like underlining text.

Letter-shape vs. drop caps

LET'S BEGIN with a simple example in which the shape of the letter and the word of which it is a part will have an effect on the way in which the letters after the drop cap are handled. In this paragraph, we have had to back up the first line so that the word 'Let's' will be a recognizable unit. We also had to kern the drop cap itself into the margin very slightly to make a cleaner-looking left margin.

Indefinite article at the start of a paragraph

WE MOVE ON to an example that demonstrates that we must sometimes move the drop cap quite a bit into the margin to get the right effect. For such instances, the principle seems to be that the lower-left corner of the letter must align harmoniously with the left margin.

WHAT HAPPENS when we don't move the drop cap to account for its shape? As you can see in this example, an unsightly hole or 'tooth' has developed in the left margin — not attractive. If you look briefly at the next example you might ask: "But why isn't the drop cap 'A' moved into the margin so that the apex of the letter aligns with the left margin?" Well, I suppose it could. As it is, however, the shape of the letter becomes a part of the shape of the paragraph, and does not seem to create the same sensation of a "hole."

A DIFFERENT PROBLEM presents itself when the indefinite article begins the paragraph: You do not back up the first line. It is also possible, particularly in the case of automatic software drop cap creation, that you will have to move some of the line to avoid letting the text get too close to the drop cap, particularly the serifs of the drop cap, which can be quite large.

The previous examples illustrate some other points about using drop caps. (1) The text immediately following the drop cap should be either in caps or small caps. Bruce Rogers (in *Paragraphs on Printing*) preferred caps, but small caps might be better if the caps lend too much in the way of a possibly distracting emphasis to the text. (2) Both caps and small caps should be letterspaced slightly for best effect. (3) The top of the drop cap must align with the tops of the caps or small caps. (4) The baseline on which the drop cap sits must align with a baseline of the paragraph of which the drop cap is a part.

*F*INALLY, THERE IS ONE MORE possibility that actually has a couple of interesting uses. This is useful at the start of a chapter where there is plenty of room at the top of the page. It is even more useful when the first letter, as here, is ornate and would benefit from a large size. Using a standard drop cap in such a case would probably be more trouble than it is worth. This sort of cap is usually referred to as an elevated or standing cap. Notice that the 'F' has been moved into the margin: Actually, script letters like this often have a negative left (and right, for that matter) sidebearing, i.e., the letter sticks out of its bounding box on the left-hand side — designers take note.

IF YOU ARE LOOKING for a quick and easy way to dress up your text, you could create what are sometimes called "department store drop caps" such as I have devised for this paragraph and for the beginnings of chapters. The first floor, so to speak, consists of a design. You could vary it from letter to letter: some of the more involved examples, for example, have design elements that begin with the letter used on the second floor. The letter on the second floor might have to be scaled a bit in order to fit. In the case of letters that extend significantly below the baseline, you might have either to re-draw the letter slightly (shortening a *J* for example) or incorporate the descender into the design of the first floor (as in the case of a *Q*). The width should be a little greater than the width of the widest letter — usually *W.* You could vary the width of the drop cap, but this would necessitate the re-design of the first-floor ornament.

8. Font structure. PostScript fonts for the Mac are packaged into two files: (1) the bitmaps used for the screen; (2) the PostScript file containing the actual outlines — the outline file is also used for seeing the typeface on the screen when the Adobe Type Manager (ATM) is installed. The PostScript outline file is relatively straightforward and needn't detain us here: If you want more information you can consult the works listed in the Bibliography.

Of greater interest to us now is the structure of the suitcases: those files that the Macintosh operating system (OS) uses to reference the typefaces when it needs to. The following elements may be a part of a suitcase:

Suitcases & font files

FOND, FONT, NFNT, SFNT

FOND   This resource contains information about the font, the family about which the font is a part, the width table, and the kerning table.

FONT   This older resource contains the bitmaps necessary to draw the font on the screen. It could only be numbered from 0 to 255; when it became clear that this was not enough, the FONT resource was abandoned in favor of the NFNT.

NFNT   This resource can be numbered from 0 to 32,767. In addition, each number can refer to up to four style variations. e.g., Roman, Bold, Italic, Bold-Italic. The NFNT resource is recognized only by Macs that have a 128K ROM or larger, i.e., from the 512KE and after.

SFNT   This resource contains the TrueType character outlines.

❖   **9. AFMs.** Adobe Font Metrics are text files that have quite a lot of information about a typeface — just about everything except the characters themselves. They are in three parts: (1) a header giving general information about the font; (2) a list of the characters and the dimensions of the bounding boxes (width and height) that contain them; (3) and finally a list of kerning pairs with the associated kerning amounts.

❖   We will use the AFM produced by Fontographer for Goudy Italian Oldstyle — the type that you are reading right now. We'll begin with the header:

```
StartFontMetrics 2.0
Comment Generated by Fontographer 3.5 6/10/92 11:45:14 AM
FontName GoudyItalianOS-Roman
FullName GoudyItalianOS-Roman
FamilyName GoudyItalianOS
Weight Medium
Notice ©1992 Richard Beatty Designs
ItalicAngle 0
IsFixedPitch false
UnderlinePosition -174
UnderlineThickness 20
```

```
Version 001.000
EncodingScheme AppleStandard
FontBBox -85 -275 1206 896
CapHeight 693
XHeight 400
Descender -264
Ascender 736
```

❖ This information is global in nature, that is, it pertains to the entire font. Most of this is pretty straightforward. The **FontName** is the name that the **findfont** PostScript operator expects to see when it is asked to look up a particular font. There can be no spaces in this name as spaces are significant PostScript entities: this is not an optional entry. Virtually everything else in this list, except FontBBox, is optional. The **ItalicAngle** is measured positive going counterclockwise; most italic typefaces, therefore, will have *negative* italic angles. The **IsFixedPitch** entry is a *boolean* so that the word following it will either be 'true' or 'false.' Monospaced fonts such as Courier would be marked 'true.' You might need the FontBBox, CapHeight, XHeight, Descender and Ascender information to re-create exactly a specialty typeface: Fontographer can read this information and use it when building a font suitcase. Note that the optional **Version** entry is a *string* and so may contain any combination of letters and numbers.

❖ Next comes the individual character information, containing the number of the character, its width, name bounding box, and ligature information; after that, there is a section that details the kerning pairs and the amount of kerning:

```
StartCharMetrics 247
C 0 ; WX 0 ; N NUL ; B 0 0 0 0 ;
C 1 ; WX 773 ; N Eth ; B 15 -4 721 696 ;
C 2 ; WX 447 ; N eth ; B 26 -5 420 707 ;
[omitted lines]
C 99 ; WX 375 ; N c ; B 22 -11 360 408 ; L t ct ;
C 100 ; WX 485 ; N d ; B 25 -20 463 737 ;
C 101 ; WX 391 ; N e ; B 25 -13 373 408 ;
C 102 ; WX 276 ; N f ; B 23 -4 377 736 ; L f ff ; L i fi ; L l fl ;
C 103 ; WX 469 ; N g ; B 10 -273 456 407 ;
[omitted lines]
C 186 ; WX 533 ; N ff ; B 23 -4 634 721 ; L i ffi ; L l ffl ;
C 187 ; WX 353 ; N ordfeminine ; B 6 345 345 717 ;
C 188 ; WX 420 ; N ordmasculine ; B 19 345 407 718 ;
```

```
C 189 ; WX 484 ; N Omega ; B 23 -4 461 727 ;
C 190 ; WX 602 ; N ae ; B 22 -13 602 412 ;
C 191 ; WX 468 ; N oslash ; B 21 -13 446 408 ;
C 192 ; WX 354 ; N questiondown ; B 61 -10 312 649 ;
C 193 ; WX 255 ; N exclamdown ; B 87 -16 192 650 ;
C 194 ; WX 569 ; N logicalnot ; B 43 -49 500 656 ;
C 195 ; WX 717 ; N ct ; B 20 -13 712 600 ;
```
[omitted lines]
```
C 253 ; WX 507 ; N hungarumlaut ; B 119 497 402 634 ;
C 254 ; WX 441 ; N ogonek ; B 173 -81 303 111 ;
C 255 ; WX 390 ; N caron ; B 54 497 337 652 ;
EndCharMetrics
StartKernData
StartKernPairs 196
KPX less less -120
KPX greater greater -129
KPX A C -10
KPX A G -10
KPX A O -19
KPX A Q -20
KPX A S -10
KPX A T -52
KPX A U -9
```
[omitted lines]
```
KPX Y v -111
KPX Y w -102
KPX Z O -20
KPX f d -74
KPX t t -38
KPX v comma -30
KPX w comma -42
KPX y comma -42
KPX z l 1
EndKernPairs
EndKernData
EndFontMetrics
```

❖   The structure of the metrics entries is very simple. Everything has to be on one line; that is, the end of the line marks the end of the entry. The elements within the line are separated by a semicolon with a space on either side of the semicolon, a space after the last semicolon is optional.

❖   Each metrics entry begins with a **c** *number*: the number represents the location in the PostScript encoding. Then there follows the width entry **WX** *xxxx* where *xxxx* is an integral number of units showing the width of the character. Then there is the name entry: **N** *the-name* in which *the-name* may have upper- and lowercase letters, but must not contain a space character. The name element can be specified in Fontographer 4, and this is very useful particularly in the case of special characters we might have to find later in the AFM (*see below*): notice that **C 195** has been renamed to **ct** for the ligature called for in **C 99**. Next there is the bounding box entry for the character: **B** *llx lly urx ury* where the elements are, respectively, lower-left-x, lower-left-y, upper-right-x, upper-right-y. Notice that the physical width of the character itself, not including the sidebearings, can be obtained by:

$$\text{width=upper-right-x} - \text{lower-left-x}$$
$$\text{height=upper-right-y} - \text{lower-left-y}$$

❖ The final entry in a character's metrics information is optional and indicates the ligatures formed by the character. The form of the entry is this: **L** *successor ligature*. Both of the entries following the letter **L** are *names*. The *successor* is the letter with which the character forms a ligature, and the *ligature* is the name of the character where the ligature can be found. So an entry like **L t st** in the line giving the metrics for *s* would mean that when the character **t** follows **s** that a ligature is formed and that ligature can be found in the character slot named **st**.

❖❖ The interesting thing is that Fontographer has never written this information into an AFM, even for the *fi* and *fl* ligatures, which are a part of the Apple and Adobe standard encodings. Adobe has always included this ligature information in its AFMs to the point where this indication is itself virtually a de facto part of the Adobe standard encoding. Hopefully future versions of Fontographer will allow users to incorporate this information directly from Fontographer, rather than through a text editor. After all, this is vital information that should be a part of the font's database.

❖ The kerning entries are even simpler. The format is **KPX** *name1 name2 kern-amount*, where *name1* and *name2* are character names as defined in the metrics section. **kern-amount** is the amount of the kern in integer units, positive to move letters apart, negative to move them closer together.

❖❖ *10. A note for TEX users.* This book was put together using TEX using Textures from Blue Sky Research. Several issues were raised, the solutions to which might prove of interest.

❖ ❖ Encoding was the first problem. Richard Beatty uses a proprietary encoding which includes all of the *f* and *ff* ligatures as well as the less usual *&t* and *st* ligatures. This required altering the AFM—*Adobe Font Metrics*—to include the ligature comments that would provide the appropriate information to EdMetrics. The ligature comments, by the way, though rarely discussed are a standard part of the AFM format. The lines in the AFM that had to be changed are as follows:

```
C 99 ; WX 375 ; N c ; B 22 -11 360 408 ; L t ct ;
C 102 ; WX 276 ; N f ; B 23 -4 377 736 ; L f ff ; L i fi ; L l fl ;
C 115 ; WX 344 ; N s ; B 17 -13 318 408 ; L t st ;
C 179 ; WX 760 ; N ffl ; B 23 -4 717 733 ;
C 182 ; WX 669 ; N st ; B 17 -13 664 606 ;
C 186 ; WX 533 ; N ff ; B 23 -4 634 721 ; L i ffi ; L l ffl ;
C 195 ; WX 717 ; N ct ; B 20 -13 712 600 ;
C 197 ; WX 741 ; N ffi ; B 13 -4 721 736 ;
```

❖ ❖ I would note, in passing, that Richard Beatty *duplicates* the 'fi' and 'fl' ligatures in places on the keyboard that are more convenient to hand and memory. You will notice from the AFM exerpt above that I did *not* rename those positions, but used the standard locations.

❖ ❖ This done, there were two routes open to me, or so I thought. I opened EdMetrics and converted the altered AFMs to TFMs—TₑX Font Metrics—using the Computer Modern encoding option. Failure: I lost the *ff* ligatures, and for some reason there was a problem locating the left-quote character—the latter problem led to some weird spacing problems in the first released version of this book. I then thought that I would make a PL—*Property List* in TEXspeak—which is a human-readable metrics file for TEX; TFMs are not human readable, but are compressed and meant for high-speed reading. Failure again. EdMetrics was choking on PL files. It was at this point in time that Boston *MACWORLD* started, so I decided to swallow my scruples and make up some copies of the book using the first non-solution above, missing ligatures and spacing and all, on the pathetic and desperate principle that *something* is better than *nothing*.

❖ ❖ Finally, the evening before MACWORLD when I had printed up 12 flawed copies, I solved the problem, though not in a way which is generally considered to be idiomatically TEXnical. In EdMetrics it is possible to specify how both the QuickDraw (i.e., screen) encoding and the PostScript encoding are to be used by TEX. If I direct that EdMetrics is to use all 256 characters of the Quickdraw encoding, but is to make no assumptions at all about the PostScript encoding or how the PostScript and Quickdraw are to be mapped into a TFM, I will be able to use any character in any place that I like — ligatures and all. That worked perfectly. What makes this solution slightly un-TEXnical is that quotation marks must be specified explicitly instead of by the use of the more usual TEX method.

❖ ❖ The whole purpose of this exercise is twofold. First, of course, anyone who uses TEX does so in order to take advantage of a line-breaking algorithm that has yet to be bettered, giving an unusually even typographic color. Second, the rich ligature set of this typeface can be used to the fullest effect with the greatest ease: I never have to type an explicit ligature — TEX takes care of all the substitutions (and hyphenations within ligatures, if necessary) quite automatically. A side benefit of this last feature is that my spelling-checker never queries spellings rendered strange by ligature substitutions.

11. Character count. It is of interest to be able to predict the number of characters that will fit into a line of given length. All approaches to this begin by taking a sample of text and measuring its total width. The sample must be statistically valid: The distribution of letters in the sample must accurately reflect the distribution that occurs in the language (e.g. English) for which the sample is being prepared. Obviously, all calculations for all typefaces being examined must be based on the same sample of text. For English the distribution is as follows, based on a thousand occurrences of the letter 'e':

e	1000
t	770
a	728
i	704
s	680
o	672
n	670
h	540
r	528
d	392
l	360
u	296
c	280
m	272
f	236
w	190
y	184
p	168
g	168
b	158
v	120
k	88
j	55
q	50
x	46
z	22

With the sample in hand, you now measure its total horizontal length. At this point you have two alternatives open to you. You can count the number of characters and divide that by the width of the text in picas: This gives you the traditional characters-per-pica count. Such a measure will vary with both the typeface and the size of the type: the bigger the type, the fewer the characters there will be in a pica of text width. Or, you could take the character-per-pica figure and multiply it by the size of the type in points: this is the principle of Bruce Brown's "type factor." This cancels the effects of the size of the font on the character-per-pica count — the smaller character-per-pica figure for a large font will be cancelled out by being multiplied by a larger type size — and makes the "type factor" purely a function of the typeface itself.

Bruce Browm's "type factor"

Typeface identification

12. *Identifying a typeface.* This can be a surprisingly challenging task, particularly for text type (as opposed to display typefaces), and more challenging still for different versions of the same typeface — Simoncini Garamond, say, as opposed to Stempel Garamond. Whatever you do, *don't* just look through dozens of examples searching in a general way for a match: A few minutes of that sort of thing, and all typefaces start to look alike.

You need a plan. Look for important and distinguishing characteristics that set the typeface apart from all the others. For instance:

1. Look at the letters that usually reflect a revealing individuality. For the uppercase, this would be *G*, *Q* and *W*. In the lowercase you might look at *a*, *e* and *g*.
2. In particular, look at the *ampersand* — & — this is a character upon which designers generally lavish a good deal of inventiveness.
3. The numerals are occasionally distinctive enough to indicate the identity of a typeface.
4. Note the size and shape of the serifs — this, obviously, won't help in the case of a sans serif face.
5. Note the x-height.

13. *The commercial context.* The typefaces that you design and/or modify exist within a complex and at times ethically or legally ill-defined context. Before you thrust yourself into the commercial side of typography and design, here are some potential possibilities and problems that you might want to keep in mind.

14. Legalities.   When you buy a typeface, you are merely buying a license to use it, you are not buying the typeface itself to do with as you choose. That is, you have permission to use the typeface, but are restrained by the terms of the licensing agreement from doing certain things with it. Generally speaking, you will be on safe ground if, having made changes to a licensed typeface, you attempt neither to sell the typeface (that is, it remains solely for your own use) nor to rename it. When in doubt, read the license carefully and/or call the manufacturer.

   If you are making a typeface based on one that does have a registered name, then you must be careful not to use the same name for your version. Quite aside from legalities, giving the typeface the same name given to it by its designer imples that you have the designer's blessings, and, more important, original drawings, which would further imply that your versions is, in every respect, entirely what the designer of the face wanted. For example, when I digitized Goudy's Bertham, I renamed it Goudy Hundred. Whether there would have been legal problems is open to question, and, anyway, beside the point — it would have been tacky and tasteless for me to have used the same name.

15. Copyright.   This is a vexed issue in the United States, where it is not possible to copyright a typeface. You can register the name as a trademark, but you cannot copyright the type itself. You *can*, however, copyright a computer program. On this basis, Adobe has successfully argued that a PostScript typeface is, in essence, a computer program that produces type and is thus subject to copyright laws. This is a situation that ought to change. Typographic designers ought to be able to protect their work in the same way that a musician or writer can. Still, we must be grateful for small blessings: at least if you work in PostScript you have some protection.

International
Typeface
Corporation

ITC, submitting
a type face
to

16. ITC.   The International Typeface Corporation was founded in 1970 for the express purpose of offering to the print industry the high quality typeface designs, while at the same time offering to typeface designers the legal, marketing and development services which would otherwise be difficult to find. Although ITC does sell typefaces, it also licenses the designs to others (e.g. Adobe) who then produce the typeface in some usable form (e.g. as software) and license the typeface in that format to individuals for use. The interesting thing about this is that the ITC is thereby not committed to a particular technology, but to any technology that can reproduce type at an acceptable level of quality, and to designers who are stimulated to produce new and useful designs. The designer receives a percentage of the licensing royalties.

If you find that you have designed a typeface that you think may be marketable, then you might consider submitting it to the ITC for marketing. The process of submitting a typeface to the ITC is relatively simple (an extended discussion is found in an article by Allan Haley — see the _Bibliography_). You begin by submitting your typeface in the form of a keyword to the ITC Review Board: for the ITC (and many others as well) a useful keyword is 'Hamburgerfonts.' If the Review Board is satisfied with the design, the designer is then asked to supply 120 characters of the roman and italic in the lightest weight; payment is made to the designer for this work. The roman and italic then form the basis of full text tests which are used to evaluate the typeface further. The board then undertakes marketing research to see how widely the typeface will appeal to the print community. If everything has gone well up to this point, the board then commissions the designer to execute the typeface in the boldest weight of the roman and italic. The extreme weights are digitized in a CAD (*computer aided design*) environment; the intermediate weights of the typeface are created by interpolation, and the number of characters is brought up to 250.

The typeface design can be rejected at virtually any point in the decision-making process, at which point the designer is free to submit the designs elsewhere, or to resubmit the designs to the ITC at a later date. Upon acceptance, however, the designer is given a portion of the ITC revenues as a royalty, both for the original light and bold versions and the CAD-produced intermediate weights. The designer is also afforded such legal protection as the ITC can offer.

17. *Other approaches to marketing.* There are other ways of distributing your fonts. You could declare them shareware and distribute them on-line through CompuServe, AOL or GEnie, for example. Or you could set up in business and distribute them yourself, in the manner of Richard Beatty and Judith Sutcliffe. They publish periodic catalogues of their work and make available a wide variety of font materials, often unavailable elsewhere.

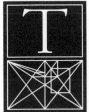THIS IS IN NO WAY to be considered a complete and exhaustive listing of terms. It is simply a convenient listing of and commentary on terms used in the body of this book and should help to make clear the meaning of any unduly technical passages. For further assistance in finding useful sources of information, see the Bibliography.

Ampersand	The character '&'. A word of nineteenth-century invention, short for 'and per se and.' Interestingly, there are a number of versions of the word in various British dialects: *ampussy, ampusand, amsiam.* The character itself was originally a ligature of the 'et,' the Latin word for 'and.' This character has traditionally afforded type designers an opportunity for exuberance and/or whimsy, which Frederic Goudy, for instance, never resisted. Robert Slimbach designed some 50 ampersands for his typeface Poetica.
Arm	A horizontal stroke.
Ascender	The extended stem of *b, d, f, h, k, l, f.*
Ascent	The distance the ascenders of a typeface extend above the baseline.
Crossbar	The horizontal stroke of *e, f, t, A, H, T.*
Baseline	The line on which characters such as *H* or *x* rest.
BCP	Bézier Control Point The point at the end of a handle and which is used to move the handle.
Bézier curve	A highly flexible curve used by PostScript for drawing.

Bowl	A curved line that completely encloses an area.
Brackets	(of serifs) The connecting curve between a stem and a serif.
Capital	The uppercase letters.
Cap height	The height of the capital letters.
Cap height numerals	Numerals whose height lines up with the caps of a typeface. Also called "lining numerals" (q.v.). As opposed to x-height, or text, numerals.
Contrast	The difference in weight between the thick and the thin strokes.
Control points	Points that influence the shape of Bézier curves. They are located at the ends of handles (q.v.) and are used to manipulate the length and direction of handles.
Counter	The area enclosed by a bowl, or by the closed tail of *g,* or by the bar of *A;* or partially enclosed as in *v, n, c, a* (two counters), *e* (two counters) and *c.*
Critical points	Points associated with templates that require the placement of drawing points. In better than 95% of cases, critical points on a template curve occur when the template curve is momentarily parallel (or, if you like, perpendicular) to the x- or y-axis. Discontinuities (sudden changes in the curve's direction) also require drawing points.
Depth	As used by Donald Knuth (and as usually followed by me), this is the distance a character extends below the baseline. *See also* Height.
Descender	The extended stem of p, q; and the tails (except R).
Descent	The distance from the baseline to the descender line.
Diagonal	A stroke between vertical and horizontal.
Diphthong	Sounds represented by the ligatures œ, æ, Œ, Æ.

Drawing points   Points associated with Bézier curves that are placed at important ('critical') points on template curves.

Ear   The small stroke to the right of the bowl of *g*.

Face   *See* Typeface.

Font   Derives from the French word *fondre*, to melt metal and pour it into a mold — to cast, as for example a typeface; now taken to mean a complete set of letters and numbers in a given size, weight and posture of a typeface.

Hairline   (Of serifs) Much thinner than the stem, and unbracketed.

Handle   The line that issues from a drawing point in the creation of a Bézier curve; moving the handle using the BCP controls the shape of the curve.

Height   As used by Donald Knuth (and followed by me, usually), this applies to the distance a character extends above the baseline; this is as distinguished from depth (q.v.).

Inscriptional   Forms deriving from stone-cut letters.

Kern   Originally part of a piece of type overhanging its shank (the shoulder of f, the tail of j, Q; now refers to the adjustment of character pairs so that they are closer together or farther apart in order to maintain even character spacing.

Leading   This term originally referred to strips of lead that were placed between lines of metal type to open up the text, i.e., increase the distance between baselines. Depending on who is using the term, therefore, leading could mean the *extra* space between lines of text, or it could mean the *total* distance between baselines — the latter being its more usual DTP meaning.

Ligature   A joining of two or more letters such as fi, fl, &, etc.

Lining numerals	Numerals that have been monospaced (q.v.) so that they will line up in columns of numerals. Such numerals are invariably cap height.
Lowercase	*See* Uppercase.
Majuscules	*See* Capitals or Uppercase.
Minuscules	Synonym for Lowercase; *see* Uppercase.
Monospaced	Characters (usually cap height numerals) that are given identical widths. Some typewriter-like typefaces such as Courier are entirely monospaced.
Orthogonal	At right angles: applied to the orientation of the handles in a PostScript Type 1 font, and refers to their orientation to the x and y axes.
Pilcrow	The paragraph sign ¶. This odd word is, apparently, an unexplained fifteenth century mangling of the word 'paragraph.'
Point	A unit of typographic measure, the point comes in many forms. There are 72.27 standard Anglo-American points to the inch. For PostScript, this has been simplified to 72 points to the inch. In Europe, the Didot point is used, of which there are 67.54 to the inch.
Point size	The size of a typeface in points. This does not refer to the size of the letters themselves, but, traditionally, to the size of the body on which they are carried.
Rule	What a typographer calls a drawn line. Rules may be of any thickness and can be composites of two or more lines of the same or different thicknesses. "Scotch rules" are a thick and thin composite (or multiple) rule. A 1 pt rule is actually rather thick; a half-point rule is more common. There are also dotted and dashed rules.
Sans serif	Without serifs

Serif	A cross ending a main stroke; serifs may be single (on one side only) or double (on both sides); *see also* Brackets, Hairline, Sans serif, Slab.
Set	Traditionally, the width of the metal shank on which the types are cast; now would make reference to the size of the em-square of a typeface.
Shoulder	The curved stroke springing from the stem(s) of *a, f, h, m, n, r*.
Sidebearings	The space at the left of a character represented by the distance between the origin line and the leftmost part of the character; or at the right of a character represented by the distance between the width line and the rightmost part of the character.
Slab	(Of serifs) Thick and unbracketed.
Small caps	Capital letters that have been scaled down, usually somewhere between cap height and x-height, but redrawn so as to maintain even typographic color.
Spur	A small projection, usually pointed, from a stroke or terminal.
Stem	A vertical stroke.
Stress	The directional tendency of contrast (stress is diagonal when one set of diagonals — usually those running from upper left to lower right — are thick and the others thin, the vertical and horizontal strokes being intermediate in thickness; and is vertical when the vertical strokes are thick, the horizontals thin, and the diagonals intermediate).
Stroke	A single line, straight or curved.
Tail	The parts below the base line of *g, j, y, J, Q*; also for the diagonal of *R*.

Template	A template is some form of representation of a character that is in turn traced in Fontographer. Templates may be physical, as from type specimen books; or they may be cerebral, formed in the heart and mind and held before the inner eye as a guide to drawing.
Terminal	Stroke-endings other than serifs, described as bulbous, pointed, or sheared; sometimes cupped or hooked.
Titling	Originally this referred to capitals cast full on the body, without room for descenders; formerly called two-line letters; now it frequently refers to fonts that have been scaled and proportioned in such a way as to be particularly suitable for relatively large sizes.
Typeface	The uniform design of a set or sets of letters, numerals, signs, etc., for printing.
Uppercase	Chests of type were divided into two "cases", upper and lower; the capital letters (among other things) were located in the upper case; the other letters were kept in the lower case.
Weight	The degree of contrast of a typeface, described as light, medium or bold.
x-height	The distance between the baseline and the average height of the lowercase letters (without ascenders); also called the 'mean height.'
x-height numerals	Numerals that line-up with the x-height of a typeface. Also called "old style," or text numerals. *See also* Lining numerals and Cap height numerals.

1. Typeface classification. It is extremely useful to have some sort of system of typeface classification fixed in your mind. This is not merely an arid scholarly exercise, but rather a set of "memory hooks" that you can use to distinguish the characteristics of one typeface from another. It also allows you to develop an approach to the creation or manipulation of a typeface more efficiently and properly by reminding you of the salient features of that typeface.

Alexander Lawson's scheme for the classification of type is as follows:

1. – Blackletter
2. – Oldstyle
   a. – Venetian
   b. – Aldine French
   c. – Dutch-English
3. – Transitional
4. – Modern
5. – Square Serif
6. – Sans Serif
7. – Script-Cursive
8. – Display-Decorative

Here follows the DIN classification of typefaces:

1   Romans

1.1   Renaissance styles (Venetians). Only minor differences in stroke thickness, inclines axis for curved portions of characters.

1.11   Early types and styles (Jenson, lower case *e* with diagonal crossbar).

1.12   Late styles (Polophilus, Garamond; horizontal crossbar in lower case *e*).

1.13   Modern styles (Palatino, Weiss, Vendome; types designed after 1890).

1.2   Baroque Styles   Strong contrast in strokes, more angular serif formation, almost vertical axis for curved portions of characters.

1.21   Dutch styles (Van Dijk, Janson, Fleischman).

1.22   English styles (Caslon, Baskerville).

1.23   French styles (Fournier)

1.24   Modern styles (Horizon, Diethelm, Times Roman)

1.3   Classical Styles   Horizontal initial strokes for lowercase characters, strong contrast in stroke thickness, right-angle serifs, vertical axis to curved portions of characters.

1.31   Early styles (Bodoni, Didot, Walbaum).

1.32   Late styles (Bulmer)

1.33   News styles (Excelsior, Candida, Melior).

1.34   Modern styles (Corvinus, Eden).

1.4   Free Romans   Romans with calligraphic modifications, etc.

1.41   Victorian styles (Auriol, Nicholas Cochin)

1.42   Non-serif romans (Steel, Lydian, Optima)

1.43   Individual styles (Hammer Uncial, Verona, Matura)

1.5   Linear Romans   Grotesques and sans serif types of optically uniform stroke thickness.

1.51   Early styles (Annonce Grotesque, Grotesque 9)

1.52   Modern styles (Futura, Spartan, Gill).

1.6   Block Styles   Egyptians and antiques. Types with slab serifs.

1.61   Early styles (nineteenth-century styles)

1.62   Late styles (Clarendon)

1.63   Modern styles, no brackets (Beton, Memphis, Rockwell, Stymie, Landi)

1.64   Typewriter faces.

1.7   Scripts

1.71   Stress variation (Legend).

1.72   Expanding strokes (Bernhard Cursive, Copperplate Bold, Invitation Script).

1.73   Uniform stroke (Signal, Monoline, Swing Bold).

1.74   Brush Stroke (Mistral, Catalina).

2   Black Letter

2.1   Textura (Black Letter Gothic).

2.2   Rotunda (Wallau).

2.3   Schwabacher (Alt-Schwabacher, heavy-looking types).

2.4   Fraktur (Unger).

2.5   Kurrent (Chancery).

3   Non-roman Characters

3.1   Greek

3.2   Cyrillic

3.3   Hebrew

3.4   Arabic

3.5   Others

2. Font size systems.   This is a vexed area of discussion as there are many systems of measurement, both over time and space. Let's start with the basics as they are currently found. The following list is comprehensive and ought to enable you to translate any system of measurement into any other system of measurement.

1 inch	=	2.54 cm
1 pica	=	12 points
1 cicero	=	12 Didot points
1 inch	=	72.27 points
1 inch	=	67.54 Didot points
1 agate	=	5.16pt = 14 lines/inch

3. Historical systems of measurement.   This is an interesting chart from *Fonderies de caractères et leur matériel* by Charles Enschedé (Haarlem, 1908). Notice the interesting similarities and differences between the systems.

French	*Dutch*	*German*	*English*	*Points*
Diamant	Diamant	Diamant	Diamond	4
Robin	Robyn	—	Pearl	4.5
Parisienne	Parel	Perl	Ruby	5
Nonpareille	Nonparel	Nonpareil	Nonpareil	6
Jolie	Joli	—	Emerald	6.5
Mignonne	Collonel	Colonel	Minion	7
Petit texte	Brevier	Brevier	Brevier	7.5
Gaillarde	Galjard	Petit	Bourgeois	8
Petit romain	Garmond	Bourgis	Long primer	9*
Philosophie	Dessendiaan	Corpus	Small pica	10
Cicéro	Mediaan	Kleine cicero	Pica	11
Saint Augustin	Augustyn	Cicero	Pica	12
Gros texte	Groot augustyn	Mittel	English	14
Gros romain	Text	Tertia	Great primer	16
Petit paragnon	Kleine paragon	Text	Paragon	18

Gros paragnon	Groote paragon	Grobe text	Two-line small pica	20-22
Petit canon	Kleine kanon	Doppel cicero	Two-line pica	24
Canon	Kanon	Doppel mittel	Two-line English	28
Gros canon	Groote kanon	Kleine kanon	Two-line great primer	32
Trismégiste	Parysche kanon	Kanon	Three-line pica	36
Sabon	Sabon	Kleine missal	Four-line pica	48
Missel	Missaal	Missal	Four-line English	56
			Five-line pica	60**
			Six-line pica	72**

(* Many authorities suggest 10pt for long primer.)
(** Not a part of the original table.)

Figure 9.1   Page Sizes and Proportions

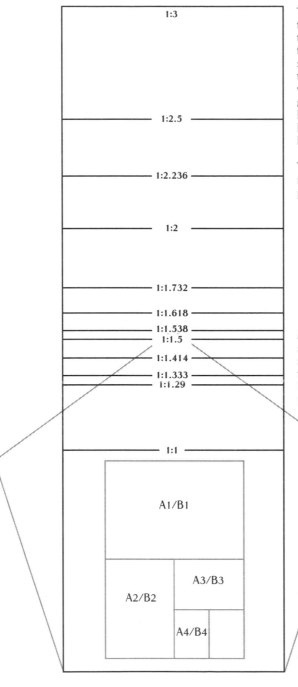

The shape of the page has an important impact on the shape of the text on the page, and even on the type used for the text. Very generally, the eye seems to prefer rectangular shapes that are distinctly taller than they are wide, without being skinny. The region of greatest interest seems to lie between 1:1.4 and 1:1.7, actually a fairly narrow range. The diagram at the left shows a variety of proportions.

The table below gives some of the common sheet names, sizes and their proportions.

Letter	8.5x11″	1.29
Legal	8.5x14″	1.647
DIN (A&B)	Many	1.414
Tabloid	11x17″	1.545
√3		1.732
√5		2.236
Pentagon		1.538
Golden Mean		1.618

Many sheets are variations on those shown above. If you take a piece of letter-size paper in landscape position, and fold it in half on the short side, each half (5.5″ by 8.5″) will have the same proportions as an 11″ by 17″ page. The DIN pages come in many sizes and are based on the square root of 2. The two principal series are the A-series and the B-series. The basic sheet is called A0 or B0; the A0 sheet is 841mm by 1189mm, and the B0 sheet is 1030mm by 1456mm. Dividing the sheets successively in half (as shown in the inset at the left) results in the A1 or B1, A2 or B2, A3 or B3, etc. Note that all of the cut sheets have the same proportions as the original A0 or B0 sheets: 1:1.414.

The proportion 2:3 (or 1:1.5) is important in traditional design. The Golden Mean is often thought of as the pleasing rectangular shape.

FIGURE 9.2   A TRADITIONAL LAYOUT

We begin with an opening, that is, we are looking at the left and right (or verso and recto) pages.

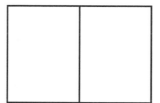

Next, draw all of the diagonals, both for the opening and the pages.

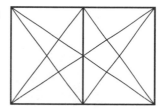

Draw the remaining lines as shown. Draw the text areas so that the upper-inside and lower-outside points align with the short diagonals; the upper-outside points align with a long diagonal. Drawn this way, the inside and top margins are one-ninth of the width and the height of the page, respectively; the outside and bottom margins are double the size of the inside and top margins, respectively.

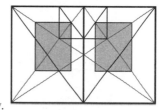

Here is the diagram in all its glory. This construction allows the margins to be a specific fraction of the width of the page, such as one-ninth, or one-eighth or one-seventh.

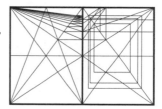

The text areas can be of an arbitrary size, so long as the inside-top and outside-bottom points align with a short diagonal, and the outside-top points align with a long diagonal. The outside margin will always be twice the inside margin, and the bottom margin will always be twice the top margin. This construction is discussed in Tschichold (1991), pp. 36–64.

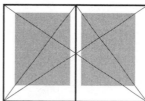

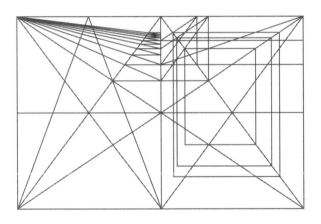

I HOPE that you find the following to be entertaining and thought provoking. I intend it to be a welcome relief from the rigors of reading the rest of the book. Come here when you want to rest and reflect for a moment. I offer this varied collection of typographic remarks in place of epigraphs at the head of each chapter: Now you can pick your own. As the margins are large, you can add your own quotations as well. I've also included a few items here simply because they make me laugh.

In my apprentice days, when I aspired to be a typographer and was learning about typefaces, I realized after a time that the accumulation of facts about them, squirrel-fashion, was not enough. It was necessary to acquire a sense of values and to develop the ability to make judgments about the quality of the type faces I was using. I was therefore grateful to Updike, Morison, Johnson and others who, in their writings, not only explained the history of type designs but expressed opinions about them. If I sometimes found it difficult to accept a particular comment I was at least pleased that the writer had made me think about the matter.

Walter Tracy

If I were asked to say what is at once the most important production of Art and the thing most to be longed for, I should answer, A beautiful House; and if I were further asked to name the production next in importance and the thing next to be longed for, I should answer, A beautiful Book. To enjoy good houses and good books in self-respect and decent comfort, seems to me to be the pleasurable end towards which all societies of human beings ought now to struggle.

William Morris

The printing works is not a place that hires out fancy dress. It is not our task to fit out any literary content with a fashionable costume; we have done our job if we see that it gets a dress in the style of our day. For what we want is typographical life, and not a typographical theatre or masked ball.   *Paul Renner*

In Typography, Function is of major importance, Form is secondary, and Fashion is meaningless.   *Aaron Burns*

Typographic arrangement should achieve for the reader what voice tone conveys to the listener.   *El Lissitzky*

The type of the future will surely more and more strip away the historic style elements of the past, yet without descending to the geometric abstract form of letters. For the optical requirements remain the same so long as the letter images are still received by the human eye and not exclusively by an electronic reading machine.   *Hermann Zapf*

Letter-forms have changed because of the designer but also because of changes in the materials, tools and technology which he has to use. Today he is faced with the technology of digital letter design, that is with the task of designing within the limitations of a grid, for computer generation. Questions of changes in form and of letter-identity have become urgent in a new way. If we want to maintain legibility should we not draw on the immense variety of ideas offered by the past? There is no need to embark on designing a new alphabet.   *Nicolete Gray*

Printing does not want primarily to be art but the most responsible part of our social, economic and intellectual structure.   *Stanley Morison*

Some typographic designers and printers shun legibility research because they regard it as a threat to the freedom of action. But typography is a means to an end, and not an end in itself, and it is subject to certain restraints. By defying those constraints which have relevance today, legibility research is likely to provide the designer with greater rather than less freedom – releasing him from many of his present inhibitions, enabling him to avoid fruitless innovation, and directing his attention and energies into more fertile fields of exploration.   *Herbert Spencer*

Type is one of the most eloquent means of expression in every epoch of style. Next to architecture, it gives the most characteristic portrait of a period and the most uncompromising testimony of a nation's intellectual status.

Peter Behrens

Typography has one plain duty before it and that is to convey information in writing. No argument or consideration can absolve typography from this duty. A printed work which cannot be read becomes a product without purpose.

Emil Ruder

Typography is the efficient means to an essentially utilitarian and only accidentally æsthetic end, for enjoyment of patterns is rarely the readers' chief aim. The laws governing the typography of books are based upon the traditions, explicit and implicit, prevailing in the society for which the printer is working. Every character, every word, every line should be seen with absolute clearness.

Stanley Morison

The function of typography, as I understand it, is neither to further the power of witches nor to bolster the defenses of those, like this unfortunate parliamentarian, who live in terror of being tempted and deceived. The satisfactions of the craft come from the elucidating, and perhaps even ennobling, the text, not from deluding the unwary reader by applying scents, paints and iron stays to empty prose. But humble texts, such as classified ads or the telephone directory, may profit as much as anything else from a good typographical bath and a change of clothes. And many a book, like many a warrior or dancer or priest of either sex, may look well with some paint on its face, or indeed with a bone in its nose.

Robert Bringhurst

Type is a thing of interest. It is sometimes a serious and useful tool, employed to deliver a message, sell a specific article or give life to an idea.

At other times it is a plaything that affords personal amusement and recreation. It is fun to produce a fresh design and unexpected ideas with letters and numbers – by themselves, or together with graphic objects. Type is a medium of philosophical enjoyment. It is interesting to discover typographic rules containing inconsistencies in logic, which are in use only because of tradition. It is also interesting to ponder the origin of these errors, the practical reasons for their perpetuation, and to suggest remedies.

An interest in Type provides a broader knowledge of history, including the appreciation of such related arts as painting, architecture and literature – and even business and politics. This affords opportunity for pleasant romantic indulgence. At the same time, it develops confidence in one's practical ability to specify appropriate typefaces to accompany creative work of specific periods.

In short, Type can be a tool, a toy and a teacher; it can provide a means of livelihood, a hobby for relaxation, and intellectual stimulation – and a spiritual satisfaction.

I believe an avid interest in Type necessarily includes a zest for everyday life.   *Bradbury Thompson*

The typographer who can serve his art modestly and with a sensitive understanding of the special demands made by each typeface will be the one to achieve the finest results.   *Paul Renner*

It is not enough simply to recognize a type instantly, something which can be done by memorizing characteristics or by tracing alphabets. The purpose of knowing types is their effective use in the production of the printed word. If they are to be used with a sympathetic understanding of their structure, it is necessary to learn their evolution. Historic grouping not only serves to assemble types of like attributes but also provides a key to their rational use.   *Alexander Lawson*

Of all the arts, architecture is nearest akin to typography. Both are equally related to their function. In both, that which wholly fulfills its purpose is beautiful.   *Helmut Presser*

Time flies like the wind, but fruit flies like bananas.   *Seen on Internet*

Make no little plans: They have no magic to stir men's blood, and probably themselves will not be realized. Make big plans: Aim high in hope and work, remembering that a noble, logical diagram one recorded will never die, but long after we are gone will be a living thing, asserting itself with ever growing insistency. Remember, our sons and grandsons are going to do things that would stagger us. Let your watch word be *Order* and your beacon *Beauty*.
                                                                Daniel H. Burnham, Architect

No other art is more justified than typography in looking ahead to future centuries; for the creations of typography benefit coming generations as much as the present ones.

Letterforms may well begin with geometry, but only the sovereignty of eye and hand can transmute a diagram into a work of art. *Paul Rand*

A man who would letterspace lowercase letters would steal sheep. [Quoted by Roger Black in *Roger Black's Desktop Design Power.*] *Frederic Goudy*

You don't draw an 'A' and then stand back and say: There, that gives you a good idea of an 'A' seen through an autumn mist, or: That's not a real A but gives you a good effect of one. Letters are things, not pictures of things. *Eric Gill*

When we seek legibility only, we obtain a readable type which is stupid and monotonous; when we seek alone beauty of form, we obtain a type of great charm in individual letter forms but tiring in mass, because the element of design is too consciously apparent. In Caslon we have the product of a master designer who made drawing the servant of readability rather than its master. *D.C. McMurtrie,* The Book

Precision of communication is important, more important than ever in our era of hair-trigger balances, when a fault, or misunderstood word may create as much disaster as a sudden and thoughtless act. *James Thurber*

Typefaces – like people's faces – have distinctive features indicating aspects of character. *Marshall Lee*

The most important element if beauty in bookmaking is PROPORTION: that is, proportion of type to page, proportion of leading and spacing to type, proportion of page to paper, proportion of margins to each other – it pervades the whole process. *Bruce Rogers*

Now that authors have for the first time the power to invent new symbols with great ease, and to have those characters printed in their manuscripts on a wide variety of typesetting devices, we must face the question of how much experimentation is desirable. Will font freaks abuse this toy by overdoing it? Is it wise to introduce new symbols by the thousands? Such questions are beyond the scope of this book [*The METAFONTbook*]; but it is easy to imagine an epidemic of fontomania occurring, once people realize how much fun it is to design their own characters, hence it may be necessary to perform fontal lobotomies. *Donald Knuth*

In the cultural history of mankind there is no event even approaching in importance the invention printing with movable types. It would require an extensive volume to set forth even in outline the far-reaching effects of this invention in every field of human enterprise and experience, or to describe its results in the liberation of the human spirit from the fetters of ignorance and superstition. The mighty power of the printed word to influence human though and action, for good or ill, has seldom been more clearly shown than in our own day and age, when we see the governments of great nations enforcing a rigorous control or even supression of the press as a necessary means of controlling the opinions and activities of their people. Since printing has exerted so immense an influence upon the course of civilization, the question of who invented it becomes one of high historical interest and importance.   *D.C. McMurtrie*

The use of words – their sounds, their meanings, and their collective letterforms – has been an intriguing aspect of design since the invention of the alphabet. Contemporary designers continue to use this play with words in their design concepts. A picture may be worth a thousand words, but as one wit pointed out: It takes words to say that.   *Allen Hurlburt*

Geometry can produce legible letters, but art alone makes them beautiful. Art begins where geometry ends, and imparts a character transcending mere measurement.   *Paul Standard*

Q: How many Bill Gates does it take to change a light bulb?
A: None — if you are Bill Gates, you simply define darkness as the industry standard.   *Noted on Internet*

In every period there have been better or worse types employed in better or worse ways. The better types employed in better ways have been used by the educated printer acquainted with standards and history, directed by taste and a sense of the fitness of things, and facing the industrial conditions and needs of his time. Such men have made of printing an art. The poorer types and methods have been employed by printers ignorant of standards and caring alone for commercial success. To these, printing has been simply a trade. The typography of a nation has been good or bad, as one or another of these classes had the supremacy. And today any intelligent printer can educate his taste, so to choose types for his work and so to use them, that he will help printing to be an art rather than a trade.   *D.B. Updike*

Each single letter is a small, well-balanced figure in itself. There are bad types, too; however, in a good type-face each letter rests complete in itself. To us, who are used to reading, a letter has become an abstract idea, a mere means of understanding.   *Romano Guardini*

The contemporary typographer regards his work from the design point of view and concentrates on the true essence of his task, to create graphic design.
Emerich Kner

Machines exist; let us then exploit them to create beauty – a modern beauty, while we are about it. For we live in the twentieth century.   *Aldous Huxley*

Neither may the clarity of the single letter be given up for the sake of rhythm, nor may formal beauty be sacrificed to mere clarity or misconceived utility.
Jan Tschichold

It's true that typography is freer. There is a proliferation and availability of types and of new ways of setting. And, in special cases, the particular way type is used makes the difference in the communication. But unless typography is being used as central to the communication, as the pivotal illustration, what makes the communication work is always the content.   *Saul Bass*

Printing is the source of practically all human evolution. Without it the tremendous progress in the fields of science and technology would not have been possible.   *Valter Falk*

If in finding a solution to his problems of arrangement, the typographer can produce a piece of work that, though not necessarily spectacular, has a quality of absolute correctness in the way it does its job, an aesthetic appeal which will induce the ordinary reader to read and arouse a sense of covetousness in the sophisticate; whether the setting be centered or asymmetric, decorated or plain, it may fairly be called a piece of inspired typography.   *Alan Dodson*

Typography is the voice of the printed page. But typography is meaningless until seen by the human eye, translated into sound by the human brain, heard by the human ear, comprehended as thought and stored as memory.

R. Hunter Middleton

Printing is fundamentally a selection of materials already in existence, and an assembling of these different varieties of types and papers and ornaments; and it is the way they are assembled that counts in the effect. One can take almost any kind of type and produce extremely varied results by different methods of handling it, by different combinations of ornaments, and by choice of various papers.

Bruce Rogers

Printing should be invisible. Type well-used is invisible type. The mental eye focuses through the type and not upon it, so that any type which has excess in design, anything that gets in the way of the mental picture to be conveyed, is bad type.

Beatrice Warde

The outlook for typography is as good as ever it was – and much the same. Its future depends largely on the knowledge and taste of educated men. For a printer there are two camps, and only two, to be in: one, the camp of things as they are; the other that of things as they should be. The first camp is on a level and extensive plain, and many eminently respectable persons lead lives of comfort therein; the sport is, however, inferior! The other camp is more interesting. Though on an inconvenient hill, it commands a wide view of typography, and in it are the class that help on sound taste in printing, because they are willing to make sacrifices for it.

D.B. Updike

Each letter should have a flirtation with the one next to it.

Mac Baumwell

Typography is the craft of endowing human language with a durable visible form, and thus with an independent existence. Its heartwood is calligraphy – the dance, on a tiny stage, of the living, speaking hand – and its roots reach into living soil, though its branches may be hung each year with new machines. So long as the root lives, typography remains a source of true delight, true knowledge, true surprise.

Robert Bringhurst

As a traditionalist I have taken the essence (as I saw it) of the early craftsmen's work to intensify my own handicraft; but I insist that I have no allowed myself to be "enslaved by the work of bygone days," nor have I attempted to impose on my own productions the superficialities of the past. "I have never marched in the wake of the latest movements of type design, nor have I been seduced into following the slimy trail of 'art nouveau'." I passed every design I made through the refining fire of study and research, and trusted that the result might bear the stamp of reason. The vagaries of the fadist have never had even a casual interest for me. I have endeavored always to produce thoughtful, dignified typefaces of legibility with a degree of distinction and beauty, "freshly risen from the canons of good type design"; attempting to secure in them the negative quality of unpretentiousness and avoiding any fantastic exhibition of self-conscious preciosity.

Frederic Goudy

The underlying idea of typography is that it should be the messenger, which conveys the thoughts of one individual to the minds of many others. Legibility and harmony are fundamental requisites.

C. Volmer Nordlund

In centered typography, pure form comes before the meanings of the words.

Jan Tschichold

Typography is not an independent Art: it is a means to an end, not an end in itself. It must always be subservient to the text which is its 'raison d'etre'...

Herbert Spencer

The more uninteresting a letter, the more useful it is to the typographer.

Piet Zwart

> The common problem, yours, mine, everyone's
> Is – not to fancy what were fair in life
> Provided it could be – but, finding first
> What may be, then find how to make it fair.

Quoted by Eric Gill

With increase of knowledge has come increasing refinement and style. For style, in the true sense of the word, is not something which can be taught. It is, or ought to be, the finest flower of a man's intellectual growth. He arrives at it by laborious process of choice and selection; the more he knows, the less liable he is to exaggeration; the more ready are his illustrations, the greater his erudition. The richer and more varied his material, the more intricate and lovely will be the pattern into which he will be able to throw it.

Frederic W. Goudy

The graphic signs called letters are so completely blended with the stream of written thought that their presence therein is as unperceived as the ticking of a clock in the measurement of time. To try to learn and to repeat their excellence is to put oneself under training in a simple and severe school of design.   *William Addison Dwiggins*

Architecture began like all scripts. First there was an alphabet. A stone was laid and that was a letter, and each letter was a hieroglyph, and on each hieroglyph there rested a group of ideas.   *Victor Hugo*

Decisive, too, for the quality of a letter is that its various parts, though of limited expressiveness in themselves should combine into a harmonious unity charged with imagination and feeling.   *Albert Windisch*

It can be considered a special merit of our time that creative forces are again concerned with the problem of type design – a problem which has been faced by the best artists of every age.   *Walter Tiemann*

Browsing through Collins Dictionary, I just found an interesting hyphenation in a reference to "... Australian hor-semen's skill". Seemed appropriate as a definition of "camp drafting".   *Collins Dictionary*

The practice of typography, if it be followed faithfully, is hard work – full of detail, full of petty restrictions, full of drudgery, and not greatly rewarded as men now count rewards. There are times when we need to bring to it all the history and art and feeling that we can, to make it bearable. But in the light of history, and of art, and of knowledge of man's achievement, it is as interesting a work as exists – a broad and humanizing employment which can indeed be followed merely as a trade, but which if perfected into an art, or even broadened into a profession, will perpetually open new horizons to our eyes and new opportunities to our hands.   *D. B. Updike*

One of the most expressive measures of each epoch of style is script. It gives, next to architecture, the most characteristic picture of a time and a sharp testimony to the spiritual ladder of development. As the fuller reflection of the surges of a time is reflected in Architecture, so writing reveals the inner inclinations, the pride and humility, the faith and the doubt of the generations.
                                                                    Peter Behrens

Good books ever give, and ask nothing in return; they speak when we would hear, and are silent when we are tired, they wait patiently through the years for us, and are not offended when finally we take them again into our hands, on the contrary they bestow precisely the same joy as on the first day. He who has books, and is possessed of the intelligence to read them, can never be entirely unlucky, and has surely the best company that can be found on earth.   *Paul Ernst*

Type is the raw material of all printing. He who has no eye for type, cannot appreciate composition. Type could be and should be the most direct and personal expression of our conception of form.   *Peter Jessen*

Saving paper by avoiding visual rubbish is worth its weight in environmental gold... A good typographer resists the mindless blather and torrents of verbal emptiness... Typography was not meant to make things which hide their secrets. Just the opposite – it should reveal all the secrets: by sensible word and sentence arrangements which appropriately convey the message to the recipient.   *Kurt Weidemann*

Like architects, typographers are more interested in their own satisfaction than that of the public.   *Fritz Spiegl*

Give me the luxuries of life and I will willingly do without the necessities.
Frank Lloyd Wright

Across the page the symbols moved in grave morrice, in the mummery of their letters, wearing quaint caps of squares and cubes. Give hands, traverse, bow to partner: so: imps of fancy of the Moors. Gone too from the world, Averroes and Moses Maimonides, dark men in mien and movement, dashing in their mocking mirrors the obscure soul of the world, a darkness shining in brightness which brightness could not comprehend.   *James Joyce, Ulysses*

Until quite recently it would have been *de rigueur* to include a sans serif in any range of typefaces for text setting, but this usage is increasingly being recognized for one of the cardinal design sins of the 1960s, quite worthy to be placed alongside residential tower blocks in its arrogant refusal to address human needs and preferences, expressed or implied. There would be more gain than loss if it were to be resolved to ban the use of sans serif for continuous reading purposes, as distinct from its role as an ancillary to the seriffed face for such purposes as captions, tables or headings where appropriate.   *Douglas Martin*

Rules or substitutes for the artist's hand must necessarily be inadequate, although, when set down by such men as Dürer, Tory, Da Vinci, Serlio, and others, they probably do establish canons of proportion and construction which afford a sound basis upon which to present new expressions.   *Frederic W. Goudy*

> Blot out, correct, insert, refine,
> Enlarge, diminish, interline;
>   Be mindful, when invention fails,
>   To scratch your head, and bite your Nails.
>
>   *Jonathan Swift*

The pen, probably more than any other tool, has had the strongest influence upon lettering in respect of serif design… It is probable that the letters [of the Trajan column] were painted before they were incised, and though their main structure is attributed to the pen and their ultimate design to the technique of the chisel, they undoubtedly owe much of their freedom to the influence of the brush.   *L. C. Evets*

Our transition from barbarism to civilization can be attributed to the alphabet. Those great prehistoric discoveries and inventions such as the making of a fire, the use of tools, the wheel and the axle, and even our modern marvelous applications of steam and electricity pale into insignificance when compared to the power of the alphabet. Simple as it now appears after the accustomed use of ages, it can be accounted not only the most difficult, but also the most fruitful of all the achievements of the human intellect.   *Otto F. Ege*

Remember that it takes time, patience, critical practice and knowledge to learn any art or craft. No "art experience" is going to result from any busy work for a few hours of experimenting with the edged pen. Take as much time as you require, and do not become impatient. If it takes a month to get it, then be happy it takes only a month.   *Lloyd Reynolds, Italic Calligraphy & Handwriting*

At first, the master printer was also a publisher, till the trade began to expand a bookseller as well, and sometimes, like Caxton, translator or author. Nor is it surprising that printing and bookselling still preserve the professional outlook of the medieval craftsman far more than any other contemporary commercial undertaking, with *mores* peculiar to themselves. Today, as throughout the past four centuries, there is still a place for the small-scale high-quality firm in printing, publishing or bookselling alike. Throughout the five centuries of printing from movable type the small proprietor has ever been the ally of novel thought; and the book trade still thrives on the free expression of views which are anathema to big business, oil politicians and Wall Street tycoons.   *Lancelot Hogben*

[Do not] put too much confidence in experimental results until they have been confirmed by theory.   *Sir Arthur Eddington*

Measure twice, cut once.
Honesty to self is a top priority.
Everything in life is a matter of opinion.
You are a part of your times and society. Your designs will reflect various aspects of your culture. If you practice slavish reproduction of design from another period without the benefits of the societal influences of that period, your work will prove to be an exercise in style which is seldom memorable. If you build your designs on the solid foundations of earlier work and bring to your designs a full reflection of yourself and your societal influences, your designs have a chance to be memorable. If you are honest to your time, you will make the job of future historians easier.   *Richard Beatty*

The old artists of the classical school were never egotists. Egotism has been and remains responsible for many defects of modern typography.

Talbot Baines Reed

The printer carried on into type the tradition of the calligrapher and of the calligrapher at his best. As this tradition died out in the distance, the craft of the printer declined. It is the function of the calligrapher to revive and restore the craft of the printer to its original purity of intention and accomplishment.

Thomas J. Cobden-Sanderson

The only thing that never looks right is a rule. There is not in existence a page with a rule on it that cannot be instantly and obviously improved by taking the rule out.   *G. B. Shaw*

Writing is one site of the struggle between individual autonomy and social control, and the resulting compromise produces identifiable styles. The pattern of stability and change continued after printing first emerged and is evident in newspapers today. Most newspaper typefaces are Roman in origin and laden with meanings that depend on historical roots as well as recent uses, and newspapers contribute new meanings to the typefaces they employ.

Kevin G. Barnhurst

Printing in its childhood was an art. The highest period of any art is its childhood, because childhood moves by spontaneous inner urge, not by rules and intellectual bondage that runs all into fixed moulds. It is an accepted truth that as skill and elaboration creep into development of an art, simplicity, feeling and beauty decline. The early printers were not weighed down with rules, formulas and theories that have smothered us today. With but one font of type, a wooden frame with a screw attachment and a crude inking device, they have given us books of strength and beauty that we have never equalled.   *Edwin Grabhorn*

However important letterforms are in our culture, printing types hardly seem to be influenced by cultural developments. Apart from some fashionable display types, letters seem to be immune to changes in the world. Whereas modern man dresses himself in a jogging suit, excessively big sneakers and a baseball-cap, drives a sports car and has rap conversations, most contemporary typefaces look as though their makers still live in the Baroque era.

(…With professional type designers, I seldom observe a preference for unmelodious sounds. Almost all type designers I know are decent people who meet the requirements for the average bourgeois.)

…So nobody has to be surprised that nothing sensational ever happens in the world of type design. On the one hand, the character of the type designer is not suited to that; on the other hand the business does not leave much room for experiments. Typefaces are meant for transmitting information. Therefore, shapes that differ too much from traditions and conventions are undesirable. This archaic trade is only appropriate, indeed, for designers who are conservative in nature.

Frank Blokland

BorderMaker. *Monotype Corporation* [Version 1.0] A flexible and useful tool for the creation of borders, type that is to be used by it must conform to certain standards: I discuss those in Chapter 2. The same standards also happen to be useful for the use of border typefaces in other programs as well. Needs some work: it is a little unstable and quirky.

Canvas. *Deneba Systems, Inc* [Version 3.5.2] A very flexible and useful drawing program. I used it to open TIFF files and then cut and paste the letters into Fontographer. I relocated the origin of the ruler and drew a selection rectangle of a standard size to preserve the relative dimensions of the original characters when pasting into Fontographer's background layer. I also used Canvas to edit screen shots for the illustrations.

Collector's Edition I. *Adobe Systems, Inc* [Version –] I used this as a source of letter forms for illustrations.

The Electric Typographer. *2216 Cliff Drive, Santa Barbara, California, 93109; (805) 966-7563* [Font materials] Judith Sutcliffe provides a delightful, beautifully crafted and varied collection of font materials. A catalog is available.

Flash-It. *Nobu Tage (Shareware)* [Version 3.02] This is an excellent screen-capture utility. The shareware fee is $15: Nobu Tage, P. O. Box 7114, Menlo Park, California 94026 USA.

Font Chameleon. *Ares Software* [Version 1.0] An interesting concept in typeface creation. Descriptors of any available typeface can be altered in a variety of ways, and can be blended with other descriptors to produce yet more descriptors and typefaces. Used intelligently, this could be a very useful tool.

Fontographer. *Altsys Corporation/Macromedia* [Version 3.5/4.1] The first and still best of the tools available for font creation and manipulation. The deceptively simple interface is in reality extremely powerful by virtue of being both transparent and supple.

FontMonger. *Ares Software* [Version 1.5]   Font manipulation from the people who wrote Letraset's FontStudio. Now a very powerful program that includes drawing tools.

FontStudio. *Letraset* [Version 2.0]   Potentially a very fine program for the creation of typefaces, with numerous functions – even auto-kerning. Problems in interface continue to plague the program and make it harder to use than it ought to be. Letraset's support is also less than stellar: the program deserves very much better. Now officially declared *dead* by Letraset. Too bad. As of this writing, the source code for the program has reverted to Ares Software: time will tell the outcome of that.

FreeHand. *Aldus/Macromedia* [Version 3–5]   A fine update to an useful program. Like Illustrator, FreeHand can now do hanging punctuation. FreeHand was particularly useful in preparing the illustrations for this book: it quietly and with no fanfare converted the screen-shot PICT files into TIFF format which was of incalculable utility in scaling and printing the illustrations.

Ikarus M. *URW* [Version 2.5]   Powerful tool with, relative to the rest of the font tools available, a non-standard approach. This program is intended for use with a digitizing tablet.

Illustrator. *Adobe Systems* [Version 5.5]   Version 5 of this classic is a treat and a joy to use. Illustrator and Freehand are still the only widely accessible programs that can hang punctuation, though their primary function is illustration. PageMaker? XPress? Aldus..., Quark..., are you listening? Version 5.5 has a number of powerful filters that would be useful in creating typeface variations.

Incubator Pro. *Type Solutions* [Version 2.0]   A program that can manipulate the x-height, descent, weight, slant, etc. of a TrueType or Type 1 font. Used with caution can be very useful. No longer in development, it is also not supported.

Kernus. *URW* [Version x.x]   Creates about 1000 kerning pairs easily and quickly. Very configurable. Expensive – $400 or so – considering that Fontographer, which can do it all, retails for about $300.

Linus M. *URW* [Version 3.0]   Auto-trace module for the Ikarus system. Very good, and flexible.

Metamorphosis Professional. *Macromedia* [Version 2.03]　The Swiss Army knife of font conversion programs. An invaluable tool in the DTP arsenal.

PageMaker. *Adobe Corporation* [Version 5.0]　The page layout program that started it all. I used it for some of the illustrations, as well as one of the type specimens ('Fleuron').

Photoshop. *Adobe Corporation* [Version 2.5.1]　An amazing tool that can do just about anything to an image. My own simple use of it was to clean up some scans. Can also be used to alter type, often with the help of Streamline: see Chapter 6.

Richard Beatty Designs. *2313 Laurel Park Highway, Hendersonville, North Carolina 28792; (704) 696-8316* [Typefaces]　A wonderful source of magnificent typeface materials. A catalog is available. A strong showing in Goudy's typefaces, and an extraordinary collection of border and ornament materials.

Spectacular. *Omega Systems* [Version 1.2]　A fine program that produces a wide variety of type specimens. Very useful and highly recommended. Omega Systems, P.O. Box 7633, Chico, California 95927-7633; (916) 894-6351.

Streamline. *Adobe Systems* [Version 3.0]　Dedicated auto-trace program for PostScript. Probably more attractive as a possible first step now that version 4.x of Fontographer can "Clean Up Paths."

System 7. *Apple Computer* [Version 7.5.1]　This work has been carried out entirely under System 7.5, which I have found is a complete delight. I have had no problems installing it or using it, with the exception of some older programs that failed to function as they ought to. Overall, more stable than any version of System 6.x.

Textures. *Blue Sky Research* [Version 1.7]　TEX for the Macintosh. A wonderful implementation of TEX fully integrated into the Macintosh environment. TEX sets text better and more flexibly than any other available page layout environment. Originally intended for the typesetting of technical documents (it is very good at typesetting math), it is now used for a wide variety of typesetting tasks in the humanities as well as the sciences. *Lightening Textures* – essentially see-it-as-you-type-it WYSIWYG TEX – is about the most breathtaking thing I have ever seen. This work was typeset in TEX using Textures. [I am occasionally asked why I use TEX, renowned as it is for its enormous learning curve, and given its usual association with the sciences generally and especially mathematics. There are several reasons. (1) No other piece of desktop software I know of has a line-breaking algorithm based on the paragraph: TEX reads an entire paragraph before it typesets anything, and can juggle the line-breaks in such a way that a tight line will not be set immediately above or below a loose line, for instance. All other pieces of DTP software are line-based: Once a line has been typeset they become brain-dead about all that comes before and after. In TEX, on the other hand, changing a word in the next-to-last line might alter the way in which the entire paragraph is set in order to maintain consistent typographic color. (2) The basic files for TEX are simple ASCII text files, which can be taken to virtually any computer platform. (3) Ligatures (such as ct, st, ff, fi, fl, ffi and ffl) are handled automatically by TEX – the ASCII text file itself contains no ligatures whatever: they are assembled only when the document is actually typeset by the program. (4) Because TEX is essentially a computer programming language that specializes in typesetting, complex 'programs' can be written that solve extremely difficult typographic problems, but which are used by merely issuing a simple command. (5) Pairwise kerning is built-in. (6) I find the use of TEX to be utterly exhilarating: typesetting for the thinking person. (7) Blue Sky Research is to be warmly congratulated for its superb support, including an 800-number.]

The TypeBook. *Golden State Graphics* [Version 2.37] A useful and flexible source of type specimens. Supports color. Freeware, although for $45 you can have aspects of the program customized for you. Jim Lewis, Golden State Graphics, 2137 Candis, Santa Ana, California 92706; (714) 542-5518. CIS: 71650,2373; AOL: JimXLewis.

XPress. *Quark, Inc.* [Version 3.31] One of the leading contenders in the WYSIWYG page-layout line up. Superb control and an interface much improved over earlier versions. I used it to set up some of the type specimens of Chapter 7.

Bibliography ❏ 12

Adobe Systems. *Adobe Type 1 Font Format* [Addison-Wesley, 1990]   A technical document that made public the details of the Type 1 format.

——. *Adobe Font Metric Files Specification, Version 2.0* [Adobe Systems, 1989]   Available from the Adobe area on CompuServe.

——. *Adobe Font Metric Files Specification, Version 3.0* [Adobe Systems Document LPS5004, 1990]   Available from the Adobe area on CompuServe.

——. *Font and Function* [Issued quarterly]   Adobe's catalog of typefaces. An indispensable reference, and invariably fun to look at.

Anderson, Donald M. *Calligraphy – The Art of Written Forms* [Dover, 1992; originally copyright 1962, Holt, Rinehart and Winston, Inc.] Tremendous amounts of information (well researched) that sheds much light on typographic forms, often explicitly discussed.

André, Jacques and Hersch, Roger D. *Raster Imaging and Digital Typography* [Cambridge University Press, 1989]   Proceedings of the International Conference Ecole Polytechnique Fédéral Lausanne, October 1989. A collection of fairly technical articles dealing with the digitization and printing of type by electronic means.

Apple Computer. *The TrueType Font Format Specification* [APDA M0825-LL/A]   Available from Apple Computer.

Barnhurst, Kevin G. *Seeing the Newspaper* [St. Martin's, 1994]   This is an interesting exploration of the philosophical, technical, artistic and typographic problems that attend newspaper design. The author argues that the form of the newspaper influences the way we interpret the news it contains.

Beatty, Richard. *A Designer's Remembrancer* [Printed by the author: Richard Beatty Designs, 2312 Laurel Park Highway, Hendersonville, North Carolina 28739; (704) 696-8316]   "The thoughts in the *Remembrancer* are from my experiences in architectural design and are not about types but about an attitude toward design of any kind and the sometimes-delight in learning from experience."

————. *On the Just Spacing of Letters* [Obtained from the author–see above] An excellent method for establishing good type spacing.

Beaujon, Paul. "The 'Garamond Types': A study of the XVI and XVII century sources" *The Fleuron* [No. 5, 1926]   Beatrice Warde, writing under her pen name. An early but important study of the Garamond problem.

Bennett, Paul A., ed. *Books and Printing: A Treasury for Typophiles* [Frederic C. Beil, 1951, 1991]   A wide-ranging and excellent anthology of typographic writings, from just about everyone who wrote anything about typography. Highly recommended.

Binns, Betty. *Better Type* [Watson-Guptill, 1989]   Superb treatment of the use of text type. The book is better that 90% examples. Required reading: would seriously reduce the amount of poor typography commonly found in DTP.

Black, Roger. *Roger Black's Desktop Design Power* [Bantam, 1991]   There is a lot of information in this book on a very broad range of subjects, accompanied by good taste and common sense.

Bringhurst, Robert. *The Elements of Typographic Style* [Hartley & Marks, 1992]   This book is of a value far past reckoning. At once lyrical and useful, it gives insight both to the joyful spirit and practice of fine, conscientious typography.

Brown, Alex. "Type Renaissance – A Primer on Digital Type" *MacWorld* [July 1991]   The first in a series of four articles on the present state of digital typography, particularly on the desktop. This article lays the groundwork with some history and technical background. Also brief introductions to some of the important people in the field: Warnock (Adobe), Knuth (TEX), and Carter (Bitstream).

Brown, Bruce. *Brown's Index to Photocomposition Typography* [Greenwood Publishing, 1983]   This interesting reference work has a glossary, list of photocomposition machines, and an index of typefaces based on Brown's typefactor. An interesting work. The typefactor is discussed in chapter 9.

Bruckner, D. J. R. *Frederic Goudy* [Abrams, 1990]   A long overdue appreciation of the one of the greatest typographic designers America has ever produced. Very highly recommended as an antidote to the still-fashionable pastime of "Goudy-bashing."

Catich, Fr. E. M. *The Origin of the Serif* [Davenport, Iowa, The Catfish Press, 1968]   From Nicolete Gray 1986 (see below): "Father Catich, in his book, argues that [the design of the Trajan letter] derives from the square-cut reed pen of the *ordinator* [the person who planned and sketched-out the inscription] and owes nothing to the chisel of the carver. In his view the serif is a Roman invention, drawn or carved from the point inwards towards the stem of the letter. This seems to me to be an unnecessary and unproven simplification. There is no reason why the *ordinator* and the carver should not have been the same person... The 'Trajan' alphabet was evolved by master craftsmen who were probably both *ordinators* and carvers, perhaps working in the same workshops, surely working together. It does not seem to me to be profitable to try to eliminate or even to separate the relative contributions [of the *ordinator* and the carver.]"

Designer's Guide to Type. *Various* [Step-By-Step Graphics, Vol. 6, No. 2]   An interesting collection of articles concerning many aspects of typography. Particularly interesting is an article about Roger Black's design of a typeface in Fontographer.

Dowding, Geoffrey. *Finer Points in the Spacing and Arrangement of Type* [Wace & Company, Ltd., 1954]   A delightful, valuable and thoroughly informative book.

——— . *The History of Printing Types* [Wace & Company, Ltd., 1961]   This is a very good introduction to the subject. It contains a wealth of examples.

Drogin, Marc. *Medieval Calligraphy* [Allenheld and Schram, 1980; Dover, 1986]   This is a practical, how-to book that gives much insight to the letterforms (and their predecessors) that were current at the time that printing was first practiced.

Dwiggins, W. A. *Layout in Advertising* [Harper and Brothers Publishers, 1928]   Dated? Well, yes, perhaps a bit. Still, there is a timelessness to good design that keeps this book fresh and useful. Wonderfully practical and insightful, with an unfailing charm and humor. Though type is not specifically the focus of the book, there is much good advice.

Eckersley, Richard et al. *Glossary of Typesetting Terms* [University of Chicago Press, 1994]   A worthwhile addition to the literature of typography. Very complete, and the definitions are clear and useful.

Enschedé, Ch. *Fonderies de Caractères et leur matériel dans les Pays-Bas du XVe au XIX siècle* [Haarlem, 1908]   A magnificent and luxurious book that could provide enough raw material for a gaggle of Fontographer-mavens for decades.

Felici, James. "PostScript versus TrueType" *MacWorld* [September 1991] The third in a series of four articles on the current state of desktop typography. Compares and contrasts the strengths and weaknesses of the two formats. Opinions/profiles include Jeff Level (Monotype), Ernie Brock (Aries Software), and Jim Von Ehr (Altsys Corp.). Jim points out the advantages of PostScript as a type development medium, even for TrueType: Bézier curves are easier to manage than quadratic splines).

Fenton, Erfert. "Desktop Foundry – Forging Fonts on the Mac" *MacWorld* [August 1991]   The second in a series of four articles on the present state of digital typography, particularly on the desktop. This article examines the principal pieces of software for creating type on the Mac: Fontographer, FontStudio, TypeDesigner and Ikarus-M. Also introduces some of the users of this software: Sumner Stone (Adobe), Charles Bigelow and Kris Holmes (Bigelow and Holmes Foundry) and Judith Sutcliffe (The Electric Typographer).

————. *The Macintosh Font Book* [Peachpit Press, 1991 (2nd edition)]   This has become one of the standard references, and rightly so. It contains a great deal of timely and pertinent information. The second edition contains information on System 7.0 and TrueType.

Firmage, Richard A. *The Alphabet Abecedarium: Some Notes on Letters* [David R. Godine, Boston 1993]   A real treasure, and fast becoming one of my favorite books. A kind of anecdotal history of the alphabet, yet meaty with lots to think about. There is a congenial air of creative reflection about the book that makes it positively charming. Lots of information, and a delight to read.

Gaskill, Philip. "A Nomenclature for the Letterforms of Roman Type" *Visible Language* [X 1 (Winter 1976)]   A really excellent and rational approach to the naming of the parts of letters. Should be better and more widely known. Consists of a brief but exhaustive glossary, and a large number of illustrations and examples of the nomenclature put to use.

Gill, Eric. *An Essay on Typography* [David R. Godine, 1988]   A feisty and irritating though sound and influential (and very personal) view of typography. Gill's contributions to the field are tight word-spacing and the advisability of rag-right margins.

Goudy, Frederic. *A Half-Century of Type Design and Typography 1895–1945* [The Typophiles, 2 volumes, 1946]   Goudy discusses each of his type designs in more-or-less chronological order. A sample of each is included. Very useful.

Grafton, Carol Belanger, ed. *Pictorial Archive of Printer's Ornaments* [Dover Publications, 1980]   A magnificent collection of ornaments and fleurons that cry out for digitization. The same editor has produced a number of equally interesting and useful collections.

Gray, Nicolete. *A History of Lettering* [David R. Godine, Boston 1986]   A brilliant account of the art of lettering, which contrives to give the reader a real feel for the letterforms, and the people and times that devised and used them.

Haley, Allan. "How to Submit a Typeface" *U&lc* [Vol. 18, No. 2]   The author, Chairman of the ITC Typeface Review Board, outlines the process whereby an individual can submit a typeface to the ITC. See chapters 4 and 9.

Harling, Robert. "The Early Alphabets of Eric Gill" *Alphabet and Image* [December 1946; No. 3]   Beautifully reproduced drawings of Gill's roman and italic types.

Hosek, Don, editor. "Serif" *The Magazine of Type & Typography* [Quarterly; Dept. S-1, 555 Guilford Avenue, Claremont, California 91711-5439; (909) 621-1291; US subscription 1 year $28, two years $50.]   Huzzah huzzah! Finally a really excellent journal of typography, both practical and philosophical.

Hussmann, Heinrich. *Über die Schrift* [Guido Pressler Verlag Wiesbaden, 1977]   A superb and informative book about the history of writing and type design. The book is dedicated to Jan Tschichold.

———. *Über das Buch* [Guido Pressler Verlag Wiesbaden, (1968)]   This book is excellent and should make an appearance in an English translation. It is a fine introduction to the art of the book.

Jaspert, Berry and Johnson. *Encyclopedia of Typefaces* [Blandford, 1970, reprinted 1990]   An excellent and richly informative source. Typeface samples are accompanied by a brief outline of its history and origins.

Karow, Peter. *Digital Formats for Typefaces* [URW Verlag, 1987]   An interesting and informative account of the various approaches to the digitization of type. Also an exposition of the Ikarus program for typeface digitization, created by Karow. This translation by Mike Daines and Dietrich Buglass is very good and enjoyable. Recommended reading.

Kindersley, David. *Optical Character Spacing for New Printing Systems* [Lund Humphries Ltd. for the Wynkyn de Worde Society, second edition of 1972]   An interesting examination of various approaches to letterspacing based on the application of the principles of mechanics to letterforms.

Knuth, Donald E. *Mathematical Typography* [MIT, 1960]   An interesting and early essay (dedicated to Pólya on his 90th birthday) which outlines not only TEX but Metafont as well.

———. *The METAFONTbook* [Addison-Wesley, 1989]   The basic textbook for the Metafont type design system. If only Metafont were easy to learn, alas. Still, as with all of Knuth's books there is much to learn here. A fascinating book.

———. *The TEXbook* [Addison-Wesley, 1989]   The basic textbook for the TEX typesetting system. It is a unique blend of the informative, the entertaining and the infuriating.

Lange, Wilhelm H. *Schriftfibel* [Franz Steiner Verlag GmbH, Wiesbaden, 1951 3rd ed.]   Excellent history of type from its origins in handwriting. Also much information about German typography.

Lawson, Alexander. *Anatomy of a Typeface* [David R. Godine, 1990]   If you don't have access to Updike's *Printing Types…*, then you should have this treasure of typographical information.

———. *Printing Types* [Beacon Press, revised and expanded version, 1990] This book is an outgrowth of the authors teaching at the School of Printing at Rochester Institute of Technology. Compact and packed with information.

Martin, Douglas. *Book Design, A Practical Introduction* [Van Nostrand Reinhold, 1989]   A concise but tremendously informative overview of the subject. Erudite and well written, yet approachable and enjoyable.

Martin, Judy and Miriam Tribley. *Calligraphy: Skills and Techniques* [Macmillian, 1994] Contains examples of characters that show their architecture in such a way as to make them useful for gaining insights into the drawing of letters for type.

Matthies, Hurt W. G. and Hogan, Thom. "7.0-Friendly Persuasion" *MacUser* [April 1991, pp239–40] Gives some information on the use of fonts in System 7.0 from the viewpoint of programmers.

McLean, Ruari. *Jan Tschichold: typographer* [David R. Godine, Boston 1975] A wonderful book about one of the greatest typographic thinkers and doers of the twentieth century. Also contains translations of some of Tschichold's writings. A good select bibliography is included.

——. *The Thames & Hudson Manual of Typography* [Thames and Hudson 1988] A compact and informative overview of typography.

McMurtrie, Douglas C. *The Book; The Story of Printing & Bookmaking* [Oxford University Press, 1943] A vast compendium of information, as fascinating as it is useful.

Morris, William (Peterson, William S., ed.). *The Ideal Book* [University of Southern California Press, 1982] This beautifully produced book contains a collection of Morris' writings on typography and book arts generally.

Morison, Stanley. *Memorandum on a Proposal to Revise the Typography of 'The Times'* [The Times, London, 1930] A wonderful summary of the history of type, with particular reference to newspaper typography. A very enjoyable read.

——. *Politics and Script* [Oxford University Press, 1972] The subtitle sums up this fascinating and scholarly work: *Aspects of authority and freedom in the development of Graeco-Latin script from the sixth century B.C. to the twentieth century A.D.*

——. *The Roman Italic & Black Letter Bequeathed to the University of Oxford by Dr. John Fell* [Oxford (for the Typophiles)] These magnificent and important types are examined in this beautiful, small volume, which is set in the Fell types.

——. *A Tally of Types* [Cambridge University Press, 1973] Morison was the typographic consultant for the Monotype Corporation. Walter Lewis was the director of the CUP, and a supporter of Morison's drive to improve the state of British typography by means of a program of typographic restoration, renovation and creation. This *Tally* makes particular reference to the typefaces used for machine composition at the CUP.

———. "Towards an Ideal Italic" *The Fleuron* [No. 5, 1926]   This is a wonderful discussion of the development of italic type, and what constitutes a good one.

———. "Towards an Ideal Type" *The Fleuron* [No. 2, 1924]   A brilliant, wise and quite readable essay on the aesthetics of type.

———. *Type Designs of the Past and Present* [The Fleuron, Limited, 1926] Morison wrote a great deal for (and edited much of) the important annual *The Fleuron.* This is a scholarly and delightful historical essay.

Morison, Stanley, and Day, Kenneth. *The Typographic Book 1450 – 1935* [London, Kenneth Benn, Ltd., 1963]   A sumptuous book that illustrates some of the greatest examples of printing, superbly reproduced. Brilliant and concise introduction sums up and says much about the history of the book and typography.

Osley, A. S. *Scribes & Sources* [David R. Godine, 1980]   The subtitle says it all: "Handbook of the Chancery Hand in the Sixteenth Century." There is also an essay by Berthold Wolpe on John de Beauchesne.

Parker, Roger C. *One Minute Designer* [Que, 1993]   An interesting series of over 200 design topics tackled with imagination and good sense. A wonderful book. Also has an extensive "pre-flight" list of things to remember when putting a publication together.

Petzendorfer, Ludwig, ed. *Authentic Art Nouveau Alphabets ...* [Dover, 1984] A fascinating collection of typographic raw materials. Well reproduced, but never giving a complete font (often omits punctuation, for instance).

P·I·E Books Editorial Staff. *Business Card Graphics* [P·I·E Books, Tokyo, 1990] A delightful book containing some 1200 examples of business card design. There are many pointed lessons here about effective, small-scale typographic design.

Rodenberg, Julius. "Karl Klingspor" *The Fleuron* [Vol. V, 1926]   An interesting account of the founder of the Klingspor foundry (formerly the Rudhard foundry) and his great influence on German typography. The work of Koch and Tiemann is discussed (among others). Most important, there is a table showing the types issued by the Klingspor foundry from 1900 (the famous *Eckmannschrift*) to 1926 (Koch's

Klingsporschrift). There is a lot of material here for anyone interested in type revivals carried out with Fontographer: some 29 alphabets. Some cry out for revival like the Behrens Medieval and Hupp-Antiqua.

Rogers, Bruce. *Paragraphs on Printing* [Dover Publications, 1979]   This classic is as pertinent now as ever it was. Covers in a compact yet humane way a rich variety of topics with perfect good taste and clarity. A necessary part of any typographic library.

————. *Report on the Typography of the Cambridge University Press* [Cambridge University Press, 1950]   This became a very important document, in that it clearly expressed what good, scholarly typography should look like, and the materials (type in particular) that are necessary to make it look good.

Rookledge, Gordon and Perfect, Christopher. *Rookledge's International Type Finder* [Moyer Bell Ltd, 1991 (revised edition)]   The most exhaustive tool of its kind. Not only are there samples of hundreds of typefaces, but there are exhaustive tables of distinguishing characteristics that enable you to find a typeface.

Ruder, Emil. *Typographie* [Arthur Niggli Ltd., Switzerland, 1967]   Ruder was a brilliant Swiss typographer and teacher. This book beautifully sums up the typography of the 50s and 60s, much of it an outgrowth of "die neue Typographie" championed by Tschichold in the late 20s. There is much here that is very dated – style, mostly – but there is also much technique and attention to detail that is extremely valuable.

Shepherd, Margaret. *Learning Calligraphy: A Book of Lettering, Design and History* [Collier Books (Macmillan Publishing Co.), 1977]   Highly recommended introduction to the subject. Very clear, with excellent instructions and examples.

Shushan, Ronnie and Don Wright. *Desktop Publishing by Design* [Microsoft Press, 1989]   Well-written compendium of techniques and applications for DTP, focusing on PageMaker 3.0.

Solo, Dan X. *(Various volumes of type samples)* [Dover, various dates]   These wonderful collections are perfect sources for templates and inspiration. Very reasonably priced and well reproduced for the most part.

Spiekerman, Eric and E. M. Ginger. *Stop Stealing Sheep & find out how type works* [Adobe Press 1993] A very interesting and (thought-)provoking little tome. Very finely produced, and an example of current typographic praxis.

Stone, Sumner. *On Stone; The Art and Use of Typography on the Personal Computer* [Bedford Arts, 1991] This wonderful book is every bit as useful as it is beautiful. Instructional as well as inspirational.

Thomson, George L. *The Calligraphic Workbook* [Sterling Publishing Co., 1985] Shows how to use a broad point pen. Interesting in that it shows both the path of the center of the nib – the 'backbone' of the stroke, if you like – and the *outline* of the shape produced by the nib. Gives roman, gothic and italic forms.

Thorp, Joseph. *A Suggested Nomenclature for the Forms and Parts of Letters* [London, The Monotype Corp., 1934] This is a fascinating examination of the problem of what to call the parts of letters. Illuminating and thought provoking.

Tracy, Walter. *Letters of Credit* [David R. Godine, 1986] This book begins with an examination of the problems associated with typographic design. The author then discusses the work of: van Krimpen, Goudy, Koch, Dwiggins. There is an interesting study of Morison's Times Roman. A very clear-headed and well-informed study. The discussion on character spacing (pp70–80) simply could not be improved upon. Tracy was head of type design for 30 years at the UK Linotype Company; to his credit are the typefaces Maximus, Modern and Times Europa.

Trudgill, Anne. *Lettering Workbooks* [Watson Guptil, 1988] A series of books dealing with the techniques and applications of calligraphy. The individual titles are: 1) *Basic Skills,* 2) *Traditional Penmanship,* 3) *Applied Lettering,* 4) *Designing with Letters.* An excellent series that teaches both what to do and what to avoid doing. The first volume, *Basic Skills,* gives an excellent sense for the shape of letters and how they are formed.

Tschichold, Jan. *Asymmetric Typography* [Faber & Faber, 1967] This is Ruari McLean's translation of Tschichold's 1935 call to modern typographic arms: *Typographische Gestaltung.* A magnificent and inspiring treatment of 'The New Typography' by the man who, even if he did not invent it, was certainly its most lucid champion. Tschichold later altered his views somewhat.

———. *The Form of the Book* [Hartley & Marks, 1991]   A much needed and excellent translation of Tschichold's *Ausgewälte Aufsätze über Fragen der Gestalt des Buches und der Typographie*. Vintage Tschichold, and an endless resource for typographic good taste and excellence. Mandatory reading.

———. *Treasury of Alphabets and Lettering* [Design Press/McGraw-Hill, 1992]   A long overdue English translation of *Meisterbuch der Schrift*, containing matchless insights into letterforms and typography. Ruari McLean says of this work: "A book that has to be possessed by every student of the arts of lettering, typography, book design and graphics – for its beauty, its usefulness as a work of visual reference, and not least for Tschichold's introductory essay, showing with brilliant illustrations how to use type..." This edition is absolutely beautiful, and faithfully recreates the look of the original.

Updike, Daniel Berkeley. *In the Day's Work* [Harvard University Press, 1924] A practical and sound introduction to the business of type as well as the art. Contains interesting echoes of the present debate between traditional typography and DTP.

———. "On the Planning of Printing" *The Fleuron* [No. 2, 1924]   Something like an abbreviated *In the Day's Work*. An excellent view of the printer's work.

———. *Printing Types, Their History, Forms, and Use: A Study in Survivals* [Harvard University Press, 1922; Dover, 1975]   This is the standard source for information about printing types. Though now, sadly, out of print, it is still essential reading.

———. *Some Aspects of Printing – Old and New* [New Haven, William Edwin Rudge, 1941]   A brief but superb collection of essays that examine some of the problems of the typographer/printer.

V & M Typography, Inc. *The Type Specimen Book* [Van Nostrand Reinhold, 1974]   A huge and well produced book of type samples. As well as alphabets, it contains a large section of ornaments. A good source.

Wallis, Lawrence W. *Modern Encyclopedia of Typefaces 1960–1990* [Van Nostrand Reinhold, 1990]   A wonderful collection of recent type design. There is also information about the designers.

Warde, Beatrice. *The Crystal Goblet* [The World Publishing Company, 1956] Sixteen magnificent essays on the subject of typography. The first essay ('The Crystal Goblet') is pure gold, and ought to be read by anyone with any interest in typography.

Weidemann, Kurt. "Biblica: Designing a New Typeface for the Bible" *Visible Language* [XVI 1 (Winter 1982)] A fascinating study of the design of a typeface as it is influenced by the purpose for which it is to be used.

White, Alex. *How to Spec Type* [Watson-Guptill, 1987] To 'spec' type is to *specify* how it is to be arranged on the page: margins, line length, leading, drop-caps, runarounds, color, indents, rules and boxes, typeface and weight, word spacing, letterspacing, etc., etc. This excellent and compact book does all that, and is also a source of interesting ways to use type.

White, Jan V. *Graphic Design for the Electronic Age* [Watson-Guptill,1988] A complete reference for general DTP. Much good sense, and highly recommended.

Williams, Robin. *The Mac Is Not a Typewriter* [Peachpit Press, 1990] This wonderful little book packs more sound advice and typographic wisdom into its mere 72 pages than heaps of other books many times its size. It should probably come with the Mac as standard equipment. In any case, buy it. Read it. Buy it for your friends, and quiz them to make sure they've read it.

Williamson, Hugh. *Methods of Book Design* [Yale, 3rd ed., 1983] Quite simply, a magnificent, useful and fascinating work that must be in the collection of anyone who has anything to do with typography. This is a classic work that has justly earned a very high reputation among a very broad range of critics and professional typographers and book designers.

Woodcock, John, and Stan Knight. *A Book of Formal Scripts* [David R. Godine, Boston, 1992] Intended for calligraphers at virtually any level of expertise, this book also has much that is extremely valuable to Fontographer users about letter forms, spacing, calligraphic techniques, historical background, and much more. Highly recommended.

Zapf, Hermann. *Typographic Variations* [Museum Books, 1964] A beautiful book that demonstrates a large part of Zapf's design palette.

———. *About Alphabets – Some Marginal Notes on Type Design* [MIT Press, 1970]   Valuable observations from one of the greatest masters of typography.

Zapf, Hermann and John Dreyfus. *Classical Typography in the Computer Age* [William Andrews Clark Library, 1991]   A fascinating pair of papers which look at the present state of computer-assisted typography from two very different standpoints. Very interesting.

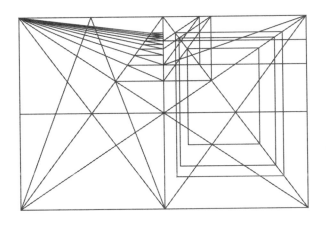

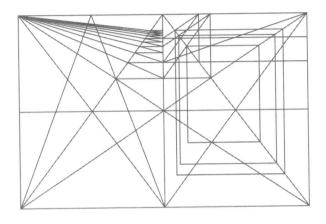

The following tools were used in the preparation of this work: Software — Fontographer versions 3.5 & 4.1; FreeHand 3.1, 4.0 and 5.0; PageMaker 4.2 and 5.0; Canvas 3.5.2; Illustrator 3.2 and 5.5; Photoshop 2.5.1; XPress 3.31; ReadySetGo 6.0; Metamorphosis Pro; Font Chameleon; and Textures 1.7. Hardware — Macintosh IIsi, se/30, Classic II and Plus; StyleWriter, Laser-Writer IINTX, IIg and Pro 630. Typefaces — *Livingston* (designed by Richard Beatty) and Goudy's *Italian Old-style* (provided by Richard Beatty & altered by him at my request for a lowercase *y* with a longer descender) were used for the entire book, except where noted.